To Olive

Lots of love

Tina Gn

GOLDEN GIRL

D1435455

TRINA GULLIVER

WITH PATRICK CHAPLIN

Golden Girl

The Autobiography of the Greatest
Ever Ladies' Darts Player

JOHN BLAKE

Published by John Blake Publishing Ltd,
3 Bramber Court, 2 Bramber Road,
London W14 9PB, England

www.blake.co.uk

First published in hardback in 2008

ISBN: 978 1 84454 500 1

British Library Cataloguing-in-Publication Data:

A catalogue record for this book is available from the British Library.

Design by www.envydesign.co.uk

Printed in Great Britain by CPI Bookmarque, Croydon, CRO 4TD

1 3 5 7 9 10 8 6 4 2

Papers used by John Blake Publishing are natural, recyclable products made from
wood grown in sustainable forests. The manufacturing processes conform to the
environmental regulations of the country of origin.

Every attempt has been made to contact the relevant copyright-holders, but some were
unobtainable. We would be grateful if the appropriate people could contact us.

Dedication

To my hero, my mum, Muriel.

Mum, you have been, and continue to be, my rock. Your patience, understanding and unconditional love are special qualities that you offer, not just to me but to all the family. You have always taught me to be the best person I can be. You have sacrificed so much in your life for all of us. You're an amazing lady and I'm proud to call you my mum. If I become half the person you are in my lifetime, then I'll be really proud of myself.

I dedicate this book to you, Mum. I love you so much.

X

Foreword

by the 'Golden Girl'

Friday, 12 January 2007, is a date that will live in my memory forever, for it was on that day that I rewrote the history books and became the first woman darts player to achieve seven successive world titles.

The British Darts Organisation (BDO) had introduced the Ladies Embassy World Professional Darts Championship to the darts calendar in 2001. Held at the 'Home of Darts', the Lakeside Country Club in Frimley Green, Surrey, I won the world title in that inaugural year, beating my good friend Mandy Solomons 2–1 in the final and I have retained the world title every year since. This, and numerous other wins in major competitions, has led to the darts press dubbing me the 'Golden Girl'.

From that very first world championship win I became very possessive of the title and have fought tooth and nail to ensure that no one will ever take it away from me. I am a naturally determined person and that applies to anything I do, whether it is on the oche, in my former trade as a carpenter/joiner, or anything else I set my mind to, including writing this book.

Losing my WINMAU World Masters Ladies title at Leisure World, Bridlington, in October 2006 was the wake-up call I needed. I was dumped out of the competition at the semi-final stage by Holland's number one (and another great friend) Francis Hoenselaar. I had held the WINMAU title for four consecutive years (five in all) and was angry with myself when my poor form and Francis' consummate skill and consistency denied me five wins in a row. That drab performance made me realise that, if I didn't pull myself together, I could well be on the verge of losing *my* world crown. I wasn't prepared to let that happen.

Despite all the problems I had experienced in my personal and professional life in recent months, I stepped onto the world stage in January 2007 and retained my title. I admit that my performance in the final was probably my worst ever on the Lakeside stage, but I battled hard against Francis and against my personal demons and overcame them all. I lifted the Lakeside Ladies' World Championship title for the seventh time! OK, so I hadn't been firing on all cylinders in that final, but I did the business.

I always do.

Trina Gulliver
Wantage, Oxon
October 2007

Acknowledgements

So many people have helped me through my life and career:

To my sponsors: Graham & Julie Reeves of Reeves Boatbuilders – your support has been simply wonderful and I'm certain that I wouldn't have achieved the success I've had without your support and friendship. You have every faith in me and that I'm truly grateful for. I love you both. Xx

Richard and Shirley Wright of Car Consultants – you have been fantastic. You're always there for me whatever comes my way; always willing and ready to help. Thank you. Xx

Ian Flack of the WINMAU Dartboard Company – Ian, I've really enjoyed my time with you and WINMAU. You're always there to offer your support and advice and, more importantly, I value our friendship. Thank you. X

Peter and Vera Linguard of Westpoint Shirts – You make me look good! Vera, you always know what I like. You've not been wrong yet. Thank you. Xx

Special thanks to Peter Prestidge, Sheila Alford, Tina Metcalfe, Anna Saunders and Gail and Roy Marshall, the late Jack Cundy and the late Dennis Roberts for their guidance in my career. Xx

Patrick – I've really enjoyed writing this book with you. Thank you for your patience. X

To Wayne Baker – for continually chasing me every month for my *Darts World* column and giving me encouragement when I have felt like not bothering anymore.

Many thanks to Clare-Louise Photography, Yvonne Andrews of Double Top Dart Shop, Steve Daszko Photography and Mark Sandom for kindly giving permission for their photography to be used in this book.

To all my friends – you know who you are, but in particular, Helen, Crissy and Fran. I've had some amazing times with all of you. I'm so lucky to have fantastic friends that I know I can call upon anytime, laugh with or moan to, friends who never judge. I love ya loads. X

And Clare – God we've had some mad times! Thank you for being patient and strong for me when I've needed you most. I know I'm not the easiest person to live with, but then neither are you. (Only joking ... kind of!! Lol) I'm not sure where I would be now without your love and support. I will always be there for you, too. Whatever and whenever you need me. Love Ya. X

To some of my favourite men, a big 'thank you' to Andy Fordham, Martin Adams, and the 'Fatman', Martin Fitzmaurice, for making me feel safe and looking after me whilst on the road. Fatman – you can be the biggest, moaning, pain in the arse ever, but I luv ya. X

It would be wrong of me not to thank the British Darts Organisation, Olly, Lorna and Sam, to name but a few, for giving me, and indeed everyone, a system of darts to play in from grassroots.

Julia – I'd love to be able to give you a copy of this mate. I miss you. X

Gully – thank you. Be happy. X

Last, but by no means least, my family – You have always been there for me, WHATEVER! I've caused you all plenty of worry and you have guided me, and bollocked me on many an occasion. Character building they call it. (Lol.) I'm blessed with a beautiful family of which I'm very proud. I love you! X

Contents

Introduction by Dr Patrick Chaplin, Darts Historian   xv

Chapter 1   Early Days, First Darts   1

Chapter 2   Loving Linley Road, Hating School   9

Chapter 3   High School, and Guess What?   23

Chapter 4   Besotted   33

Chapter 5   In Among the Lads   39

Chapter 6   'Trina Gulliver – Carpenter and Joiner'   53

Chapter 7   Those who can, Teach   59

Chapter 8   Devastation   67

Chapter 9   Serious Beginnings   83

Chapter 10   The Happiest Day of My Life   93

Chapter 11   The Year of the Cat(rina)   101

Chapter 12   Beauties and the Beast   123

Chapter 13   Where Would I be Without Them?   133

Chapter 14   I Aim to be Master of the World   145

Chapter 15   Champion of the World   155

Chapter 16   The Aftermath   163

Chapter 17   The Defence of My Titles   171

Chapter 18   World Champion Again ... but Only Just   179

Chapter 19   Hat-trick   189

Chapter 20   Putting a Family on Hold   199

Chapter 21   Four Up!   209

Chapter 22   From Stamford Bridge to Las Vegas   219

Chapter 23   Happy Times, Sad Times, Five Times   231

Chapter 24   The Most Difficult Decision of My Life   243

Chapter 25   Same Old Faces?   253

Chapter 26   Hit for Six   261

Chapter 27   The Magnificent Seventh   271

Chapter 28   What's Next for Me ... and Ladies' Darts?   279

Introduction

'Has there ever been a more successful women's darts player?'
(Olly Croft OBE, Director, British Darts Organisation)

When Olly Croft wrote those words in *Darts World* magazine in September 2004, he was not expecting the readership to answer.

By then, Trina Gulliver had won four Embassy/Lakeside World Championship titles, become the Ladies WINMAU World Master four times, won the first ever BDO Grand Slam title and the inaugural (and gruelling) Women's British Pentathlon. This exceptional sportswoman has won countless other darts titles, including the Las Vegas Desert Classic, and there appears to be no end in sight for Trina's supremacy of her sport.

Compared with the men's game, the emergence of ladies' darts is a recent phenomenon. Men had played the game (as it was described then) in English public houses in one form of another for many centuries, but it was not until the interwar years that opportunities arose for women and girls to participate. High profile participation, in particular a 'one-off' game by Queen Elizabeth the Queen Mother at a social centre in Slough in the late 1930s, led to women in their thousands approaching the offices of the British Darts Council in London demanding to know the rules of the 'royal game'. Some brewers in the southeast of England introduced women's darts leagues during the 1930s and – believe it or not, but it's true – before the outbreak of the Second World War, a woman made it to the grand finals of the *News of the World* Individual Darts Championship in London.

Throughout the 1950s the National Darts Association of Great Britain (NDAGB) organised Ladies Pairs competitions and then, in 1967, introduced a women's individual tournament. The first winner was Marjorie Drabble of the Marston Moor Club, near Chesterfield. However, it was not until the 1970s that the British Darts Organisation (BDO), with Olly Croft at the helm, dragged the game of darts kicking and screaming into the twentieth century and the first real *names* in ladies' darts began to appear.

The most popular men's darts champions of the 1970s and 80s immediately spring to mind – Eric Bristow, John Lowe, Jocky Wilson, Leighton Rees and Bobby George. Ask anyone in the street to name three darts players and their reply will be a combination of these four, plus perhaps the name of Phil Taylor. For, when someone is asked to 'name three darts players', they never ask, 'Men or women?'

Maureen Flowers was arguably the best woman darts player in the world during the 1970s and early 80s, winning numerous Open titles and captaining England. Other leading lady darts players that have made, and in many cases continue to make, their mark on the sport over the past three and a half decades include Linda Batten, Sharon Colclough, Sandra Gibb, Deta Hedman, Sharon Kemp, Jayne Kempster, Mandy Solomons, Jane Stubbs, Anne Kirk, Barbara Lee, Jan Robbins, Crissy Manley and

Clare Bywaters. America's Stacy Bromberg remains a key threat in major competition, as do Holland's number one, Francis Hoenselaar, and Russia's Anastasia Dobromyslova. However, none of these lady darters have achieved what Trina Gulliver has achieved – and it is unlikely that, in the future, anyone ever will. (Now *there's* a challenge for you!)

Trina is the first female darts player to write her autobiography. How she achieved her success in a sport where the men's game far outstrips the women's in terms of press attention, sponsorship and television exposure reveals much about the frustrations felt within the women's game for proper recognition and reward. I believe anyone reading *Golden Girl* will come away admiring Trina's resolve in making it to the top of her chosen sport against the odds.

Seven-times World Champion, Trina has earned her place in sport history.

I am proud to have been associated with this project and to have had some input into Trina's fascinating, and sometimes disturbing, life story. I believe *Golden Girl* will go down in the annals of sports writing as one of the most honest and groundbreaking autobiographies of all time.

Dr Patrick Chaplin
Darts Historian and Consultant
Maldon, Essex
October 2007

Chapter One

Early Days,
First Darts

I was born at 3.15 a.m. on 30 November 1969 at the Warneford Hospital in Leamington Spa. My parents, Muriel and Geoff Jones, named me Catrina Elizabeth; Catrina for no reason other than my mum loved the name – which was quickly shortened to Trina – and Elizabeth which was my maternal grandmother's middle name. I was Mum and Dad's fifth child, arriving in the world to join my older brothers Steve, who was born in 1953, and Andy (1956), and my older sisters Denise (born 1959) and Jeanette, who was born in 1961. So there were eight years between Jeanette and me which was quite a gap. I asked Mum about it once and she said that I had been 'an accident' and then quickly added, 'but a lovely one.' At the time I was born Mum and Dad were licensees of a pub called The Bowling Green in Southam, a small market town about ten miles north east of Warwick. It was in The Bowling Green that I would throw my first darts at a very early age, much to the disapproval of my mum.

1

Of my grandparents I know very little. To be honest, on my dad's side, the Jones' side, I didn't see a lot of my nan and granddad but there was a good reason for that. Dad walked out on the family when I was only four years old. All I can remember is that Dad's mum's name was Gertrude, always shortened to 'Gert', and that Granddad Jones was named Richard but was always known as 'Dick'. Mum told me that Dick owned a business, Jones Coal Merchants at Goodyears End Lane, Exhall, Bedworth, a town outside Coventry, and that he had brothers named Sidney and Walter and a sister called Maud. Dick was the oldest and had to take over the running of the business with his mum when his dad died. He was just eleven years old at the time. He died at the age of seventy in May 1974. I was only four years old then so any other personal memories of him are only impressions gained from old family photo albums. Nan died at the age of eighty-five in 1989.

To be truthful, I didn't really see a great deal of my nan and granddad on my mum's side either: Sidney and Ann Bilson. However, I do recall Sidney having a wicked sense of humour. He was a very funny man, but he did tend to favour my mum's sister, Auntie Bett, and her children more than us, which I think was due more to them living just down the road from him than anything else. I do know that my granddad didn't want my mum to marry Geoff. I've never been told why but it seems that Granddad was proved absolutely right when Geoff eventually walked out on the lot of us. The combination of Dad leaving us, Mum not being able to drive and having five kids to look after meant that contact with my maternal grandparents was all but lost, visits being very much dependent on them coming over to see us.

The only thing I do remember clearly from the very occasional weekends when we visited them was that Nan and Granddad always used to have the wrestling on the telly ... Big Daddy, Giant Haystacks and all that lot. They loved it. If we kids said anything while that was on – even if only in a whisper – Granddad would put his finger to his lips and go 'Sssssssh!' and we'd say, 'All right! Sorry!' You had to be quiet. Nothing – absolutely nothing – was allowed to interrupt their wrestling on a Saturday afternoon. Although those visits were few and far between, I did over time become close to my nan. It was later, when I was fourteen: Nan was diagnosed terminal cancer and my mum nursed her throughout that time. I often went along with Mum and I would sit and chat with Nan for ages. Nan died on 10 February 1983.

My mum, Muriel, grew up in a little cottage in Baginton, near Coventry. It was one of a pair of cottages right next to the ancient Roman fort and between Whitley airport and Baginton airport. Mum's nan, my great-nan, Mary Bilson, and great-grandpop William lived in the cottage next door. During the Second World War my granddad worked on the land, tractor driving and ploughing for Coventry Corporation. He was also a member of the Home Guard, while my nan worked in a local munitions factory. They lived in the little cottage throughout the whole of the war. It all sounds so sweet and quite picturesque and I suppose it must have been, but the things that stick in my head from when I was a young girl are Mum's stories of the war years when she was a child and how scared she was of the bombers that attacked Coventry and the surrounding area seemingly every night.

The cottages were only a short distance anyway from the airport, which was targeted regularly. Not far away was Rowley Road, which ran alongside the airport buildings and runway. False wooden tanks had been manufactured and loads of them were placed along the road and around the airport to give the enemy pilots of spotter planes or bombers overhead the impression that it was well protected. The Whitley bombers were also made nearby and so the area received a lot of attention from the Germans.

I remember Mum telling me how, as a little girl, she saw 'the Blitz' from the window of her home in Baginton, when Coventry was hit over and over again and so much death and destruction was caused to that once beautiful city. Mum was about five when war broke out. Whenever there was a raid on, the whole family used to hide underneath the stairs. This happened regularly. Even from their hiding place they could hear the 'ack-ack' guns being fired at the enemy from the nearby Memorial Park and Stoneyfields.

I remember Mum telling me of an old saying that went something like, 'If a bomb stops whistling, then it's got your name on it'. One night, while crouched under the stairs, they heard a bomb falling; heard the whistling – and then the whistling stopped. Mum thought that was the end. No whistle. As she waited for the bomb to hit the cottages, she put her hands over her head and started to cry. Then there was a huge explosion. It shook the whole building, but Mum soon realised that it had not actually hit the cottages.

Everyone was safe. Fortunately, the bomb had landed in a field directly behind them and thankfully had caused little damage to the cottages. Mum soon recovered from the shock and the very next morning was out in the field with her friends collecting shrapnel. However, Mum's sister was reacting badly to the incessant raids and so, in 1943, the three of them were evacuated to their nan's (Mary Yapp's) home in Cannock where they would be safe. The enemy never dropped bombs on Cannock as there was a German war cemetery there.

I am so grateful that the bomb hadn't got Mum's name on it. I have often thought how different things would have been if that bomb had fallen on the cottages. Chances are that there would have been no Catrina Jones. I would never have had the life that I have had and continue to enjoy.

It was my mum's brother Alan who was instrumental in

bringing my mum and dad together for the first time. Geoff was working as a driver for Morton's Transport hauling coal for the gasworks near Exhall. Alan was a driver there, too. One day, Alan came home to lunch and asked Mum if she'd like to come out for a drive. They stopped off at the gas works and Muriel was introduced to this young driver named Geoff Jones. It was only a brief 'hello' but Geoff wasted no time at all. The next time Geoff saw Alan he asked him to ask Mum if she'd go out with him – and that was that. They were married on 20 December 1952. My brother Steve was born almost a year later to the day on 19 December 1953.

Later, Dad worked for my granddad in his coal merchant's company, but he didn't earn very much, so, despite having five children to care for, my mum had to go out to work. She worked really hard; so very hard. When we were kids it was seasonal work, like potato picking. Where she was allowed to, she would take us kids along with her and we'd help (if 'help' is the right word!) as best we could. When we were all at school, Mum worked during school hours, usually cleaning jobs, including one down at the local pub, but she always made sure that she was back home to be there when we arrived home from school. Dad eventually stopped working for my granddad, coming out of the coal merchants and working as a boiler man at GEC in Coventry. This lasted for two or three years and after that he and Mum decided to go into the pub trade.

I asked Mum why they decided to go into the pub business and she said, 'We must have been mad, but it was just something Geoff wanted to do.' Mum and Dad had friends who ran a pub and they had helped them out from time to time so they weren't exactly new to the business when they decided to have a go. Their friends were impressed with their work and one day said to them, 'Why don't you try it?' So they did!

Their first pub was the Black Bull at Kidderminster in 1967. The pub was to be demolished to make way for a new road and so Mum and Dad took it on as a temporary arrangement, just for the short period of time before the licence ran out. The business-side was basically run from home by Mum, while Dad managed the pub all week. Mum then brought us all over to the pub for the busier weekend periods. At the beginning of 1968, Mum and Dad moved the family to the Hope Tavern in Leamington Spa. They stayed there for eight months. 'Just enough time for me to clean up the previous tenants' mess,' Mum told me and then, at last, in September 1968, they took over a pub of their own, The Bowling Green in Southam, where they stayed for six years.

Although it was something Dad wanted to do, Mum really enjoyed it, too. From what I've heard, they were very good at it. My mum's always been very good at catering and things like that; she did lots of weddings and that sort of thing and Dad was a good landlord. He never used to drink much himself. However, looking back, Mum told me recently, 'I'd never do it again. Babies and pubs don't mix.' Those were really tough times for the whole family, especially with a new baby. During the day Mum would care for me, but in the evening, when the pub was busy, my older brothers and sisters looked after me. Mum told me they were great.

Being just a baby at the time, I can't remember anything about those days at The Bowling Green, but I've been told stories of what I used to get up to. Apparently, I'd be sat on someone's lap in the bar and customers would take my dummy out of my mouth, dunk it in their beer and pop it back in. Mum became very angry with some of the customers about this. In particular, there was a baker who used to deliver to the pub every morning at 8.00 a.m. and at the same time stop and have a tot of rum. Mum told me that as soon as I saw the baker walk in I'd spit the dummy out in readiness for him to dunk it in his drink. Mind you, I was also well known, while sitting on a customer's lap, to simply lean over and stick my nose in their Guinness or whatever without any assistance at all! Come to think of it, that's probably why these days I like a drink every now and again.

On at least one occasion, when I was still only about three years old, I upset a customer. I was sitting on someone's lap and suddenly shouted to my dad across the crowded pub, 'He's bald, Dad! He's got no hair!' I don't know who the customer was but it really upset him. He really had a go at my dad. Then he drank up, left the pub and didn't come back for weeks.

In those days, of course, where there was a pub, there was a dartboard and The Bowling Green was no exception. Although I was far too young to play darts, there was one customer who gave me my earliest encouragement. When I was about three years old, Bill Calcutt, who is now ninety years young and has run the Southam Darts League for sixty-odd years, used to stand me on a chair and put a dart in my tiny hand so that I could throw it at the dartboard.

So that's where it all started!

By the time I was four, Mum and Dad had left the licensed trade and Dad had left the family. Why did he leave? Well, basically it was a troubled, strained and sometimes violent relationship brought about mainly by the fact that Dad was a womaniser. He's calmed down now, bless him, but he had lots of affairs at the time. Mum knew what was going on, but she seems to have just got on with it for the sake of me and my brothers and sisters. One of the people Dad had an affair with was actually my mum's best friend at the time, Rene. Dad's married to her now.

So Dad was gone, and Mum was left with the job of bringing up five kids by herself. Fortunately, at the time, my eldest brother Steve had just got a place to live with his wife Cathy. It was a three-up, two-down flat above a supermarket just across the road from the pub in Coventry Street. We all moved in with them. This made a total of eight most of the time, but often

Cath's sister would live there, too, and added to all this was the fact that Cath was pregnant!

I've been told that I caused some trouble one night. Cath's dad John had come over to the flat and was helping Steve decorate the hall, stairs and landing. I got up at five o'clock one morning and decided to help out. I walked across the landing to the paint pots, picked up a paintbrush, dipped it into the pots and started to paint. I got paint over everything – the carpet, the walls, me – everywhere. My brother Steve did his nut. When he discovered my artwork, he screamed, 'I'll bloody kill her!' But fortunately for me he didn't carry out his threat.

We stayed at Steve and Cath's for about six months until a Council property became available. At that time the Council was building lots of new properties on an estate on the outskirts of Southam so we were very lucky in that, when we did move, it was into a brand new house. I can see it now. The Council were still building around us when we all moved into 94 Linley Road.

It is from this time in my life that my real memories begin.

Chapter Two

Loving Linley Road, Hating School

I can remember moving into Linley Road as if it were only yesterday. Although the area looked like a bomb site, our new home shone out across the street at us like a beacon as we arrived in the removal van. Number 94 was a brand new, mid-terrace, three-bedroomed house. Just over the way from us the Council subcontractors were still busy building flats.

All the sights and sounds you'd expect from a building site – the diggers, the dumpers, the shouting of the site foreman – filled my head and, as a kid, I was immediately attracted to it. I know now that children and building sites don't mix but back then, well, it was an adventure and it took me no time at all to decide to explore. Before long, I was over the road and examining the flats. I wandered into one. The rooms were still in a raw state with no windows or doors and no plaster or paint on the walls. A gentle breeze blew through the space where the windows should have been and gently brushed my face and hair. The smell of paint and wood stain wafted through the air.

The place fascinated me. I stood there for a few minutes, slowly gazing round the flat at the bare walls and floor. Did I feel that I was in any danger? (Remember children: 'Building sites bite!') No, it wasn't danger I was feeling. It was something more. It was a sense of excitement. Even at that young age I felt very safe in that environment. I scanned the room and imagined it full of people; people like Mum and my family, moving into a new home for the very first time. I looked round the room again and then I saw something lying on the floor in the corner.

At first I hesitated. I stood and stared. Whatever was it? Whatever it was it was more or less totally hidden from view by shadows, so much so that less sharp eyes than mine might never have spotted it. Without further thought I walked confidently over to the corner, knelt down and, without hesitating, picked up the object. I was quite surprised by its weight. It was heavy but what was it? I brought it out of the shadows and into the light and examined it closely. I saw a brand name on the side. I turned it round at various angles like a university professor examining a rare find from an ancient Egyptian tomb. I really had no idea. Whatever it was I am certain it looked totally out of place in the hands of a young girl. Nevertheless I decided to keep it – 'Finders Keepers' as they say. I hid it in my coat, walked out of the flat and took it home.

It was a pin hammer.

On arriving home I took the pin hammer – which I learnt later was used by carpenters for securing beading – out of my coat and began looking around for something to load the hammer with. At that point I was guessing it was a gun of some kind and therefore began searching the house for some nails or similar ammunition to put in it. Then my mum appeared and I proudly showed her my new possession. She asked me where I'd got it from. I said, 'I found it.' Whether she believed me or not I don't recall, but I handed it over to her and I think it ended up in our tool box. Well, when I say 'tool box', you know, it was one of those boxes all households have where all kinds of miscellaneous oddments, odd tools, screws, electrical fuses, small pieces of wire, etc are stored on the off-chance that at some time in the future they might be useful.

Ironically, in my late teens, I actually turned my hand to carpentry, which later became my profession. I know that's an unusual occupation for a girl, but more of that later. I often wonder whether it was in that empty flat that I was first subconsciously attracted to that kind of work. That was certainly my first taste of the carpentry profession – 'borrowing' a carpenter's pin hammer – so I like to think that's probably where it all started.

We had some lovely neighbours in Linley Road. Next door to us on the left-hand side lived a lady named Mrs Paul. She was the widow of a vicar and was – not surprisingly – a very religious person. But, for all of that, she was a lovely, lovely lady. On the other side of us were Graham and Jean Hirons and their children Shaun and Mandy. Shaun was a couple of years older than me, and Mandy was a little older still. Then on the other side of Mrs Paul were another lot of Joneses – no relation to us – named Les and Margaret. They had four kids. Karl was the eldest, then Debbie, then Roy – who for some unaccountable reason was always called 'Fred' – and the youngest, Mark. When they moved in, it was just Karl and Debbie; Roy and Mark were born later. Debbie was a year younger than I was and we became best mates and used to hang about a lot together.

Debbie and I used to play games out in the street, like chase and football, and we even did a bit of skateboarding. The street was safe – well, as safe as any cul-de-sac could be, but then as kids we didn't consider danger and, in any event, if any cars came through we just stopped playing and moved out of the way. Even at that age, I was a bit of a tomboy, more so than Debbie. I used to play football with Shaun and Karl, mainly kickabouts in the street. I used to enjoy the rough and tumble with the lads and when it came to tackling I always gave as good as I got. Debbie used to play football with us as well, but I have to say she was rubbish. But all in all it was great fun. Life was so uncomplicated then.

I was almost five when all that fun seemed to grind to a halt. It was time for me to begin my schooling. I hated school with a vengeance. How can I put it?

I HATED SCHOOL! HATED IT! HATED IT! HATED IT!

Is that clear enough?

Right from day one I hated school with a passion. Southam Infants School was the establishment blessed with my presence. Every day, from the very beginning, Mum used to drop me off at school and I'd start up. I kicked, stamped and screamed. It took at least two teachers and my mum to grab hold of me and physically drag me yelling and flailing my arms about into the classroom. Then they would try and sit me down and, while the teachers were whispering reassuring words into my ears, Mum would walk out. The teachers held on to me until she'd gone. I guess Mum could hear me screaming at the top of my little voice 'Mum, don't leave me!' as she walked down the corridor and out of the school building. My screams must have been ringing in her ears all the way home. I know now that my mum used to be very upset about this happening all the time, day after day after day. I'm sorry for that but every day she left me in that classroom I felt as though my heart were breaking; such was my detestation of school. Then, after a while, I'd settle down a bit and look as though I was paying attention, but the teachers' words just rattled around the room and very little knowledge sank in.

Without realising it, by being so demonstrative in class and making such a fuss every day, I made a rod for my own back. I

12

became a victim of bullying at school. The girls seemed to be fine with me, and perhaps some even shared my view of school, but it was the lads who picked on me. One boy in particular, named Nigel Adair, was very nasty to me – not physically bullying me but always taunting me – and very spiteful. He was like that all the way through Infant and Junior School, but when he went up to high school he started to grow up a little bit. Perhaps he met his match there and was bullied a bit himself. I'd like to think so. I still see him wandering about Southam now and again. We speak and we're fine, but he was a bit of a bugger back then.

Even though I hated school, I wasn't a complete failure and I still recall a number of my teachers with affection. One of them, Mrs Thomas, was recently Mayor of Southam and she was the one who arranged a civic reception for me in 2003 in recognition and celebration of my third successive Embassy Women's World Professional Darts Championship title. Try as they might, Mrs Thomas and others did their best but, I have to say, I didn't respond too well.

My only real interests at school revolved entirely around sport; all sport. Anything to do with sport was fine with me. I reacted well to sport. At both the Infant and Junior Schools I excelled at sport – football, running, you name it, I was great at it. I particularly loved sprinting. In those days, as a kid in primary school, it was the egg-and-spoon race and flat racing over short distances. I was in the relay as well. I didn't realise it then, but I was being what grown-ups called 'competitive'. I was learning to win and, more than anything, learning how it felt to be first across the line, how it felt to be a winner. Nowadays, I can't understand people not being competitive. To me, whether it's work, sport or whatever, being competitive is just the most natural thing to be. Apparently, Mum was very good at sport when she was at school, so perhaps I've inherited some of her competitive spirit. She certainly needed some competitive spirit bringing up all of us on her own!

Apart from sport – and I think I may have mentioned this before – I absolutely *hated* school. I wasn't interested in any other subject; not maths, not English, nothing. I struggled with maths and reading, but looking back at the latter, I blame the system. One minute I was being taught to read, write and spell by a new method based on phonetics and then half way through a term the curriculum was changed and a new teaching method introduced. It threw me completely. (I'm sure I wasn't the only one, but it certainly felt like it at the time.) It was absolutely terrible, and I was so confused. I'll admit it now; I'm not and never have been very academically minded. However, when I do decide to put my mind to something I usually succeed. Sport was where I excelled at school and in the rest I was pretty average. Well, you can't be expected to excel at everything now, can you?

I suppose it took me a good year or two to settle into the infants' school and then I was a bit better about things in general. I was never *really* naughty, just not interested in being educated. It also didn't help that I hadn't any close friends in the classroom. Debbie Jones, my best friend from Linley Road, was in the year below me. But it wasn't important to me at that time to be surrounded with friends, and gradually, oh so gradually, I became used to school.

At the age of seven, just as I was settling down, I left Southam Infants School and went up to the junior school, which nowadays is called Southam Primary School. It wasn't in the same building but it was in very close proximity, more or less just across the playing field. I was mostly interested in the field that the school shared with the infant's school because it had not only a football pitch but also a running track.

My first teacher at the junior school was Mrs Edkins. She was very strict but a very good teacher. By 'strict' I don't mean to say that she resorted to violence or anything like that – oh no – I mean that you had to get on with your work, keep your head down and no messing about or you received a good telling off. With Mrs Edkins you never ever felt that you were in the wrong class. You always felt you belonged and she taught us that if we didn't understand something, 'you must ask' and then if you still didn't understand, she would explain it again. She wouldn't make you feel uncomfortable or snap 'Oh for God's sake!' in frustration. No. She was very strict but very fair and if all the class worked hard, she would reward us with a story. I remember we would all sit on a mat around her and she would read us the loveliest stories. At that time, when I was about eight or nine years old, and with all due respect to her, Mrs Edkins seemed old, bless her. She's still about today and still lives in Southam.

Mrs Edkins was followed next by Mrs Carry. She was a really lovely person and a very good teacher. Pupils could even have a laugh and a joke with her but only as long as you worked hard. Then there was Miss Rowland. Oh, that Miss Rowland! She and I just didn't get on. She had it in for me. I'm certain of it. I don't know why. It was probably because I was quite a popular girl in the infant's school, sporty and that sort of thing, or maybe it was because I was a tomboy and therefore perhaps not feminine enough for her. We had absolutely nothing in common; not even it seemed my education.

There was one particular incident involving Miss Rowland that sticks in my mind. One day, one of the girls, Brenda Johnson, came to school wearing a fabulous new jacket. It was silver – a sparkly, silver thing – really nice and we were all out in the playground and – like kids do – everybody was admiring and feeling the jacket and talking about it and taking it in turns to wear it. Anyway, it came round to my turn so I put the jacket on and everyone said I looked really good in it. I gave Brenda's jacket to the next girl and I walked off to do something else. A little later Brenda came up to me crying her eyes out. Quick as a flash, out of nowhere, Miss Rowland appeared, assumed that I had upset Brenda about this bloody jacket, and herded me into her office. Once in the office she yelled, 'Right, you're on detention.' I was flabbergasted. What was she on about? ('Planet Earth to Miss Rowland – is there anyone there?') She wouldn't listen to a word I said. I told her, 'I haven't done anything,' and she snapped back at me, 'Yes you have! You've made Brenda cry.'

I said, 'No, I haven't. I've not ...' and Miss Rowland interrupted me mid-flow yelling, 'You have! You have!'

She kept me in her office for ages until eventually there was a knock at the door. Miss Rowland called, 'Come in!' and the door opened and a red-faced Brenda entered the room. She had understood what was happening and had followed us back to the office and had come to set the record straight. She told Miss Rowland, 'It's not her.'

Did I get an apology?

Did I –

The truth of the matter was that Nigel Adair, who had come up in the same year as us, had been picking on Brenda and upsetting her. Brenda had run away from him, seen me and come up to me crying and saying 'Nigel's just been picking on me'. Perhaps because I could relate to the boys better, or perhaps I was just that little bit tougher, a little more street-wise than the other girls, they did tend to come to me if they were in trouble. If a girl said to me, 'So-and-so lad's picking on me,' I used to go with her to find the lad and have a word. I'd sort the problem out, but I never caused a fight, never ... I think perhaps somehow I had earned the lads' respect and could talk things out with them. I think that's what it was. Not surprisingly, half the time the lad responsible was Nigel bloody Adair who continued his practice of being a particular bugger.

In the end, Mum came down the school to see Miss Rowland

about the Brenda business. Mum said to her, 'You've had it in for my daughter for ages. Why? It seems like it's any little thing at every opportunity.' I don't remember the final outcome. I certainly don't recall receiving an apology. To this day, I don't know why Miss Rowland treated me that way. I was OK with her. Although I struggled academically, I was a good, well-behaved student and I was never naughty at school – *never*. Whether that frustrated her I don't know.

Maybe it was because I used to ask her more questions in class than anyone else. I would put my hand up and say 'I don't understand that', or 'Could you explain that again?' So perhaps she simply became irritated by what she perceived to be my inability to absorb knowledge, to understand what she was saying, when in fact I was only seeking clarification just like Mrs Edkins had previously taught us to do. Believe it or not, I was trying to learn. However, I did finally reach the point with her where I just didn't ask anymore because I thought, 'She's just going to have it in for me.'

In those days the usual length of time spent at the junior school was four years but my class had to do an extra year because the curriculum changed *again*. At that point our headmaster was Mr Hales. I remember him as being very tall. As far as his teaching was concerned he was, like many of the others, firm but fair and, of course, because he was the headmaster he automatically commanded respect.

I think by that time I was really beginning to enjoy school, after a fashion. Sport was still my favourite subject. I played every sport in which I was allowed to participate. Mrs Adair was the girls' sports teacher and a teacher named Mr Hawker was in charge of the boys. Mr Hawker and I got on really well. I used to go to school football practice all the time and, with his approval, I played in the lads' team when I could. However, I was only ever allowed to play in friendly matches with the lads because the rules of the school football league banned girls from participating. But don't get me wrong; I wasn't playing football with the lads because they were lads. I mean it wasn't a plot on my part to get me into close contact with them. I just wanted to play football. To be honest, I wasn't particularly interested in lads at the time and my first boyfriend was still a couple of years away. With hindsight, I often wonder if that was my first taste of taking on the 'men' at their own game; a first rehearsal for when I eventually entered the competitive world of darts which, in the early 1990s, was still dominated by men.

In the last year of junior school a girl named Helen King moved into Southam from Southampton and lived just round the corner from me. She joined my class and we became firm friends. I had already lost touch with Debbie as she was a few years below and on a different playground to me. Helen and I became the very best of friends and have remained so since the day she arrived. Helen used to call for me every day and we would walk to school together. I've got a picture of us in our blazers on our first day of high school. We wore blazers that were about six times too big. The reason for this was that they were so expensive, parents bought a blazer you could grow into, one that would last you all year and, if possible, throughout your entire school life. I remember Helen laughing at me when I arrived at her house one day.

She stood in the doorway and gasped, 'Oh my God! You've got your blazer done up!'

I said, 'So? What's wrong with that?' and she replied, 'You don't have your blazer done up. It's not cool.'

I went, 'Oh, all right then.'

Helen was a lovely girl and she tried her best to help me as much as she could. She was brighter than I was. We were actually in the same maths group together, although that's probably because I used to copy her work half – if not all – the time. Helen used to help me a lot since most of the time I was only thinking of sport – any sport – cricket, football, table tennis, athletics ...

During the last years of junior school Mrs Adair encouraged me and other girls to excel at sport. She also taught maths and actually played darts in the same Southam darts league as my mum and my sisters. It was she who, knowing that most of my family played darts, encouraged me to become more interested in the game as an aid to improving my arithmetic. This was yet another instance of my interest in the sport of darts being nurtured without my really knowing it.

One of the school sports I was best at was throwing the rounders ball. (You see? Here's *another* target sport I was good at!) There were three girls there who used to throw the rounders ball for the school. Of the other two, one was named Vanessa Gascoigne who was in the year above me; in the year below me, there was Tracy Gearon. We all used to represent the year above us because we were all so good. At Emscote, which was the local athletics club in Leamington Spa, the schools used to meet for athletics competitions and that's also where we used to throw the rounders ball for our county, Warwickshire. I think all three of us threw for Warwickshire at one time or another – but I was better than the other two!

I loved the school sports day and held the record for throwing the rounders ball for years. Like most schools, the pupils were split into 'houses' – in our case there were three, namely Ragbourne, Stoneton and Hodnell. I was in Stoneton and our house colour was blue. I will always remember one year I was ill on sports day and so was unfit to attend and throw the rounders ball. The team needed me so badly that Mrs Carry actually rang my mum at home and said, 'We've got the rounders and we desperately need Trina.' Mum replied, 'I know, but Trina's *really* ill. She's really poorly.' Mrs Carry didn't accept Mum's reply and begged her to drag me out of my sick bed and attend the sports day. She said to Mum, 'We need her. We desperately need her. Please, just bring her down to throw the ball and then take her home.'

Well, Mum came up to my room and told me that Mrs Carry was on the phone pleading with her to send me down to the school, whatever condition I was in. Mum asked me, 'Do you feel up to it?'

I thought about it – for about three seconds – and replied, 'All right. I'll go down and throw the rounders ball and then come back to bed.' Mum went back to the phone and before she could get a word in Mrs Carry, more or less crying in desperation, said again, 'Honestly. We really need her. We *really* need her. Please –' When Mum managed to speak she told Mrs Carry that I had agreed to clamber out of my sick bed and come down the school as soon as I could. Mrs Carry gave out a deep sigh of relief and thanked my mum several times before Mum put the phone down.

I dressed quickly and Mum and I went down to the school where I changed into my sports gear and prepared for my throw. Mrs Carry stood with Mum on the sports field and watched me prepare. As I was about to throw, Mrs Carry nudged my mum, nodded in my direction and said, 'Right. Now watch this. This is why we need Trina.' I threw the ball as hard as I could. For a moment I didn't think it was ever going to land. My mum was amazed. 'Bloody hell!' was all she could say as the ball sailed through the air for what seemed like a mile. Mrs Carry turned to my mum and said, 'See? I told you.'

It was a super throw. When it eventually landed and the distance was measured, it was announced that I had thrown twice as far as any other competitor that day. With my arms in the air and smiling in celebration, I ran over to Mum and Mrs Carry who congratulated and hugged me. Mrs Carry then turned to my mum and said, 'Right. Trina can go home now.' But I was having none of it. The adrenalin was coursing through me. I said, 'Well, I'm feeling a bit better actually.' So I stayed for the rest of the day.

My final memory of junior school is of the other sport I used to love to play at that time – netball. I started off as goal attack and was then moved to wing attack which at the time I wasn't too impressed with because I liked scoring the goals. (See? That's my competitiveness again!) Mrs Adair said, 'But I want you to play wing attack because you feed the ball so well.' So I played wing attack and she was so impressed that she made me promise there and then that when I left junior school I would continue with my netball. She was convinced that I would eventually become good enough to play netball for England. I replied, 'Yes. OK. I will.'

I didn't.

Chapter Three

High School, and Guess What?

I hated that too.

When I went to Southam High School in 1982 it was like an attack of déjà vu. I hated school all over again. I don't know why. I had been relatively happy and content during my last couple of years of junior school but the high school was, well, so big and so different to junior school and I guess it disorientated me and I ended up back at square one – hating it.

Southam High School was huge; a massive place that swamped me completely. I loved my sport, but when I was asked to take part in school sporting events and undergo compulsory training in the lunch hours, I refused to participate. For some reason, I wasn't happy. My reputation as a top girl of sport at the junior school had preceded me and when I acted up and only reluctantly took part, the teachers were surprised – or perhaps 'stunned' would be a better word. They couldn't believe that the person described on the records as a top sporting type, whose name had been bandied about by my previous school as being a potential star sports pupil of the future, and the girl standing in front of them was the same person. They said, 'Well on your record you're down as being really sporty and you love sport and everything ...' and I replied, 'I *do* love sport but I'm not doing it.'

High school was so completely different. I just could not settle in at all. I felt the same as when I started infants school. OK, so this time there were no tears and my mum and the teachers didn't have to drag me kicking and screaming into the classroom. But I hated it. Maybe I was a little frightened. I don't know. Perhaps it was because I was starting all over again. Throughout my time at junior school, especially in the last couple of years, I'd fought hard, worked hard and earned respect and was, quite literally, on top of my game – any game. I was the bee's knees and the best sportsperson there. At the high school I was bottom of the heap again, literally a 'new girl'. All of a sudden I'm not the best anymore. The sheer size of the school swamped me. Similarly, the size of the imagined task ahead of me – of becoming best in school – seemed to disable my competitive spirit. I was overwhelmed by the whole thing and responded in a very negative way to all my teachers and especially those who tried to encourage me to take part in school sports. As a result, my first couple of years at Southam High School were really tough.

But, as usual, there was one teacher who was able – eventually – to coax me round. Her name was Mrs Clarke. She was my head of year throughout high school and had previously been head of year for my sisters, Jeannette and Denise, too. The school had a policy of keeping family members in the same 'house' and in the Jones' case the house was Arden. Mind you, she was Miss Banfield back then. Jeanette and Denise had warned me that Mrs Clarke was 'really strict' but I saw none of that. She was absolutely lovely to me and so helpful. It was Mrs Clarke who helped me to settle down. I remember her saying 'Any problems you've got, Trina, just you come to see me'. She was very patient with me. She said, 'Why don't you want to take ...?' and I replied, 'Because I don't!' Then she calmly asked, 'But why?' and then we'd sit together and talk things through. She was really, really nice and quite a calming influence on me.

Despite Mrs Clarke's kindness and patience with me, no one could convince me to participate in serious sport for at least the first two years. That's not to say that I didn't do any sport. I had to take the PE lessons that were a statutory part of the curriculum but when they wanted me to play netball, hockey, do athletics or throw the javelin, discus or rounders ball for the school, I wouldn't do it. When the teachers asked, 'Would you represent the school at so-and-so Trina?' I always replied, 'No. I don't want to do it', and that was that.

But this attitude of non-cooperation wasn't restricted to just school sports. I responded badly in all other classes, too. I admit it. I struggled. I was struggling to settle in and my mind just wasn't on anything; sporting or academic. At one stage, I was actually put into a lower class so that I would feel more comfortable. That was the teacher's bright idea to help improve my educational chances, to feel more comfortable and try and fit in a bit better. However, I found that too easy and then I got bored so then they put me into different classes to suit my level of aptitude and that – very gradually – began to work.

I was thinking of describing those early days as a lull but that would be lying to myself. I just really felt completely out of my depth and then, as with junior school, in the last two years I began to grow up. Just before it was too late, I realised that if I didn't put some effort in soon, I'd leave with nothing. At last, I said to myself, 'Trina, these are the most important days of your life and you've got to knuckle down.'

The inspiration came as a direct result of all Mrs Clarke's hard work and – at last – my own personal resolve. Mrs Clarke was very good and helped me out as much as she could. She was invaluable because I always knew that if I had a problem I could go to her and not feel stupid. She would listen and if I was struggling with anything she advised me and even on occasions made other teachers aware of my situation.

In those final couple of years I settled down properly and made new friends. I started to play a bit more sport but not a great deal to be honest. Even though I had promised Mrs Adair I would continue to play netball and perhaps even play for England, it never happened. I only ever played netball in PE lessons. Looking back, that's quite sad really. I mean, I *did* promise, but back then I suppose it wasn't that important; either netball or my promise to Mrs Adair. I only hope that my eventually captaining the England Ladies' darts team compensates in some way for my letting her down on the netball front.

Once I was back into sport at school, I began to improve, but I never represented the school at anything while I was there – oh no – except once, when I threw the javelin for Warwickshire. I turned up for the event full of confidence and even my competitive spirit had returned. I had three throws all of which landed two to three metres ahead of everyone else's efforts. Unfortunately, my technique was not quite right and on all three occasions the javelin landed flat. Because of this they were all judged to be 'no throws'; such was the rule then. I thought 'Chuffin' 'ell! Three no throws!' It's changed now. Today, if it lands flat, I think it counts – but that's irrelevant to my story. I wasn't asked to represent my county again in that sport.

Academically, I continued to struggle. If I had read a lot more books, I'm sure my English would have improved. I didn't – and still don't – enjoy reading. I'm an active person, a sporty person, not an academic, so I've always found reading quite boring. I've probably read only three or four books in my entire life and two of them were at school. One of them was *Hobson's Choice*, but ask me today what it was about or who wrote it and I wouldn't be able to tell you. I don't think to pick up a book. It's not something that comes naturally to me and never has.

Other subjects I studied at high school included history and geography, which were compulsory, as was one language. The brightest in the class took German while the rest of us learnt French – well sort of. English language, English literature, general science, art, metalwork and technical drawing completed the list. It's strange – given my eventual profession as a carpenter and joiner – that I took metalwork as an option at school and not woodwork.

When I was about twelve years old, I became interested in making things, building things. I was always doing something in the back garden. Mum encouraged me to be creative in this way. At that time Mum worked at Supra Automotive on the Kineton Industrial Estate on the outskirts of Southam, where she used to pack and parcel car parts, brake shoes and things like that. She used to bring home materials for me in the form of timber pallets. I'd gather my tools together in the garden and just make things. I wouldn't use a plan or anything – just knock things up. I made tables and all sorts of other things from the wood and I also made a greenhouse. Yes, a greenhouse! Both Mum and I liked growing tomatoes so I built a greenhouse. Mind you, when I say *I*, I have to admit that my real dad, Geoff, who had recently returned to the Southam area having been away in Coventry for some years, did help me a bit.

But my skills were not simply restricted to making items from wood. Oh no. One day Mum came home from work and discovered a great big hole in the back garden. I stood proudly beside the hole, leaning on a spade, my face beaming with pride. 'What on earth are you doing?' asked Mum. I smiled and replied, 'I thought we'd have a pond.' After a short pause, Mum said, 'Well done Trine,' and went indoors. She didn't really want a pond but then she didn't have the heart to tell me to fill it in. Mum knew it had taken me all day to dig it and didn't want to hurt my feelings. Yet given all the skills I was honing at home, when I came to choose my options in the penultimate year of school, why did I choose metalwork over woodwork? (Mum still has a table with a tiled top that I made at school as part of the course work.) I took technical drawing, too, because, at that point, I really wanted to become an architect.

I found out that to qualify as an architect I needed to obtain high grades in all my exams and then undertake seven years training after school. Seven years! Eventually I decided that, realistically, given my track record of academic endeavour and the likely outcomes of my examinations, I probably wouldn't stick it.

After that I toyed with the idea of some kind of career involving working with my hands. I was thinking along the lines that, if I could build a greenhouse, then I could probably build a house. I was much more 'hands on' than academic and I'd always wanted to build things or make things, so I thought I would become a bricklayer and I pictured myself at some stage in the future building my own house. That's why, when the options came up, I was offered the chance to go to college one day a week and do a general building course. Bricklaying was included and I was keen. Bricklaying it was then. I thought it was a great idea. I told my mum of my latest career choice and she was not impressed. 'Oh, our Trine,' she said, 'Your hands'll be terrible if you do that. You'll be out in all weathers. You'll be freezing.' That short argument seemed to deter me from a life as a brickie, so I thought for a moment. I thought about the pallets, the wooden table and the greenhouse and then said, 'All right then. I'll be a carpenter.' Again Mum argued, 'But Trine, that still means you're going to be out in all weathers, out in the same ...' But I said, 'Yeah, I know, but I can do that. I can be a carpenter who only works indoors.' This major career decision was made in my last year in high school and by then it was far too late to opt for woodwork.

For a short while, before deciding to become a carpenter, I had considered other career options including joining the police. That came to nothing. Another road I nearly travelled down was to go into the Navy as a Wren but the idea was short-lived. I smile to myself now as I write this because the whole idea of joining the WRNS was futile: I suffered from sea-sickness! I realised this when I was in my penultimate year of junior school and went on a trip to France with other pupils from the school. It was actually for the pupils in the last year of school but there were some places left so they offered them to pupils in the next year down and luckily – I thought – Mum could afford to pay for me to go. I very much looked forwards to the adventure but ended up hating it.

We went by coach from Southam down to Southampton and on to the ferry to Le Havre. I felt very uncomfortable all the way across but was not ill. When we stepped off the ferry in France, I thought, 'That wasn't so bad after all,' and in minutes of setting foot on solid ground had convinced myself that I had easily acquired my sea legs. Oh, how wrong I was! We stayed somewhere around Normandy for four or five days and had day trips out and about. The day trip to Paris, which I must admit I was quite excited about, was crap – absolute crap. The coach driver drove us into the heart of the city and parked at the side of the road for about two minutes. We got off the coach, looked at the Eiffel Tower and that was it; back on the bus and away. In fact, the whole trip was horrible. I hated it, plus I was becoming more and more homesick. I hated everything about that trip. The food was crap. It was quite scary for me actually, being so young and away from home for the first time.

On the return trip the English Channel was much rougher than the outgoing journey. I was sitting inside rocking and rolling about in my seat feeling nauseous and desperately trying to concentrate on anything other than the fact that the contents of my tummy were rocking and rolling about, too, but it was no good. I put my hands over my mouth, got up and rushed outside and up to the rail where, clinging on, and looking down into the water, I vomited over the side. I felt dreadful. I pulled myself away from the rail and wiped my mouth with my sleeve. As I was trying to regain my bearings, I noticed this lad – who I didn't recognise as being from our school – a little further up the boat from me. I felt so embarrassed. Had he seen me? Had he been watching me? Was he going to help me? Was he going to ask me if I was OK? Absolutely not. Do you know what that little bugger did? He spat at me. I turned as quickly as I could but the wind-assisted saliva hit me on the side of my head! I shouted, 'You dirty git!' and if I had got hold of him at that moment, I would have thrown him over the side, but I was feeling sick all over again. I walked back to the rail and ...

I hated the whole experience; homesick and sea-sick, which seems strange now looking back, as being a professional darts player I spend so much of my time away from home and travelling on ferries. Perhaps I should have pursued a career in the WRNS after all.

I think not.

I eventually sat eight CSE exams and passed the lot. Although I always achieved 'A's in metalwork, I decided in my last year not to take the exam as it was no longer relevant to my career choice. Nobody was more surprised than I was when I found that I had passed CSE English Language at grade 1, which meant that it was equivalent to GCE 'O' level standard at grade D! Art and Craft was my next best subject at grade 2 and something about *Hobson's Choice* must have registered as I also passed English Literature at grade 3; the same grade as I obtained for Geography. I didn't do very well at all in what I called the 'clever' subjects, namely maths, science and history. Three grade 4 CSEs came as no surprise to me. However, the grade 3 in technical drawing pleased me and would help equip me for my chosen profession as a carpenter.

I just don't make things very easy for myself, do I? A female carpenter! Now come on! I'm talking 1986 here. What chance would I have of making a career for myself in such a male-dominated profession?

Well, I liked a challenge...

Chapter Four

Besotted

I had my first boyfriend in the first or second year of junior school. His name was Daniel Walker. Well, when I say 'boyfriend'... I mean how serious can it be at seven or eight years old? God that sounds really young! Let's say eight. It sounds better.

Daniel – or 'Danny' as he was better known – had a sister, Sharon. They were twins and were in the same classes as me at school more or less all the time. Danny used to play football. He usually played in goal and I knew him fairly well when I used to play football with the lads in the playground and then later when we played in friendly matches for Southam Town. Our relationship was hardly anything serious. In fact, it was only a quick kiss behind a tree. Like most kids our age, a group of us used to play 'Kiss Chase'. Me? I loved it. I just wanted to get caught all the time but, having said that, I guess that very much depended on who was chasing me. Sometimes, I'd deliberately feign injury, or simply slow down to give the lad a better chance of catching up with me.

Despite all this feverish activity, I had no serious boyfriends throughout my entire school life and then, in 1985, when I was sixteen and had just left school, I fell hook, line and sinker for the man I was to spend nearly twenty years of my life with.

His name was Paul Gulliver.

By the time I was sixteen, I was playing serious darts. I was in the Warwickshire County side and also playing darts with my mum and my sister Denise at The Bowling Green pub, the one that my mum and dad used to run. It was our local too, our social point, so we were often in there. 'Gully', as Paul was always known (it's only his family that call him Paul), used to drink there, too, with his friend Ted Collett. Gully and Ted had been best mates right through school. To begin with, I didn't take a lot of notice of Gully. He was actually five years older than me – quite a gap – and, in any case, I fancied Ted first off. I actually went out with Ted for a week or two but I wasn't that experienced and Ted was – how can I put it? – a bit too far advanced for me at that point. In fact, it scared the shit out of me and I didn't know what to do to finish it. In the end, I told my sister Denise, saying something like 'I can't ... Ooh, no.' Denise understood and asked, 'Do you want me to tell him?' I was so relieved and said, 'Yes please,' before she had time to finish her sentence. So off she went and broke the news to Ted. 'She doesn't want to see you anymore,' she told Ted. 'She's just too young.'

Ted replied, 'Oh. Right. OK, that's fine.' And that was it. Job done. Thanks Denise. So, relationships took a bit of a back seat after Ted. Maybe I was unsure about things. (You know what I'm talking about.) But New Year's Eve 1986 changed all that. Up until that time I hadn't really looked at Gully. Never thought...

I was at a New Year's Eve party with some friends in the back room of The Bowling Green when Gully walked in. He was wearing a very smart grey suit, white shirt and red tie and I thought to myself, 'He looks all right.' Then I looked down and, bless him, he was wearing trainers. I smiled and thought, 'Well, bloody hell.' I didn't do anything else at that time but Gully just stuck in my mind. That was the first time I really took any notice of him, trainers and all.

We didn't actually go out together for another couple of months. Again, I held back, but not for much longer. After New Year's Eve I still saw him at the pub. I often played him at pool. On one occasion, I played him in the final of a pool tournament at The Bowling Green. I was playing OK but he deliberately missed the black so I beat him. He was quite a gentleman like that really. I remember Ted saying afterwards, 'You could have beat her easy!' I was really pleased with that pool trophy which went up on the shelf with all the darts trophies I was accumulating.

I asked Gully out on Valentine's Day. I'd plucked up the courage the day before and phoned him and said, 'There's a do on at the Stoneythorpe Hotel tomorrow night; a Valentine's party thing. Do you fancy going?' Quick as a flash he replied, 'Oh, I can't. I've got basketball training.' I knew how sporty he was. I think that was part of what attracted me to him in the first place. Being a sports lover myself, I understood how important training was, so I just sighed and said, 'That's OK. It was just a thought.' I paused and then said, 'Another time ...'

It had taken me ages to make that call. I was about to put the phone down when Gully said, 'Whooooah! Hang on a minute.' I hung on. 'I'll finish early. I'll pick you up at half eight.' I said, 'Good. All right then.' I replaced the phone and punched the air.

Result!

Gully picked me up right on time, told me I looked great, and off we went to the Stoneythorpe Hotel. He was so nice to me. Once at the venue, he behaved like a real gentleman. When we found a table he even pulled the chair out for me to sit down. Unfortunately I didn't realise he'd done that. I went to sit down, missed the chair completely and fell straight on my arse. Gully was horrified and really embarrassed. He said, 'Oh my God! I'm really sorry, Trina!' He was. It seemed that he would never stop apologising. I said, 'It's all right. Don't worry. No problem. I'm OK.' But it wasn't really OK and there was a problem. I was wearing white trousers and the floor was so dirty that when I stood up people could see I had a black arse. Despite this, the rest of the night was uneventful. Gully and I just chatted and got to know each other a little better. There's not a lot more to tell about that night. Gully continued to behave like a real gentleman all evening and, when the do was over, he took me home – and that was it.

I can't remember exactly when we next went out together. I think we probably went out for a meal. I know I should remember, but to be honest I don't. Obviously I used to see him in The Bowling Green with Ted and we'd have a drink together. Gully was a super-fit sportsman who lived for rugby. He used to play a lot, every weekend home or away, so a day or so before he'd say 'We're playing so-and-so Saturday. We're away but I'll be back in Southam early evening so I'll meet you at The Crown [or wherever] around 8 o'clock', and I'd be there waiting for him. He'd be there or come in with the rugby lads and all the other players' girlfriends and wives would meet up there, too, and that's basically how it was for a while. I used to talk to Mum about Gully and I'm not sure she totally approved. Because of the age difference Mum would say, 'Well that's ... um ... OK. But just be careful.' She knew I had a level head on my shoulders anyway. Mum was very trusting and she knew that I could look after myself, even at sixteen.

One thing I had difficulty coming to terms with was the fact that Gully never ever allowed me to go and watch him play rugby. People used to tell me how quick he was on the field and how he scored most of the team's tries and for two seasons running he had been the highest try scorer in the league. I worked with someone at Silverstones Builders who played rugby against him and one day we were talking about Gully and he asked me, 'Have you never watched him play?' and I said, 'No. I'm not allowed to go and watch.' The guy added, 'Honestly, if we get anywhere near him during a match we have to knobble him. We have to because, once he's off up the field with the ball, chances are no one will catch him. He's *that* quick.' Gully kept himself in excellent shape. He used to go running two or three times a week and never less than six miles.

God, he was fit. Very fit.

By this time my darts were becoming my main focus. Gully had his rugby and I had my darts. Whereas I desperately wanted to watch him play rugby, he simply wasn't interested in coming to watch me play darts – not at that point in time anyway – so he left me to it. That really was the sporting life we shared apart. He worked all week to play rugby at the weekends for Southam and I practised hard for those important darts matches. Despite his lack of interest in my sporting passion, I still occasionally said to him, 'I'd love to come and watch you play,' and each time he said, 'No.' So I decided that if he wasn't going to invite me to watch him play, I'd find some way ...

I was in a pub one night talking to Linda Harvey whose husband played rugby for Southam with Gully, and we got round to talking about the team and she said, 'You ought to come down and watch a game sometime. You'd enjoy it. Gully is so good.' I said, 'I can't. He'd kill me,' and she replied, 'He won't bloody know you're there. We'll turn up after the match has started. Once he's on the field, he'll be so focused, he'll not even notice you're there.'

I liked this idea very much but I still replied, 'He'll kill me.'

'That's as maybe' said Linda, 'But you've got to come and watch him, Trine cos he's just *brilliant.*'

A plan was hatched and one Saturday I managed to sneak in a few minutes after the start of a match and stood quietly on the touchline watching Gully and the team doing their stuff. Then the ball was chipped up. The girl beside me said, 'Now watch this!' and I watched Gully run – and I mean run. He was so fast; it took my breath away. (It has the same effect thinking of it today.) I couldn't believe it. I knew they said he was quick but I couldn't believe how quick he was. Apparently, that was how he used to score most of his tries. A team member would just chip the ball up knowing that Gully would be there at outside centre to receive the ball and then make a dash for the line.

Gully wasn't very impressed when he found out that I had watched him. I was in the clubhouse with the rest of the girls and he walked in and was surprised to see me. I said to him, 'I've watched you play at last!' Gully replied, 'I've told you ...' and before he could say any more I said, 'It doesn't matter. I didn't put you off, did I?' and he repeated, 'I've told you ...' I said, 'I know but – '. He wasn't happy *at all* and I think he was going to have a go at me when Linda, the girl who'd helped smuggle me into the match, said, 'Oh shut up Gully. Just shut up. Leave her alone. Don't be so bloody miserable', and that was that. No more was said.

Mind you, I never did go to see him play in a formal match again. I guess I knew that I had upset him. However, I did take part in the occasional friendly matches when the wives and girlfriends took on the lads. They were great fun. And no, they were never the walkover you might imagine. The lads were 'handicapped' having to wear wellies tied together with a yard of string. That was good fun.

The truth of the matter is that, at that time, I was completely besotted by Gully, completely. I suppose that was because he was my first love. You know, when you're at school, you always think you're in love and then you realise ... no ... this isn't it at all. Gully was *the* one. Even at sixteen I knew that as fact.

It was as simple and as serious as that.

Chapter Five

In Among the Lads

When I did my options in my penultimate year at high school I chose to go to Mid-Warwickshire College one day a week to do a general building course. It was split into three terms; the first term covered painting and decorating, the second plumbing and the third bricklaying. The third term was particularly important because, at that time, I had decided that I wanted to become a bricklayer.

Believe it or not I enjoyed my time at college and learnt all sorts of basic building skills, not only bricklaying but also plumbing, lead-burning and things like that. Then, in the last year of school, all the pupils had the option of going on work-experience placements. By this time, I had lost interest in becoming a bricklayer and favoured becoming a carpenter-joiner. However, even at my relatively young age, I could foresee potential problems.

Remember, this was the 1980s and, despite all the talk that

had been bandied around since the liberated sixties about women's rights, like many other places in the country, such concepts as equality of employment were relatively unheard of in Southam. However, I was determined that I would succeed in my plans to become a carpenter. That's where my skills lay so why should I be denied the opportunity? That makes me sound like a bit of a women's libber, doesn't it? I wasn't really. I don't believe I could have survived in a man's world – and survive I did and very successfully, too – if I'd have been a 'burn your bra' kind of girl. The lads just wouldn't have allowed it.

I envisaged all sorts of problems. I imagined trying loads of builders and joiners in the area and I could see them all scoffing at me, saying 'No. No way', and then laughing out loud as I left the building. Let's be honest, I reckon that, looking back, I was way ahead of my time. A woman looking for employment in a man's trade was really new then – especially in a country town like Southam – and I wouldn't have blamed them if they had all turned me down. After all, they were just a bunch of ignorant blokes who couldn't see the future standing there in front of them. That could have easily happened to any ordinary girl, but it didn't happen to me. I used family connections.

My brother Andy had previously worked as a foreman on Northamptonshire Council contracts at Silverstone's Builders at Brewster's Corner in Pendyke Street, in Southam, so I asked him for his help. 'Can you get me in at Silverstone's Builders for my work experience? Please?' He said he'd try and I was chuffed to bits when, a day or so later, he'd convinced the owner, Ron Sharples, to interview me for a placement there.

Mr Sharples agreed to see me one day immediately after school and so, as soon as the last lesson was over, I made my way to Silverstone's. Still in my school uniform I walked nervously into the reception, not really knowing what – or who – to expect. After a short wait Mr Sharples walked in and greeted me warmly.

I nervously shook his hand and smiled. He was a man of average height and build, dressed in his working clothes, a bit thin on top with a Bobby Charlton hair do (you know – or your parents or grandparents will tell you – where the long hair at the sides was brushed across the balding bit. I think they called it a 'comb over'.) He also wore glasses and a smile. He interviewed me then and there, informally, standing in reception. We never sat down. It was a very brief conversation that was over in minutes. The interview, if you could call it that, started with Mr Sharples saying 'So, you want to be a carpenter then?' I immediately replied, 'Yeah, and joiner.' He then asked, 'But *why* do you want to do it?' Without hesitation I replied, 'Because it's what I want to do and I've always been knocking things into woo –'

Mr Sharples interrupted with 'Yes, so Andy told me'. Then he smiled at me and said, 'And you want to do your work experience with us?' I said, 'Yeah, please,' quickly adding, 'if you let me I could then go on to a proper apprenticeship and do that Construction Industry Training Board (CITB) thing. I could do that for two years and then –'

Mr Sharples held up his hand to stop me mid flow. I stopped. He shuffled and adjusted his stance and then said, 'Right. Are you serious about this?' immediately asking me again but with greater emphasis, 'Are you *absolutely* serious about this?' I nodded my head enthusiastically and replied, 'Yeah. Absolutely Mr Sharples. Absolutely. There's nothing else I want to do.' He paused and ruminated for what seemed an age (but what was actually less than a minute) and I started to panic a little, thinking that perhaps he didn't like the idea of a girl joining his company after all. Then Mr Sharples cleared his throat and said to me, 'OK. I'll give you a go on work experience one day a week from school and then, if you are still sure that joinery is what you want to do, then, if I'm happy with your performance, I'll send you on the CITB Scheme.'

I was so pleased that I wanted to grab him and give him a great big kiss on the top of his head, but I didn't. I just muttered humbly, 'Thank you.'

Mr Sharples went on, 'I'll take you on, but on one condition.' I replied eagerly, 'What's that then?' And he said, 'You don't expect to be treated any different to anyone else.' It was the 'girl in a lad's job' thing. God knows what the other workers' reactions were going to be to my working with them and God help Mr Sharples if he were to treat me – a mere schoolgirl – any different than the lads. That was to be expected and, to be honest, if my brother hadn't have worked for him, if I had been just any schoolgirl walking into Mr Sharples' office on that day, he would have probably said, 'Thanks, but no thanks' – end of interview. I smiled at Mr Sharples and said, 'That's fine by me.' With that we shook hands. He said, 'Right. OK then,' and escorted me out of the reception and into the yard. I was so pleased to have been accepted and looked forward to my first day.

On that day Mr Sharples took me to the workshop, introduced me to the lads and told me to call him Ron. The lads were of all ages, shapes and sizes and varied in experience. These included Barry Lightowler, who became a good friend and remains so today, and Matt Sharples, Ron's nephew. Then there was Roy Clennel. He was quite an old feller – well, early sixties – but sprightly for his age. Roy knew a lot about every part of the carpentry and joinery trade but was the clumsiest and most accident-prone person I've ever met in my life. He had a total disregard for his own wellbeing, something that I had never witnessed in anyone else before or since. One day, he casually sawed through an electric cable. I thought he'd fused himself to the national grid, but no. Roy thought nothing of it; he just swore a bit and continued with the job in hand. It was all part of Roy being Roy. There was also a lad named Simon Lazzell there who was in the last year of his apprenticeship. He was good and quite knowledgeable. I learned quite a bit from Simon. Actually, I got on really well with all the lads, but it did occur to me sometimes that I had an easier time of it perhaps because they all knew my brother Andy. Possibly they had it in the back of their minds that if anyone upset me Andy might just have a word with them.

'We'll put you on that bench over there,' said Ron, pointing to one of a number of benches situated around the workshop. But it made little difference which bench I was allocated because at that time I wasn't insured to use any machinery. I could use drills and sanders but that was about it, all basic stuff. So, to begin with, my standard day consisted of tea making, sweeping up, more tea making and priming dozens of windows for homes for a major job the company had at Vernon Road, in Towcester – oh yes – and more tea making. I never tired of it though. I saw it as building the foundations of my future career.

I worked very hard at Silverstone's learning the trade. I thoroughly enjoyed myself and it convinced me that this was what I really wanted to do. While the other girls in the school were undertaking their work experience in shops and offices and hairdressers, I was in the joinery shop doing what I genuinely wanted to do and feeling just like one of the lads. In one spell, Barry, Matt and I were in the joiners' shop making and priming windows for the Vernon Road job when they suggested that I should accompany them there and help them on the spot.

As part of the day-release I was supposed to go out on site so I jumped at the chance. Silverstone's Builders had won a council contract involving sites all around the Northants area and Vernon Road was just part of that contract. I thought the job was going to be interesting, a learning process. What I didn't know at the time was that Vernon Road was full of characters; so many that it was unbelievable. An old dear on the end of one row of houses insisted we all went to hers for a cup of tea at 1.00 p.m. on the dot and again at 3.00 p.m. She was a lovely lady and got the cake and biscuits out each time. Then in the middle of the row were a husband and wife. We called her 'Co-Co the Clown' as she had long hair each side of her head but was completely bald on top. Her husband claimed to be a 'Professional Cornflake Stacker' at Asda supermarket. I nearly wet myself when he said that. He was a nightime shelf stacker but he'd changed his job title to impress us. Another good thing about working at Silverstone's – apart from getting me away from school – was that they also allowed me to work for them for a few days during the school holidays, *and* they paid me for it. At the end of my work experience, I received a certificate.

One of the core elements of my training to become a carpenter-joiner was of course the CITB course, which Ron signed me up for after I started working with him at Silverstone's when I left school. The course was run at the Mid-Warwickshire College in Leamington Spa. I attended the college full time for six weeks and then spent six weeks back at Silverstone's either at the bench or on site. Although I liked my workmates at Silverstone's and they got on with me, I had a tough time when I was at college. Not surprisingly, I was the only girl in the class. I was one sixteen-year-old girl among ten lads and you can imagine ...

All that testosterone ...

Because I had always been a bit of a tomboy I had had no problems getting along with the lads at school – better really than I did with the majority of the girls – but college was somehow different. I suppose it was this change of emphasis. You're no longer in a general school situation and, of course, at college you are there to learn a trade and, for obvious reasons, I stood out in the class. I could see the looks on the lads' faces. In some of them I read, 'What's *she* doing here? This is a man's trade,' while on others ... Well, I could only guess what they were thinking!

I didn't realise it at that time but my being there was kind of ground breaking, being a girl trying to qualify in a man's trade, but it was what I wanted to do. I felt strange. It *was* strange but it wasn't that daunting. I saw it as an opportunity to be seized and I was keen to do well. It was a new start with new people. Having said that, there were a couple of lads from school on the college course but both of them turned out to be complete dickheads, but there you go. I was there to learn and they just seemed to be there for a laugh and to piss about. They obviously hadn't started to grow up yet.

My attitude to college was so very different from my attitude to school. I had settled down and improved during the last couple of years at school but, most importantly, I wanted to get on and do something. I didn't want just any job; I wanted to learn a trade and get that behind me. Mum had drummed that into me time and time again. She'd tell me, 'Get a trade behind you. It'll be better for you. Whatever you want to do, do it. Just don't end up in a dead-end job like me.' You can hardly call raising a large family more or less on your own and keeping them fed and watered, clothing them and teaching them life skills 'a dead-end job', but I guess Mum meant the menial sorts of tasks she had taken on over the years in order to provide for us; cleaning and that sort of thing.

So there I was at college, six weeks on, six weeks off. The first six weeks consisted of practical work in an enclosed area the size of a big warehouse that was called the Barn. The space was split into little units known as 'pods' in which small groups worked. We worked on architraves, roof joints, skirting and putting in door linings. It was hard but very basic work for the first six weeks, and I absorbed it quickly. We had to work in pairs so it was inevitable that I was paired with a lad. I was teamed up with a tall lad named Andrew Knott. He was from the Wellesbourne area and I think he later went on to set up his own company. He didn't volunteer to be with me, he was just chosen by the lecturer and it was a task he accepted reluctantly. It was clear from the outset that he felt embarrassed being paired with me, which is probably why he was such a complete knob. Me? I was quite comfortable with it. I wanted to get on with the work – to get on and learn – but all he wanted to do was have a crack with the lads and, naturally, I became the butt of his jokes most of the time; his jokes and others. He used to take the piss out of me as a reaction to the rest of the lads taking the piss out of him for being paired with me. I suppose he had no choice, but he was still a knob.

Since I'd always got on well with lads in the past, this treatment made me feel very uncomfortable to start off with. Andrew felt intimidated, I felt intimidated and the rest of the lads felt intimidated, too – not to say threatened by a female interloper. But I was there and I desperately wanted to learn, to try and achieve something against the odds. It was often tough-going.

To start off with most of the intimidation was verbal which normally didn't bother me. But then the lads started to interfere with my work, especially in the joinery shop. I'd come in to find my work had mysteriously disappeared or had been damaged or even smashed up. I could never prove it was the lads in my class but I had no doubt. It eventually reached the point where I was so alienated by their inane behaviour that I felt like a complete outcast and began to lose my self-confidence and my self-esteem so much so that I decided to give it all up.

One day, I arrived home in tears and ranted on at Mum about how the lads were behaving and how they'd been treating me and how I'd let them get to me. I said to Mum, 'I'm going to jack it in.' Mum told me to sit down and calm down while she made a cup of tea. We then had a long chat during which she said she'd help sort it out. We talked and, as usual, I felt a little better. I was OK. Mum's chat had sorted it all out in my head. I felt so much better and more confident and was ready to go back to college the following week to face the lads again. But, unbeknown to me, Mum hadn't quite finished sorting it. In her wisdom, and without further consultation with me, Mum rang the college and spoke to the head of the course telling him how distressed I was and that the lads were to blame. Apparently Mum finished the conversation with something like 'That is what she's going through and it's not on. Do something about it!'

The first morning back after my chat with Mum, and not realising that she'd contacted the college, I was late arriving for class. I walked into the room, where the head of the course was giving all the lads what seemed to be a stern lecture about unacceptable behaviour. I made my way to a desk and sat down. All I heard was the head of the course say 'It's not on. Anybody found doing it will be off the course immediately. Right? Right!' and with that he turned and stormed out letting the door slam shut behind him. I turned to a couple of the lads near to me, lads I had sort of been getting on with a bit and asked, 'What's going on?' They both stared at me in disbelief and one of them scoffed and replied, 'As if you don't know!' I said, 'What are you on about?' They explained and I was stunned. They'd even believed that I'd deliberately been late into class so that the head could deliver his reprimand to them in my absence. What had Mum done? The fragile bond of friendship I had had with a few of the lads was broken and now I was completely on my own.

In all fairness to my mum, she was just trying to help, but it made things even more difficult for me. It's really nothing more than any loving parent would have done for their child, but it had done me no favours at all. When I arrived home that day, I explained to my mum what had happened and that not a single one of the lads speaking to me. I asked, 'Mum, what did you do that for?' She replied, 'Well, you're not having it. You're not putting up with it.' I said, 'But you've just made things worse!' We talked some more and had a cup of tea and I calmed down and decided to run with it, to cope as best I could and say no more about the matter to Mum.

I survived the silent treatment. The lads sent me to Coventry, never spoke to me, for ages, which wasn't very pleasant, but when they *did* speak to me – or rather *at* me – it was horrible. They were nasty little buggers. They whispered behind my back and called me names like 'slag' for no reason at all. (I wouldn't have minded if I had been a slag. I mean, I would have been having a bloody good time, wouldn't I? But I wasn't.) Little things they said and did wound me up so badly. It was endless so, in the end, I had to hit one of them.

I'm not very proud of that.

I was walking through a long corridor at college that linked the main hall to the engineering block and soon noticed that I was being followed by some of the lads from my course. They began calling me 'slag', and the more they did it, the more I got upset, so much so that within a very short time I was raging inside. I walked further and further down the corridor, and they came closer and closer, continuing their verbal abuse and laughing like the immature little knobs they were. They were still doing it when I stopped, turned round and thumped one of them. I didn't think I'd actually hit him very hard but he fell and knocked himself out on the floor. The lads with him were stunned into silence until one eventually gasped, "Kin 'ell, Trine. What have you done?' I simply replied, 'Anybody else?' Then I turned and walked away. I carried on walking, shaking like a leaf, out of the long corridor and round the corner. I was near to tears, but I wasn't going to let the lads see me and was thinking to myself, 'What have I done now?' I'd completely flipped. I'd hit a lad and knocked him out. Whatever would happen to me now?

The answer to that question was: nothing.

For a long while after the thumping incident the lads in my

class were as right as rain with me. I think I might have earned their respect or perhaps the incident made them realise that they had pushed me too far and that I could – and did – defend myself. Perhaps some of them were genuinely afraid of me. Although the lad I'd thumped said he was going to report me, he never did. I often wonder if he had bowed to peer pressure from the rest of the lads or just decided not to report it because then he'd have to acknowledge publicly that he had been floored by a girl.

Then it all began again ...

And, again, I couldn't handle it. In the end I came home from college in a state of distress once more. I sat down and Mum asked, 'What's up, Trine?' On the brink of tears I replied, 'Mum, I'm going to jack college in. I really don't like it and the lads are being complete arseholes all the time.' As usual, Mum came to my emotional rescue. She put her arms around me and said, 'Don't let 'em win, Trine. Let 'em laugh all they like. You'll be the one laughing when the exams come round and you pass them all and they don't do so well.' I smiled as she patted my shoulder and then walked towards the kitchen to make another cup of tea. Once in the kitchen, Mum repeated her advice. She said, 'Don't let 'em win, Trine, because that's what they want.' Mum certainly convinced me (again) that leaving was the wrong thing to do. That day, I decided that once and for all the lads would not beat me. Mum's advice strengthened my resolve and, from that day on, I never looked back. The lads at college felt threatened by me; that was the key. Being a girl in a man's trade I knew I had to be twice as good as any lad at college and then perhaps they would take me seriously. (Not!) I knew I could do it. Back at Silverstone's, I was working with older, more mature people. The lads at college were just ...

... knobs.

At the end of my third year with Silverstone's I completed my apprenticeship and my CITB course and qualified. (You have no idea how happy it makes me to write that.) Despite all the stuff that I had been through with the lads, I had passed and passed well. My hard work had been rewarded. With Mum's advice ringing in my ears I had soldiered on and succeeded. At the end of the three years' apprenticeship I achieved distinctions and credits in all subjects, something a lot of the lads never came close to achieving. I was really pleased. Naturally, I was distressed to discover that I had done much better than some of the lads. (Of course, I cried for days over that!) Indeed, some of the lads who had given me gyp never even finished the course. (Never mind.)

I qualified at a time when Maggie Thatcher was in power and we could sub-contract to the same company all the time then. (Nowadays you can't; the rules have changed.) Ron Sharples came up to me and said, 'Right, now you've finished your apprenticeship, you've got two options. We can take you on our books or you can go self-employed.' I thought I might have had a bit of time to think about the options, but Ron continued, 'It's your choice, but I would prefer you to go self-employed.' Being self-employed you were paid more per hour but had to do all your own paperwork and tax returns, that sort of stuff. I discovered everybody else was doing it and that if I didn't I'd be the only one that would still be on the books. So I said, 'OK. I'll go self-employed.'

By the time I had completed my apprenticeship I was living with Gully (my future husband). We had bought a house together when I was eighteen. I went home that night and mentioned to him that I was going self-employed. To my surprise, he said he didn't want me to. Having a mortgage was tough going and he thought my being self-employed was a risky business. I said, 'But Ron Sharples hasn't really given me an option. He'll take me on but he prefers his people to be self-employed and that's what I want. I want to go with his preference. He's been good to me. He's had faith in me all along. He gave me the apprenticeship. I'll sub-contract. It's beneficial to us as well. I get paid more per hour.' But Gully really, really didn't want me to go down that route and he became a little angry. I'm not so sure that he meant it as it sounded but he snapped back at me saying something like 'If you get into trouble with your tax, don't come running to me for the money because I won't bail you out!' I was stunned by his reaction and went, 'Oh. Right. Thanks very much!' All the enthusiasm I had had when I walked through the front door had evaporated. I felt gutted. Had Gully no faith in me? Did he really think that I would put myself in such a position if I didn't think I could handle it? I'd just achieved something major. Despite everything I had qualified as a joiner and now ...

Years later, Gully and I had a conversation about this incident. I can't recall the exact circumstances that brought the matter up, but I said to him, 'I'll never forget when you said that because it really hurt me. I'd just achieved so much and yet you had no faith in me going self-employed.' I was stunned when he replied, 'I didn't mean it like that.' Whatever did he mean by that? All these years on and he hadn't meant it like that? What was that all about? Even though he went to great lengths to explain the situation to me – he had loaned some money to someone and that was the last he had seen of it – I still couldn't understand why he hadn't told me earlier. For all that time I thought he didn't trust me; had no faith in me.

That aside, when Gully originally objected to me going self-employed, it was as if he'd punched my lights out. I was furious and very, very upset ... but I went self-employed anyway.

Chapter Six

'Trina Gulliver – Carpenter and Joiner'

Going self-employed is a thrilling experience. You've no one to blame if things go wrong. Despite what Gully had said, I was determined to make a success of my chosen trade, although I have to admit that, even at this stage, the darts were beginning to take hold.

My first sub-contract was with Barry Lightowler, who by then rented the workshop from Ron Sharples at Silverstone's. Barry was one of the guys who helped me through my apprenticeship. I worked for him for a good few years. It was pretty straightforward: I went in to work and Barry told me what he wanted doing. I was provided with a van and was able to use some of the equipment in the workshop, but I had kitted myself out fairly well, too, accumulating tools throughout my apprenticeship and adding to them as I learnt new skills. I was really enjoying it and then the situation changed.

I can't remember exactly what happened, but one day Barry

told me that he had decided not to rent the workshop from Ron Sharples anymore. He said something about it no longer being feasible. Then, having sub-contracted himself to another company, he left ... and that seemed to be that. For a moment, I thought I was out of work. Not a good start!

But I landed on my feet. Ron found someone else to rent the workshop, a company called Delta Joiners, which was run by a man named Jim Caddy. Jim was fair-haired, slim built and walked with a limp. When he was younger, he had spent months and months in hospital suffering with a hip complaint that resulted in the limp. But it wasn't all bad news for Jim because the hospital was where he met his wife, Pat. She nursed him. Jim had a good sense of humour and was a cheeky bugger at times; always taking the micky, but you can rest assured I always gave as good as I received.

I was asked to sub-contract to them. What a relief! All credit to Jim, though. I learnt a lot more working with him than I ever realised. He raised my awareness of the scope of the trade, taught me the secrets; in fact, he taught me more than I ever thought possible and so much about the technical side of the business. Jim had previously worked for a local company called Mazerek but left to set up Delta Joiners taking a guy named Lloyd Stewart with him. Lloyd did his apprenticeship under Jim while he was at Mazerek and joined Jim at Delta as Foreman. Now – if he's reading this – I don't want to make Lloyd blush, but in my opinion he was the best joiner ever; the best I have ever seen. He could make *anything*, absolutely anything. He also had a great sense of humour; comedy skills honed when he was at college where he was apparently the biggest clown. I learnt a great deal from Lloyd, too.

Everything seemed to be working all right but, as my darts began to take over more of my life, I became conscious that giving priority to darts might lead to potential problems in the workplace. You might think that, being self-employed, I could organise my working days and weeks to suit; come and go as I please, have time off, here, there and everywhere without worrying too much about going in the following day if I didn't feel like it. Well, it doesn't work like that – ever. I was sub-contracted to Delta Joiners and still had deadlines and targets to meet.

Jim was well aware that I was playing a lot of darts and we had agreed between us that, as far as possible, I would negotiate Mondays and Fridays off, to fit in with my commitments for the tournaments and exhibitions that I might have booked. However, it was not always possible to sort things out as best suited me and, try as he might, it was sometimes difficult for Jim to juggle the work schedule to accommodate my darts, and, of course, to fit in with whatever arrangements Lloyd wanted. On occasions, it was simply impossible. As a result, I grew a little frustrated and worried about not being able to maintain my commitment to Delta Joiners and my commitment to the sport I loved. As time went on I realised even more that I was being unfair to Jim and Lloyd – and unfair to myself. I'll also admit that there were a couple of other problems.

First, I had begun to find the atmosphere of working in a joiners' shop oppressive and it was affecting my health. I had begun to react to the timber dust by coming out in irritating rashes. What a thing for a professional joiner to admit; that I was allergic to some types of wood! It sounds crazy but it was absolutely true – daft, but true. Second, I was finding the manual work of lifting timber hard to bear. Don't get me wrong. I was fit, strong, and more than capable but I kept asking myself 'Why?' When the timber came in it was in nine-by-threes (nine inches by three inches square), six-metre lengths. Despite the length and the weight, I wasn't afraid to lift and carry the wood. I was doing that all the time. OK, so I struggled a bit with the oak – which was bloody heavy – but I always managed. I think the problems were born out of frustration more than anything else and also – perhaps – because I was a woman. How many women go home at night having spent the day in the heavy atmosphere of a joiner's workshop? Not many, right? Eventually, hardly a day went by when I didn't find myself stopping work, sighing and thinking 'This is all too much'.

Thus, it was inevitable that the day came when I had to make a decision: darts or Delta Joiners. Knowing that in my heart that it was 'no contest', I had a word with Gully. I remember saying to him, 'I'm not particularly happy doing it anymore and it's getting awkward for both me and Jim, what with me having the time off work for my darts so I've decided to go on my own. What do you think?' Gully's reaction was better than I expected. He thought it was a good idea. What helped us both reach agreement was the knowledge that, in addition to my work with Delta Joiners, I had a lot of 'foreigners' work. They're the folks who stop you in the street or ring you up at home on the off-chance and say, 'Hey, you're a chippy. Can you fit us some locks or hang some doors for us?' They were the kinds of jobs I fitted in at weekends or evenings. I'd do a good job and then they'd tell their friends and they'd ring and want work done, too. That side of my business was growing more and more and that was what was needed – work that I could schedule for myself, built round my personal commitment to darts. I did some calculations and convinced Gully that I would be financially sound. So, in double-quick time, Gully and I came to a decision that I would go completely on my own – 'One man – or rather, one woman – and a van'. When I told Jim about my decision he didn't want me to leave, but I said, 'I just think it'll be better for both of us if I leave.' Reluctantly he agreed.

The next task was to find a suitable vehicle so Dad and I went to Rugby and paid about £500 for a blue Peugeot 305 van. No, it wasn't white. I was determined not to be a 'White Van Girl'. A local sign writer emblazoned the legend 'Trina Gulliver – Carpentry and Joinery' and my mobile phone number on both sides and the rear window. I had business cards printed and advertised in local papers, such as the *Southam Advertiser*, to supplement my existing 'foreigners' and within a very short time built up a substantial and loyal customer base.

I had a couple of really excellent jobs at the beginning. Before I left Delta Joiners I had made some oak windows for a guy in Priors Hardwick, which is a village in Warwickshire near Byfield, towards Banbury. He had his own company and lived in a massive house. When the guy saw the windows before they were fitted he told Matt Sharples, who was running the job, how pleased he was with them. Matt then casually replied, 'Yeah, a woman made them,' and the guy went, 'You what?' Matt repeated, 'A woman made them.' The guy said, aghast, 'You're joking!' Matt said, 'Absolutely not.' Apparently, the guy was ecstatic and told Matt, 'I want her to work for me again. I want her to do my games room.' Matt replied, 'Well, I don't know whether she could to be honest because she works for Delta Joiners. I don't know whether she could give you the time.' What Matt didn't know of course was that, since he'd seen me last, I'd finished with Delta Joiners and was now working for myself. Matt contacted me and said, 'He wants you to do his games room.' I replied, 'All right. Sounds great,' and so I sub-contracted to Matt, so I had quite a lot of work from that which started the ball rolling and kept it rolling for a while.

So I did the Games Room. The floor was in ash and, if I remember rightly, there was panelling halfway up the wall as well with a dado rail in beaded oak, what you call 'bead and butt', which meant that it had a beaded pattern down it where it joins together. There was a bench as well to construct and a seating area made entirely of oak – and I made it all. The room also contained a snooker table, a bar area and a huge television, and adjoining that room was one lined with bookshelves which concealed a hidden door which led to a bedroom. I worked there for quite some time.

Then by recommendation I secured a second fix on a barn conversion. A 'second fix' is the detailed stuff which includes the skirting boards, architrave, hanging doors, putting in the frames, laying floors and things like that; the 'first fix' being putting on the roof, putting joists in and so on. I had a couple of lads working for me on that one because it was quite a big project.

So, right from the start, my newly found independence enabled me to plan my working week – and my life – entirely around darts. Yet I was never entirely happy. Eventually, the joinery work began to get in the way. I started doing exhibitions, being paid for throwing my darts, and I loved it and I was gradually falling out of love with my trade. It is amazing how one enthusiasm can take over to more or less the total exclusion of everything else. That's how I was with darts and so it wasn't long before another decision had to be made. Was I ready to go into darts full time? Could I make a living at the sport? I thought so, but what would Gully say?

I decided to find out.

When Gully and I sat down to discuss my transition from carpenter and joiner to full-time darts professional, he listened intently to what I had to say and his response was very positive. He had a secure job as a toolmaker-engineer and I did the sums and we agreed I should go for it. I was already working on sponsorship and was hopeful of securing key support within a short space of time. From that point on Gully was so supportive and he continued to be a big part of my darts career and my greatest fan for a good many years. He helped me to achieve my dream and I'll always be thankful to him for that.

So – decision made – I exchanged the dusty atmosphere of the joinery workshop for the smoky atmosphere of clubs and pubs as I toured Britain and Europe appearing in exhibitions and playing in numerous tournaments in search of world ranking points. These were the first steps towards my ultimate goal: to become the best lady darts player in the world.

But first, it was back to college ...

Chapter Seven

Those who can, Teach

If someone had told me when I was at school that in my early twenties I would be offered a teaching job, I would have laughed in their face and called them insane. At that time, it was as unimaginable as my becoming a nuclear physicist, a top surgeon or the prime minister. I never considered teaching as a career option and there were certainly no outward signs of any particular skills in that direction as I struggled my way through the education system. But that's exactly happened.

Life was good and I was enjoying my home life with Gully, my work and my darts. Then one day I received a telephone call from Mr Kitson, one of the department heads at the Mid-Warwickshire College where I had trained, asking me if I would consider taking on a job as part-time lecturer in a women's carpentry and joinery class that they were running. Mr Kitson had been one of my teachers at the college before he had been promoted to Head of Department.

To say I was surprised by the approach would be an understatement. I smiled to myself. This was a wind-up right? I didn't actually say that. I listened intently to what he had to say and I gradually realised that it was actually a legitimate call. He genuinely wanted me to teach at the college. I dithered a bit before answering him. I think I said something like, 'Oh, I don't know about that'. As I explained, I didn't exactly enjoy my time at college and, to be honest, I wasn't sure whether or not I could do it. It felt strange. Me? A teacher? Get away!

However, Mr Kitson was insistent. He said, 'I wouldn't be asking you if I didn't think you could do it.' He obviously had confidence in me, so why hadn't I confidence in myself? I wasn't normally like this. I'm usually up for a challenge, so why the hesitation? I think it was because I was still a bit shocked at the proposal. I mulled it over in my mind while Mr Kitson carried on talking. Eventually, I mumbled, 'Er, well. I don't know,' or something like that. He then suggested that I try it anyway – no strings attached – and added, 'If you don't like it. That's fine. No harm done.'

I was still a little unsure, but when he told me the going rate of pay – which was *really* good – I decided to give it a go. I'd nothing to lose and everything to gain and the extra money would come in very handy. Mr Kitson told me that my qualification, City & Guilds Advanced Craft, would enable me to teach practical lessons, but not theory. That suited me down to the ground. I think I would have had difficulty theorising, but the practical stuff, well, I would be fine with that. No problem.

When I told Gully he was pleased but a little anxious for me. He knew what a horrible time I had had at college. My friends were thrilled for me and encouraged me to take it all in my stride. I appreciated their support. However, it was easy enough for them to say 'Go on. Do it!' but they weren't the one who was due to stand up in front of a class for the very first time and, potentially, make a complete prat of themselves. That was the bottom line; I was afraid that I would start my lecture and then not be able to explain myself, or my subject, properly or, worse still, open my mouth and for nothing to come out!

On that first day as a part-time lecturer at Mid-Warwickshire College, I was very, very nervous – as nervous as you could get really. Given the subject I was to teach, I wore practical clothes: black trousers, a shirt, and sensible shoes. I arrived some time before my lecture was due to start and met Mr Kitson in his office. He went through the curriculum with me. I was to teach Level 1 of the National Vocational Qualification (NVQ), the system which had replaced the City & Guilds, the course that I had done at college. This included all the basics of woodwork, such as how to use tools, making mortice and tenon joints, dovetail joints, making and fitting door linings and frames, fitting locks and hanging doors; all the skills I had learned during my apprenticeship. During our conversation, Mr Kitson reminded me that he had every faith in my ability and assured me that everything would be OK. Even so, as he accompanied me to the workshop, I still wasn't certain that I could pull it off. Sure, I could make anything from timber and certainly had the necessary skills, but had I the ability to convey my knowledge to other people? Could I explain myself well enough?

Well, I was soon to find out. We left Mr Kitson's office and approached the workshop. He then opened the door and ushered me in. He introduced me to the class of about a dozen women, explained briefly what I was to do and then found himself a seat and left the rest to me. I was shaking and my nerves evidenced themselves when I opened my mouth to speak and this strange, squeaky voice came out. I stopped, cleared my throat, apologised and started again. Mr Kitson stayed with the class for a short while – just to ensure that I was comfortable in my new situation. He then stood up, smiled politely to the class, nodded to me and withdrew. I wanted to say 'Hold on, Mr Kitson. Stay a bit longer', but he'd buggered off to his office just across corridor. I thought, 'If I need him, he's just there.' But I didn't. After he left the workshop, everything was fine.

The women in the class varied in age between twenty and sixty and they were all there to learn; maybe having a woman lecturer helped. As far as I was aware, I was the only female woodworking teacher in the whole college. (There I go again: venturing into a male domain!) Perhaps my presence there even surprised them a little. However, I really enjoyed the experience and I believe my students did, too. Having learnt my trade at college with lads, it was a very pleasant experience to be among responsible and responsive adults.

The highlight of that first day of teaching was the end of it. I was so pleased with the way it had gone and how I'd got through it the way I had. At home I realised that I'd proved myself capable of being a teacher. I said to myself, 'Yes, I can do this. I have done it and quite comfortably, too.' When I first addressed the ladies in the class I had asked them to be totally honest with me and to tell me if I wasn't explaining things properly – which they promised to do. They knew it was my first teaching job and so I had as much to learn as they. I honestly believe that we helped each other through that first year.

The ladies really took to the subject. Woodworking was my job, too, so teaching it became second nature to me. Teaching the practical side of woodwork was just a matter of showing the class how to undertake reasonably simple, yet at the same time quite demanding, tasks. I was thrilled to see them construct small frames, gates and doors using the joints that I had taught them to make.

In accordance with the curriculum, I showed the ladies how things should be done 'by the book', that is, what they would find in a textbook or might be questioned on in an examination. Then I'd say 'But, if you do it this way it's far easier', and show them a faster, alternative, possibly safer, way of achieving the same thing; the practices which were commonly found in the industry; the sort of thing they would do once they were in employment or working at home, but not in front of an examiner. Because I was a woman in a man's trade, especially when it came to lifting things, there were obviously easier ways of doing things physically. Such hints were especially useful in the women's class.

On a few occasions, my pupils would say 'We're going to the pub dinner time for a drink. Do you want to come?' and I occasionally accepted. It was a great opportunity to get to know them better and I took it as a compliment that they had invited me. In fact, at the end of that first year, on my last day of teaching, they took me out to lunch as a 'thank you', which was lovely.

Mr Kitson and the college authorities were so pleased with my first year of teaching that he asked me not only to teach the women's class for a second year but also to take a class of sixteen- and seventeen-year-old lads. I reacted immediately. 'Whoooah!' I said, 'I'm very happy taking the ladies again, but ... No way! No way will I take lads!' I'd had enough of them when they were my classmates. I didn't think I could handle teaching the little buggers. Once again, the college said, 'No. No. Give it a go. If you don't like it just say.' Again, I hesitated but decided to go for it.

I thought I was mad.

It was part-time tutoring again, just every Monday – one-hour lessons – ladies in the mornings, lads in the afternoon. Once again, the women were no problem and they learnt quickly. Having agreed to take on the lads' course, too – well – I suppose I should have been able to predict how that would go. They were cheeky little buggers. I was in my mid twenties and a couple of the lads in the class even asked me out! I had to laugh. I told them, 'Look, I go out with men, not boys.' They were OK. Once they realised that I could do the job and that I knew what I was talking about, they knuckled down. Even so, there was one occasion ...

I recall a particular event that occurred one day in the Barn that consisted of the small, brick-built units within which students had to fit such things as skirting boards, architrave, door linings and doors. As a simulation of the real thing, health and safety regulations were of paramount importance and strictly enforced. However, despite my emphasising the fact that every student and member of staff on site *must* wear hard-hats and toe-tectors, there was this one little bugger who kept taking his hard-hat off every time I turned my back. I told him time and time and time again to put it back on: 'There's a reason for it. Put it back on.' I thought back to my own apprenticeship, when I was in a similar situation. I used to be like him. I couldn't see the purpose of a hard-hat; it was uncomfortable and, in any case, nothing was going to fall on me. It would only happen to someone else. I used to take my hat off, but at the time – just like this lad – I didn't realise how important a hard-hat was until I learnt first hand. I didn't want this lad to wait to have an accident to learn, as I had. I wanted him to learn *now*. I turned round again and his hat was off.

I picked up a bit of two-by-two wood which happened to be within reach and whacked him round the back of the head with it. He held his head in pain and shrieked, 'Ow! That hurt!' I replied, 'See? My point exactly and that's just from there. Imagine something like that falling on you from a great height – a plank of wood, a piece of scaffolding. It would have killed you.' The lad was really upset, hurting and annoyed. 'You can't do that', he wailed, 'I'll report you.' I was ready for him. 'OK,' I replied, 'report me then. Tell the college principal, if you like. I'll just tell them you'd got your hat off and that something fell on you,' adding with an air of confidence, 'Who do you think they'll believe? You? I don't think so. They're not going to believe you, are they?'

So there! Put that ...

Deep down, I was actually thinking 'Chuffin' 'ell Trine. You've really hurt him'. I wanted to say to the lad, 'Please don't say anything. I'll get into so much shit if you do.' Fortunately, the lad believed me and didn't report me to the college authorities. I had convinced him that he was in the wrong and that he was probably on a hiding to nothing if he had complained. I think I was lucky to get away with it. It's certainly something I wouldn't contemplate today in the same situation. The compensation culture would have sent that lad running to a solicitor, hard-hat or no hard-hat. Apart from that one incident over the course of the year, I actually built up a very good rapport with the lads – as I had done a year earlier with the ladies – and earned their respect. I loved the banter.

By agreeing to undertake lecturing work, I had to have Monday off every week. Although this suited me very well, it was beginning to become a bit of a pain for Delta Joiners, the company to whom I was subcontracted at the time. Although I was enjoying the part-time teaching, I was conscious of the fact that I couldn't continue with the lecturing work if by doing so I was letting Delta Joiners down during their busier periods. Being self-employed, I needed to maintain my main employer and not do anything that might jeopardise my position. The money from Delta Joiners was my key income at that time, while the part-time lecturing was a much-welcomed add-on. In addition, from a personal point of view, I was still keen on going completely self-employed. I wanted my own company so I could do the hours that I wanted to do and thereby balance and schedule my work and my darts. So, after the second year, rather reluctantly, I decided to quit the lecturing business.

Despite telling the college that I wouldn't be returning to teaching, I continued to receive contracts from them. Presumably, they were hoping I would change my mind, but I didn't. They even wanted me to go to Hull University and take a teaching course in order that I could qualify to teach theory as well. However, that was impractical for the reasons I've already given.

In any case, I couldn't possibly have done it because Gully had only just gone back to work after a serious illness and I had to keep an eye on him. He was still very doddery and still feeling his way back into work, so I couldn't be away from home for any length of time and a teaching course would have required my staying away. I remember enquiring if I could do the course in Coventry at night school but that wasn't practical. Even so, the college continued to send me contracts to teach practical lessons on a supply basis, which means covering for the appointed lecturer when they report in sick or can't make the class for some reason. The trouble was they would notify me perhaps only a day before they wanted me to teach or, worse still, on the actual day. That was no good to me. I couldn't let Jim at Delta Joiners down and say 'Oh, I'm off tomorrow; I've got a teaching job that pays five times more than you do'. It simply wasn't fair on him. Even though I enjoyed the lecturing, and the money was great, I had to make a decision as to what should stay and what should go. I therefore informed the college that I would no longer be available.

I look back fondly on that period in my life. It certainly built up my self-confidence, which in turn has enabled me to cope with the pressure of on-stage tournaments and noisy crowds. When the time came it helped me to deal confidently with the media as my progress in the darts world gained a higher profile.

Chapter Eight

Devastation

All of my life I've always been – touch wood – fit and healthy. Gully, too, was always very sporty and, above all, super fit. That was one of the things that attracted me to him.

We both trained hard for our sports and worked hard in our day jobs. It never occurred to either of us that things would ever be any different. OK, so our participation in sport might slow down a bit as we headed for retirement or something like that but never in a thousand years could we have foreseen the hammer blow that would be dealt to us which meant that Gully was laid up for nearly three years and brought his career in rugby – the sport he loved – to a crashing halt. Neither before nor since have I experienced such a feeling of complete and utter devastation.

There was no warning.

Gully's illness came out of nowhere, incapacitated him for many months and changed his life completely. He went from being a top local rugby player to a bed-bound invalid in less than two weeks. It was the most dreadful period of our lives. One Saturday he was running around on a rugby pitch, the next he couldn't get out of bed. *He could not get out of bed.* He was so weak and powerless that he couldn't even press the buttons on the remote control to change television channels. Because he was so lethargic he and I assumed he had an extremely bad case of flu. He had all the flu-like symptoms, but everyday he became worse, not better. Whatever I did, whatever remedies I tried, there was never any sign of improvement and Gully, being stubborn and confident that he'd eventually pull through anyway, wouldn't let me call the doctor, no matter what I said.

Then one day, after I'd gone to work, my mum went round the house to visit Gully and check up on his condition. She knew he wasn't very well and just popped in to see if she could help in any way. Mum rang the front door bell and waited. Gully literally had to crawl down the stairs on his hands and knees. Eventually, he was able to open the front door and let Mum in. She immediately saw the state he was in and said, 'Oh Gully. This isn't right. Come on. This is ridiculous. There's something seriously wrong and you've got to get it sorted.' Mum talked to him for a while longer and managed to succeed where I had failed. Gully admitted to her, 'Yeah. Yeah. You're right. It can't go on like this,' and so Mum called the doctor.

The doctor came to the house and examined Gully. As a result, within minutes of his examination, Gully was on his way to Warwick Hospital. There he was subjected to a number of tests and, while I was racing to the hospital to be with him, Gully lay in bed awaiting the outcome. Before I arrived, and without any prior warning or anyone putting him at his ease at all, a doctor walked in, stood by the bed, looked at Gully's notes and came right out with 'Right Mr Gulliver. We've done some tests and the preliminary view is that you've either got multiple sclerosis or Guillain-Barre Syndrome'. Having made that earth-shattering announcement, the doctor mentioned something about 'more tests' then turned and walked away.

Needless to say, by the time I finally walked into the ward, Gully looked absolutely awful. It was as if he'd been struck by a thunderbolt. I stood there aghast as he told me what the doctors had said, and when he ended with 'and then they just left me' I was on the brink of tears. Then Gully lay there saying over and over, 'Oh my God', while I did my best to comfort him. The doctor had disappeared without even explaining to him what Guillain-Barre Syndrome was. Thinking that he might have multiple sclerosis was bad enough but what was Guillain-Barre Syndrome all about? How serious was it? What must have been going through Gully's mind during the two hours we waited for the outcome of the extra tests? He was very, very upset. He just didn't know what was happening to him and nothing I could say or do seemed to help. I felt so helpless.

When Gully first arrived at hospital the doctor noted that he played rugby and thought that his condition might have been caused during a match. During a discussion with the doctor Gully had told him that he had been 'handed off' in a recent game, had been banged in the chest and hurt his back, but then, after further consideration, that possibility was ruled out completely. The doctor then said it was definitely something much more complex – and he was so right. The results from the second lot of tests came through and confirmed without any doubt whatsoever that Gully had Guillain-Barre Syndrome. We learned that it is a cousin of MS, but a recoverable form, named after the Frenchman who diagnosed the condition for the first time years ago. The doctor told us it was an extremely rare condition and that, although the survival rate was high, it had been known to be fatal.

Gully and I were both devastated by the news, but I wanted to know more. I asked, 'Well, what is it?' The doctor explained that it was a disease that attacks and destroys the nerve endings. Basically your body is in self-destruct mode. Bad cells are killing off your good cells. As if things couldn't be any worse, the doctor announced that, because the condition was so rare, they weren't certain themselves how to treat it! Although they were seeking advice and guidance from elsewhere, for the moment they had hardly any information available to them and would just have to do what they could with the little knowledge they had.

The doctors began Gully's treatment by putting him on a dialysis machine and cleaning out his blood to try and boost his system. It seemed to work and, after about a week, he was allowed to go home but by now he was completely bed-bound. He couldn't walk but could use a wheelchair – just about – with the help of Mum or me. Mum, as usual, was such a help to us – God bless her – and as good as gold. She knew I had to be at work so she arranged to visit Gully every day from 8.00 a.m. I had a key cut for her so she was able to let herself in and look after Gully all day; making sure he was OK. Mum lived in the next village, but every day without fail Derek, Mum's husband, used to bring her over to our house. We were so grateful to both of them. At this time I was still working for Barry Lightowler and I used to go home at dinner-time (midday) and otherwise pop in whenever I could.

To start off with, Gully slept in our bed upstairs but spent part of the day downstairs. It took him ages to find his way to the living room. I can see me now every evening giving him a piggy-back up to bed. Yes, it's true. I carried Gully upstairs. OK, so he had lost a good deal of weight, having gone from twelve and a half stone to about ten, but that's still heavy and it was very difficult for me. We used to have conversations as I carried him upstairs. On one occasion, halfway up the stairs Gully said, 'You can't keep doing this all the time, Trina,' and I said to him, 'Just get on. Let me worry about that.' I remember one time when I was on about the thirteenth step and the effort was killing me and he said, 'I'm really sorry. I'm really, really sorry.' and I shouted, 'Will you bloody shut up? I'm concentrating!' He said, 'Oh. Sorry. Sorry!'

I also had to lift Gully in and out of the bath because he couldn't do that for himself either. We had a board that was placed across the bath and the general idea was that he was supposed to sit on the board, swing his legs round into the bath and lower himself in. However, he couldn't lower himself – he had no strength in his arms – so I would stand on the bath and place one foot either side, put my arms under his arms and lower him in. Then, once he'd washed himself, I'd help him out, reversing the procedure and lifting him back on to the board. There was a lot of lifting involved. On one occasion I slipped off the bath, pushed him off the board and landed on top of him, smacking my head on the taps and on the wall as I fell. Fortunately, I was all right.

Gully would never let his mum or my mum help in that way. I can understand why, for a man, he had his pride, but on some occasions they had to insist. While he was so ill he couldn't get out of bed to go to the toilet, so he had to pee in a bottle. It was OK for me to empty it for him but not either of the mums. You know what I mean. He was embarrassed. Who wouldn't be? One day, Gully got into an argument with my mum – well, not an argument as such, more a disagreement – about the bottle. Mum would say 'Look Gully. You've got to let me do it', but he'd refuse, then she'd say 'For Christ's sake give it here! It doesn't matter. It's only pee' and removed the bottle and emptied it. It's a good job Mum had that sort of attitude because, believe it or not, it eventually made Gully feel better about it as well. After all, it *was* only pee!

After a week or so of Gully being home, he showed few signs of significant recovery. He ached and sweated all the time so I gave him lots of hot baths, but that didn't seem to do much good. However, he appeared a little happier in himself and was not in so much pain. Then, just as we thought he was beginning to improve a bit, he had a relapse and had to go back into hospital. The doctors put Gully back on dialysis, his blood was cleaned again and then he was sent back home and the routine began once more. It was good to have him home, but somehow I knew that he'd be back in hospital before long and, sadly, I was right. When Gully had his second relapse, I was called from work.

I had had to go to work and had left Mum at home with Gully, waiting for the doctor to arrive. I couldn't concentrate on my work, worrying about what the doctor might be saying – or doing. Then Mum rang me and said, 'Trine. Gully's got to go back into hospital. The doctor says Gully's not getting any better. He's getting worse again.' I immediately downed tools and jumped into my Capri. I wanted to be there at the hospital and intended to get there as fast as I could, but I found that I couldn't get out of the yard. A large timber delivery was blocking my way. So I sat there and was getting really upset, punching the steering wheel with my fists. From the nearby office window Ron Sharples' wife, Sue, saw me sitting in the car crying and rushed down to find out what the problem was. 'Trina, are you all right?' I replied, 'No Sue, I'm not. Gully's had another relapse.' She said, 'Oh dear. He'll be all right, pet. Don't worry about it,' adding 'if you need anything; anything at all. If you need any money, anything like that, you come and see us. Don't you struggle.' I said, 'Thanks very much.' The delivery lorry then moved away. I thanked Sue again and drove off to Warwick Hospital at top speed.

Sue's gesture was really appreciated. Gully was, of course, having loads of time off work (and he eventually went on to sick pay) and I was still on relatively low money and we were struggling to pay the mortgage. Yet I never had cause to take Sue up on her kind offer. I don't know how, but somehow we managed it.

Gully was in hospital for another week where his blood was cleaned yet again. The doctors were still baffled as to how best to treat his condition. They seemed powerless. A doctor said to me, 'If you come in one day and he's in intensive care don't be alarmed.' I thought, 'Don't be alarmed? Yeah, of course. Right!' I asked why. The doctor replied, 'Because it grows.' I couldn't quite get a grip of that: 'What do you mean?'

He meant that Gully's sickness grew up the body. It had already gone up all the way up from his toes, up his legs to his bladder and all the way up his arms to his neck. (At one point poor Gully developed problems with his bladder so he had to have a catheter fitted. He was in a really, really bad state, bless him.) The medical staff stuck a pin in Gully to see how far it had progressed. They started at the bottom of his arm and then once he could feel it they said, 'Right,' and put a line on him and said 'That's where it is today. That's as far as it's gone.' Then they would try again the next day and say 'It's gone a bit further' and mark that point. The doctors told me, 'It gets really dangerous when it gets to the chest. That's when it can prove fatal.'

I was frightened. Fortunately for Gully, despite affecting his arms, it didn't reach his chest. I have to say that the medical staff kept a really close eye on him and once told me that it had reached the border. That was how close Gully came to dying.

Another doctor told me, 'We can't understand why he keeps having these relapses.' As if I could help! The medical team were also looking to prevent other problems as poor Gully's body was unable to cope with even the smallest additional infection. God knows what might have happened to him if he had contracted something like MRSA! Then, just before we took Gully home again, the doctor, who had been researching Gully's condition via contacts in the USA, said, 'By the way, news from America: the patient must have no hot baths. Nothing hot must touch his skin as it will feed the virus.' Needless to say, I was distressed by that news. I said, 'Shit. That's exactly what we've *been* doing.' The doctor replied, 'Well, please stop it immediately.' So that was it; no hot baths and washing only in warm water. I was thinking 'Right, I've got to stay strong for Gully'. I said to him, 'Come on. We're more than halfway to beating this thing.'

But was that just wishful thinking?

I remember when Gully came home again from hospital. It was a nice sunny day. I pulled the sofa out into the back yard and he sat there taking in the fresh air – but not for long. The simple act of sitting outside with the sun on his face drained him and soon I was pushing the sofa back indoors. Then, after only a couple of weeks back home, or maybe less, Gully had his third relapse.

Back at the Warwick Hospital, Gully underwent dialysis again while the doctors, although knowing the prognosis, continued to puzzle over the cause of his rare condition. Then, one of the doctors revealed that an in-growing toenail might not be helping Gully's recovery process. I hear you say in amazement, 'What the f—?' but it's true. What the doctor meant was that the toenail needed to be removed to prevent it from causing any problems. Gully's condition was delicate enough without any additional difficulties that the in-growing toenail might cause. The doctors' minds were made up and Gully was taken down to theatre and returned minus *two* toenails. Those toenails never returned either. The surgeons completely removed the nails and the nerve endings, so whatever they might have caused was certainly no longer an issue. Well, not for the doctors, but it was still something else we had to deal with and that Gully had to come to terms with. This was on top of the fact that he was still exceedingly weak. He still couldn't feed himself or even grip a sandwich.

More and more, Gully convinced himself that he should give up the fight. His motivation was at rock bottom. He'd say, 'Oh, I'm never going to do it. I'm never going to get better,' and I'd reply, 'You're ill. You're doing well. You just need to put in the effort! Then he'd say, 'But I'm never going to play rugby again. I'm never going to ...' and out of sheer frustration I'd say, 'Well you might not be able to, but if you don't put the effort in now, you're not going to achieve anything.' Every night it seemed I was fighting against both the illness and Gully, but eventually the arguments subsided and we worked hard together towards recovery. Gully had been given exercises to do by the physiotherapist that included pushing his feet and certain exercises for his hands, exercises he *had* to do. He even had pads, which were put under his calves and discharged an electric shock to stimulate his nerves. Every day and every night we worked so very hard, but I have to admit that, at times, neither of us could see any end to it.

Gully was scared to death of losing me. I was nineteen when it all started and he was still in a wheelchair on my twenty-first birthday. A lot of my mates said, 'There're not many people who'd stand by somebody who's so ill. I don't know how you do it.' I did. The answer was simple. I replied, 'I love him. That's it.' And when you love someone, you don't give it a second thought, do you? You'd do anything for someone you love. At the time, although I knew how ill Gully was and I had to keep at him, it was simply the most natural thing to do, but looking back now I think, 'God. Shit.' It was obviously a big effort for him, but it was more about my keeping him positive; that was the thing. I had to be the positive one because he was so negative. Let's face it: we'd all feel the same if we were bed-ridden and in a wheelchair for months on end.

It took him another six months to learn to walk again; the first six months on crutches and then another six months on two sticks, then to one stick and then his splints were sorted out. And it wasn't just his legs. Gully had to keep his appointments at the hospital for physiotherapy to learn to use his fingers again, to learn to hold things.

It was during trips to the hospital that a few brighter spots occurred which even today make me laugh. Well, it wasn't me really; the circumstances were down to my sister Jeanette and my mum. At the time of Gully's illness, Jeanette had two kids and was at home, so she was good enough to take him to the hospital on his appointment days on a number of occasions. Jeannette's just brilliant. She's got a wicked sense of humour and she'd always done her best to lighten things. However, much to her disgust, she was once mistaken by a hospital porter for Gully's mother. Gully was standing on his crutches and the porter came up to him and whispered, 'Does your mother want a hand into the car with you?' Jeannette was out of ear shot and when Gully tried to tell her about it in the car on the way home he nearly peed himself laughing. Jeanette snapped, 'It's a bloody good job you never told me while I was there. I would've knocked that porter out.' She was marvellous with Gully, as indeed were all my family.

When Gully was learning to walk on his crutches Jeannette would be in the garden watching him carefully walking down the side of the house and on to the wide path at the back. Inevitably, but accidentally, one of Gully's crutches sank into the soft soil adjacent to path. Jeanette would then leap forwards and try to catch Gully before he toppled over. She'd make light of it before she picked him up, trying to make him see the funny side, but whether Gully thought the joking very therapeutic at the time I'm not certain. However, I am sure he'd see the funny side of it now and appreciate what Jeanette was trying to do for him.

And then there was Mum. It wasn't as though she had done anything wrong; it was just the way she informed me. When Gully was in hospital there was a big fish tank in the ward and he told us that he found it very relaxing to look at the fish swimming about. I had this great idea that I would buy one for him to enjoy at home so I went out more or less straightaway and bought a big fish tank, had it installed in the house and put loads of fish in it. Job done. When he eventually came home again, Gully was thrilled and it seemed to do him a lot of good. It was very therapeutic.

Then one day Mum phoned me at work. I was in the workshop and ran to the phone thinking the worst. 'What is it?' I asked. Mum replied, 'I think you'd better come home now.' My heart sank and I pictured yet another dash to the hospital. 'Oh God!' I said, 'He's not had another relapse!' There was a pause for just a second, but it might just as well have been a year, before Mum said, 'No, Gully's OK, but the fish tank's burst. You'd better come and get all the fish off the floor.' I said, 'You're joking!' She went, 'No. It just popped. The seal's gone. There's water going everywhere. I've got the fish out and put them in a bucket, but they keep jumping out. Gully's been laughing his head off at me running around the room after these fish.' Relieved that Gully was all right, I made my way home to view the mess. The contents of the fish tank had flooded the living-room floor; water and fish were everywhere. On an ordinary day I would have treated this as some kind of an emergency but somehow, in the light of everything else, it didn't seem that important and we had a bloody good laugh.

During that time I was working lots of extra hours – we had loads of work on – which helped to keep me busy and prevented me from worrying all the time about Gully, but also helped to make ends meet and, most of all, ensure that Gully didn't worry about money. He had enough on his plate. I was going to work at six o'clock in the morning, finishing at seven o'clock at night, going over to the hospital, seeing Gully, going back to work an hour later and then working through till eleven o'clock. I did that week after week but never noticed what it was doing to me or how tired I was every single day. I was totally focused on Gully and didn't notice what it was doing to me.

Driving home one night from the hospital after visiting Gully,

I fell asleep at the wheel. I clipped the kerb and shot across the other side of the road. I awoke as the car hit the kerb and it began bouncing back to the other side of the road. Fortunately for me nothing was coming. I parked up. I was shaking. I could have been killed. Worse still, I could have killed someone else. I said to myself, 'That's it, Trine. Enough's enough. That's it. I'm not doing silly bloody hours anymore.' As a result of that experience I knocked the big overtime on the head. There was no point in my putting myself in danger when Gully needed me so badly. Luckily, even without that extra overtime, we managed.

After many months of treatment we received the good news that, as the condition had never reached Gully's chest, recovery of a sort was eighty per cent certain. However, there was a catch. Thankfully, Gully recovered but unfortunately he had to wear splints for the rest of his life. Because of the damage the condition had caused to his nerves and because he had been in bed for so long, Gully got 'foot dropsy' and from then on had to wear splints, which go underneath his feet and up the back of his calves. It meant that he couldn't lift either of his feet voluntarily backwards so he found walking very difficult. He often tripped, especially when negotiating his way round the house and, regrettably, I wasn't always there to help him back to his feet.

Gully was never again able to play the sport he loved so much – competitive rugby – and that was a bitter blow to him. He had been so fit, hurtling round a rugby pitch and running six miles every other day. I tried to think of a sport he could play with his splints and encouraged him to take up golf. It wasn't until sometime later, strangely enough after he had lost two fingers in an accident with the cross-saw (more of which later) that Gully took to that sport, successfully overcoming both the effect of the splints and the fact that he had problems holding the golf club because he was minus two fingers on his left hand.

But at least the major struggle was finally over. Between two and a half and three years of Gully's life – and mine – had been spent in pain; his physical and mental, mine just mental. At long last the yo-yoing between home and hospital every two weeks or so was over. Gully returned to work at Automotive Products (AP) in Leamington Spa. The company had been very good: they had kept his job open for him. Before he went back I remember Gully saying 'I'm never going to be able to do it. (He was worried about standing in his splints.) They're never going to employ me'. I said, 'They *are* employing you. They've been excellent to us. Anyway, they can't sack you for being disabled.' As soon as I had uttered the word 'disabled' I knew I'd done wrong. It was stupid of me. I shouldn't have used that word. Gully didn't like being classed as disabled even though, technically, he suffers from a limited disability. He could still do a lot of things, including driving, and let's face it, things might have turned out a lot worse.

The actual cause of Gully's severe illness was never diagnosed. However, we had a lot of time to think about it during and afterwards and – although this might be an absolute load of rubbish – we eventually came up with our own theory. One night, a little time before he was taken ill, Gully, my sister Denise, my brother-in-law Ian, my mum and I were returning from a darts match in my Capri. The route involved driving through a ford. Unfortunately, for whatever reason, perhaps because the ford was high or our car was overloaded, the water reached the engine and the car conked out right there in the middle of the river. Gully and Ian leapt out and, in fairly deep water, pushed the car out of the ford on to dry land. It's the only cause we can think of – that somehow Gully caught an infection in his in-growing toenail from the dirty water of the ford, which in turn brought on that dreaded condition, Guillain-Barre Syndrome. To be honest, like the doctors, we simply don't know, but it seemed to coincide with it all.

A few years later Gully was in hospital again, but this time it had nothing whatsoever to do with Guillain-Barre Syndrome, which – touch wood – never returns, although, of course, it had left its permanent mark. On this occasion, just before we were married, Gully and I were working together on some adaptations to our house. He was using one of my saws – a cross-cut saw. I had told him not to use it. I had told him I would do that particular piece of work because that was what I was good at and, apart from that, it was a potentially dangerous piece of equipment in the hands of someone who doesn't know what they're doing. I had said to him, 'Leave it to me.' But, being a stubborn engineer, he said, 'I can do it, easy.' (Most engineers I know think they can do everybody else's job.)

What follows is not for the squeamish.

So, against my wishes, Gully started the saw up and proceeded more or less immediately to pull it across his fingers taking off the top of his wedding ring finger, his middle finger down to just below the bend before the knuckle and nearly taking off his forefinger right by the knuckle. His forefinger was hanging off.

When I saw what had happened I went into hysterics. As he ploughed the saw across his hand I heard him say 'Tch' immediately followed by 'Arrrrgggggh'! It was such a piercing scream, one like I had only ever previously heard in a horror movie. I turned round to see what had happened. I stared for a moment and went 'What the f—?' Gully just stood there staring at his bloody hand. It seemed like there were fingers everywhere. I screamed at him, 'Oh my God! I told you, but you wouldn't fuckin' listen to me,' but more or less immediately my anger turned to concern; concern to sort him out and get him to hospital as soon as I possibly could. Gully was starting to shake.

I'd been told that, when someone has an accident like that, the body releases a natural pain relief into the system so for a little while the person isn't in any pain. I rushed and found the first-aid box and bandaged it all up as best I could. Holding each other, we then ran outside. I unlocked the car and helped Gully into the passenger seat and then I drove off at top speed towards Warwick Hospital. In the rush, although I'd brought them with me, I hadn't wrapped the detached parts of Gully's fingers in anything and so they were lying on the dashboard. He looked at me with tears of pain in his eyes and said, 'I'm really sorry. I'm really, really sorry.' I don't know why I said it but I looked at the bloody digits on the dash and said calmly, 'Gully, your fingernails are filthy.'

When we arrived at Warwick Hospital, Gully was seen by doctors and nursing staff almost immediately but, by that time, the natural painkiller that his body had released had started to wear off and he was shaking almost continuously with the pain. I guessed he was going into shock. The doctors gave him loads of injections and yet Gully cried, 'No! It's not working.' So they gave him something else – morphine or something, I don't know what – and he was high as a kite. A little later, he began to calm down. Shortly afterwards, he was taken down to the operating theatre where, miraculously, the surgeons managed to sew his forefinger back on. Unfortunately, they couldn't do anything with the other two fingers because they were too damaged.

I was in the operating theatre with Gully holding his good hand, while the surgeons worked on his damaged one. I remember Gully said, 'You don't have to stay you know.' But I was going nowhere and replied, 'No, I'm not leaving you. I'm staying right here.' He looked really bad and was clearly still in a state of shock. I knew what he was thinking and then he said, 'How am I going to be able to do my job?' I said, 'You'll be all right. I know you will but ...' I paused for a moment and squeezed his hand and said, 'look, if you can't do it, then you'll just have to try something else. Just don't worry about it. We can always get round it. It's not a problem.'

Fortunately – but that doesn't seem somehow to be the right

word – it was his left hand that Gully had damaged. Even though I say 'fortunately', when you're a toolmaker, damage to either hand poses problems. With most of his fingers on his left hand missing, Gully had to learn to grip things with his thumb and forefinger and that meant that he can't pick up anything very heavy because he has insufficient grip.

Sitting by him in that operating theatre, holding his hand, I had to be strong for him. I had to be strong for both of us. I remember saying to Gully, 'We faced your serious illness together and we got through that. If we can get through that then, by comparison, this is a piece of piss.'

That was my attitude towards it.

Chapter Nine

Serious Beginnings

Even during those troubled times, I still found time for my darts, my enthusiasm for which had been growing for some years. I guess my playing helped take my mind off Gully's condition and helped me relax a little.

Without playing for your county there is no way that any darts player can gain recognition, show what they are worth and have the opportunity to achieve their dream, darts' highest accolade, that of becoming Lakeside World Champion, the major tournament organised by the British Darts Organisation (BDO).

Before standing any chance of being selected to play for your county – in my case Warwickshire – you have to prove yourself in Super League. Usually hosted at pubs and clubs, Super League comprises those darts players who have decided to take a step up out of the local pub leagues and play serious darts. When I first started playing Super League at the age of sixteen for Leamington Sureway in the Warwickshire Ladies' Super League, regular established members included Tina Metcalfe (who became a good friend of mine) and Anna Saunders, both from Leamington Spa and who had played darts for years. In fact, if I recall correctly, Anna had played at a very high level, as a member of a representative England side before the BDO set up the international squads. Then there were two girls from Warwick: Chris Glover and Pat Thornton. All of them helped me along the way and were big influences on me when I first started to play serious darts. Anna doesn't play anymore, while Tina still plays but only at pub level. Pat Thornton still plays alongside me for the Warwickshire County team.

In the late summer of 1987, I was selected to play for Warwickshire Ladies' B team. The news came just a couple of months before my eighteenth birthday and, needless to say, I was absolutely thrilled. Until then I had been in the youth team. Sheila Winterburn (now Alford) was the Warwickshire Ladies' team manager at the time and she was the one who told me. I was chuffed to bits, especially as I think at that time there had been only one other girl before me, Sharon Peasley, who had gone from the youth team into the seniors. Naturally, I told all my family and friends who were all pleased for me. Little did I know that this would be the first major step on the ladder to success that would culminate a few years on with my becoming champion of the world.

My first county match was away against Cleveland. I was drawn to play Sue Baille, a well-respected player and a tough opponent, in the second game. I was very, very nervous. (Remember, I was still comparatively young.) Tina looked after me and gave me a few words of wisdom, basically telling me to play the board not the player and most of all to enjoy the experience. As I thought, it was a really tough game, but I came out the winner two games to one, making three scores of 100, one of 125 and one 121 along the way. I averaged 23.06 per dart that equated to nearly 70 points for every three darts thrown. *Darts World* reported that the Warwickshire Men's B team 'looked nervous and somewhat indecisive from the start'. However, the report stated that the Ladies' B 'showed no such indecision as they cruised to a 5–0 win' – and this is the bit I loved – 'led by sixteen-year-old Trina Jones [as of course I was then] who won the match award in this her debut game'. A win, a crushing defeat of our opponents *and* the match award (awarded to the man and lady with the highest three-dart average) – all this in only my first match *and* the reporter had taken two years off my age!

I followed up my success against Cleveland with another victory over Anne Whitehouse of Northumberland at home in October 1987, playing fifth on that occasion and winning again by a margin of two games to one. My average had fallen to 19.44, but that was still not bad for a B player and, most importantly, I was winning my matches. The next two months saw further victories for me, 2–0 against Carol Flewitt away to Merseyside and 2–0 at home against Durham's Eileen Dinning, during which I scored my first 140 in a county match. However, the New Year initially brought disappointment, as January 1988 saw me lose my first match for the B team.

It was away to Leicestershire. For whatever reason, I was off-form, lost my concentration and fell victim to Louise Carroll by two games to nil. I scored no tons (100 points) or ton-plusses (scores over 100) and threw *thirty* darts in the first game and a massive *forty-two* in the second and still lost! What a dreadful game. I averaged 13.38 per dart; that's just over 30 points per three darts, real pub-level stuff. But it wasn't only me – losing seemed to be catching – as other team members Carol McGovern, Eunice Jones and Tina all suffered defeats at the hands of the Leicestershire Ladies. The only Warwickshire lady to win was Denise Untulis, so overall it was a very poor result for the

Ladies' B, beaten 4–1. Even though I wasn't alone in losing, I have to admit that I feared for my future place in the Ladies' A. I spoke with the men's team manager Dennis Roberts and he just said, 'Forget it.' The team had won the match 8–4 overall anyway. Although nothing more was said, I knew what was expected of me next time. As it was, that defeat against Louise was to be my only defeat during my time in the B team.

And back I came. I think I play better when I'm angry. I was angry with myself for letting the team down against Leicestershire and wanted to show what I was worth. It was Lil Bone of Nottinghamshire who bore the brunt of it when we played that county at home in March 1988. I was put on to play first for the Ladies' B and I beat Lil 2–0, averaging 17.91, hitting two tons and three ton-forties along the way. Now that felt so much better – even though the Ladies' B team was defeated by Nottinghamshire 3–2!

Then, later that same month, Warwickshire were away to Cheshire and I was again playing the first game, this time against Janet Ward. Once again, I was victorious, scoring three tons, one 120, two ton-forties and finishing one match in sixteen darts *and* I took the match award with an average of 23.06 per dart. That represented just under 70 points per three darts thrown and that, even though I say it myself, was class. It was Trina Jones at her very best (for the moment anyway).

My statistics were looking good: played 7, won 6, lost 1, games for 12, against 7, plus two match awards. But I was still stunned when, on 10 April 1988, at the tender age of eighteen, I was promoted to the Warwickshire Ladies' A team – stunned and very proud. I played my first match as a member of the A team away that month to Cumbria at Whitehaven and beat Barbara Lee, an excellent player, 2–1. I shot an average of 20.78 and won the match award. I followed that in May with a 2–1 victory over Nadine Bentley of Lincolnshire in my home debut playing for the

Ladies' A. Playing at number four, I hit a very respectable 24.66 average per dart and, again, took the match award. (Can you see a pattern developing here?) At the time of writing the only other Warwickshire ladies to have achieved match awards on both their B and A debuts have been Sylvia Kimberlee and Carol Weston. So the 1987–88 season, my first playing for the county, ended on a high, but how would I perform during my first full season in the Ladies' A?

I remember looking through *Darts World* in May 1988 and seeing the World Darts Federation (WDF) top-twenty world rankings. England ladies held the top two places with Staffordshire's Sharon Colclough in second place and Surrey's Jayne Kempster at the top. Jayne had climbed from fifth to first place in one season. The power of these two ladies in world darts was reaffirmed in July when the British Darts Organisation published its international rankings which showed Sharon ahead of the pack in the number one position with Jayne in third position, an England one-two only spoilt by Scotland's talented Cathie McCulloch. I wanted to be number one. I knew I could be number one, but that would be for later. Meanwhile, I had the new season with Warwickshire A to look forward to. However, things did not go as smoothly as I'd hoped – well not to begin with anyway.

I started badly, suffering my first defeat as an A team member at home at the hands of Cleveland's Carol Burton. Despite losing 2–0, I still produced the best home team average of the day of 20.04, but I knew I had to do better next time. Despite beating Staffordshire's Linda Mountfield in our next away match in October 1988, I lost again at home the following month against Jeanette McVitie of Merseyside but, again, I turned in the best home average, this time 20.19. I was not happy, not happy at all.

So I turned it on and was undefeated for the rest of the season taking out Durham's Margaret Stewart (away) 2–1, Brenda

Simpson (at home to Derbyshire) 2–0, Humberside's Sue Gilby (away) 2–0, Cheshire's Yvonne Whitley (at home) 2–1, Julie Pattison (at home to Cumbria) 2–1 and, finally, Lincolnshire's Gill Gillett 2–1 in the last match of the season. It is an understatement to say that I finished with a flourish. In the last five games I won no less than *four* match awards. But enough of statistics and personal trumpet-blowing for the moment; let me tell you a little about what it's like to be on the road with the Warwickshire county team.

To begin with, I didn't always travel on the team coach. Sometimes I would, but on other occasions, bearing in mind that I was only eighteen, Mum and Sam (my first step dad) would come up and watch and make sure I was OK. After a while, I felt I'd be OK on my own and so joined the coach. It was then that I experienced real life with the squad. I had no idea ...

In the beginning, my friend and fellow Warwickshire Ladies' A team member, Tina Metcalfe, sort of looked after me. We shared a room together and had what I can only describe as real good sessions at the bar. Oh no, it wasn't all serious play. The trouble was, in the early days I couldn't hold my drink at all. I used to drink halves of Guinness and blackcurrant – always a half. You'd never ever see me with a pint in my hand. No, that's not entirely true. The only time I'd be seen with a pint in my hand was if Tina Metcalfe (who drinks pints) 'accidentally' bought me a pint, too, but even then I'd have a half-pint glass and gradually tip it into there.

I remember once when the team was up in Liverpool playing Merseyside and the girls dared me to down a pint of Guinness and blackcurrant in one. I just went 'No', but they insisted – 'Go on!' For a while I wasn't prepared to do it but then I had an idea. One of our long-serving Warwickshire ladies, named Edie Foster, was quite ill so I said to the girls, 'If you put a bit of money in the middle of the table for Edie, I'll give it a go.' Well, I'd never seen them all move so fast, on or off the oche. I think there was about £60 on the table in the end.

As I was now committed to drink the pint, I tried to prepare myself psychologically for it. The pint was placed in front of me. Instead of saying to myself 'There's no way you can do it because you never drink pints', I told myself, 'It's for a very good cause. It'll help Edie and it'll show them what you're made of.' After all, it was only a pint. A pint was only two halves and I drank halves. I looked at the pint. Some of the Guinness and blackcurrant mixture was dribbling down the side of the glass. They'd certainly made sure the glass was full. All the girls were shouting encouragement and banging on the table. Suddenly, out of the blue, I was ready for it. I grabbed the glass and, to a roar of approval from the girls, brought the pint to my lips and then in one smooth operation put my head back and poured the mixture down my throat.

The last thing I remember was running to the toilet.

In the morning I woke with a headache, feeling as rough as hell. I couldn't remember a thing. I certainly couldn't remember going to bed. How did I get here? Tina must have helped me. I looked across the room. Tina's bed was empty. Then I heard a sound and she emerged from the bathroom. I looked at the clock. I sat on the edge of the bed, tried to stand up, got halfway, wobbled and sat down on the bed again. Tina didn't seem to be herself. Her 'good morning' was more of a grunt than a greeting. Perhaps she felt like I did, hung over from the night before, but then she said to me, 'Trine, you ought to apologise to Dennis' – by whom she meant Dennis Roberts, the men's team manager. I had no idea what Tina was on about. God, what had happened after I'd drunk that pint? I thought for a moment, which in my state seemed like months, and then I simply said, 'Why?' Tina frowned and replied, 'Oh no Trine. Don't tell me you can't remember! Don't say ... Oh no!'

By then I was really worried. What had I done? Fear was setting in. If I'd done something bad to Dennis, it could cost me my place in the team. I looked at Tina and said something like 'Why? I don't ... I...er ...What? I mean ... er ... How did I get to bed? I can't remember. What happened?' Tina was unwilling to make eye contact with me. She had turned slightly away from me and stared out of the window as if she was ashamed to be in my company. All she said was, 'Oh Trine.' I'd obviously done something terribly wrong. I wracked my brains – what was left of them – and tried to remember what I could possibly have done. 'Tina,' I cried, 'What happened? What did I do?' As if she hadn't heard a word I said, Tina continued peering out of the window into the distance and went on, 'He helped you. I was trying to carry you up to the room but you were dead weight. Luckily, Dennis was there. Good old Dennis. He told me to call the lift, which I did, and then he lifted you up and put you over his shoulder.' In my poor addled brain something told me that I remembered a bit about that, but which bit? Tina turned back into the room and continued, 'The lift arrived and we all got in. Then you moaned a lot and threw up all down Dennis's back.' All of a sudden, I sobered up, stood up and stomped around the room with my head in my hands. I cried out, 'YOU ARE JOKING! YOU ARE *JOKING!*' and again, louder and with more passion, 'YOU ARE *JOKING!*' Tina grabbed hold of me, looked me straight in the eyes and said, 'No, Trine. I'm not.'

I sat down. I was shaking. Was it fear, embarrassment or both? (Probably both.) I looked at Tina and said, 'I ...' But nothing else came out except, after a pause, another 'YOU ARE *JOKING!*' Tina walked back towards the window, stared out again, and repeated, 'I'm not. You must apologise to Dennis. Do it now and the worst that could happen is that you'll get the laundry bill for cleaning his jacket.' I gasped and replied, 'Oh my God!' I gathered my thoughts as best I could, as they were all over the place, and went down to breakfast to find Dennis and apologise to him like I had never apologised to anyone ever before.

I rehearsed what I was going to say to Dennis, in my mind, in the corridor and in the lift. When I walked into the breakfast room there he was, sitting at a table. Sheepishly I approached him and as I reached the table I cleared my throat. He looked up. I stopped and stood stock still. Dennis smiled and said, 'Oh. Hi, Trina.' I stood there in front of him very humbled and ashamed. 'Look, Dennis. I'm really, really, really sorry.' (Had I put in enough 'really's in there? I hoped so.) He finished a mouthful of breakfast and in his broad Brummy accent said, 'What for Bab?' and I hung my head and went, 'Because of last night.' Dennis put his knife and fork down and smiled at me and said, 'Oh, forget it. Everyone gets a bit tipsy now and again. Don't worry about it.' 'No,' I said, 'I'm really sorry about your jacket. Thank God it was only your jacket. Please, get it dry cleaned and send me the bill.' The look on his face was one of bewilderment. Dennis said, 'What are you on about Bab?' and I said, 'I was sick all down your back.' The look of bewilderment changed to a huge smile and he said, 'I don't know what you're talking about. Who told you that?' The penny dropped. I mumbled, 'Bloody hell' and then shouted, 'TINA!' and without a further word to Dennis, I rushed upstairs to our room.

But Tina was too good a friend to hit. When I burst into the room, she was already on the bed laughing her head off. At that moment, all my anger and embarrassment evaporated and I fell to the floor in fits of laughter. Eventually, Tina said, 'I thought I'd just wind you up for a bit.' She'd done that all right! 'So I wasn't ill then?' I asked. Tina replied, 'Yes you were ill, very ill, but not down Dennis' back.' I didn't ask for any more details than that and I still don't recall one single moment of that night after I'd downed that pint. Did I drink Guinness and blackcurrant ever again?

What do you think?

Chapter Ten

The Happiest Day of My Life

Shortly after we returned home from Gully's hospitalisation following his accident with my cross-saw, I knew there was something I had to do before he fell apart completely. Life was too short and so I decided that I would ask him to marry me.

Once we'd settled back at home, I ensured that we were nice and comfortable on the sofa in the living room and then I said something like, 'Right. I'm gonna ask you something now and I ain't joking and I won't ask again.' I unintentionally paused for a moment and Gully, realising what I was about to say, said, 'STOP! This ain't right!' and then jumped in with the best of questions, 'Will you marry me?' I felt like crying, but smiled and replied, 'It's taken you long enough to ask me you bastard. YES!' We hugged each other but, bearing in mind that Gully was still high on drugs from the hospital, I told him to ask me again tomorrow, which he did.

Gully and I were married on Saturday, 20 August 1994 at St James's Church, Southam.

The main event was preceded a week before the wedding by my hen night. It must have been a great night, as I remember so little about it. Even talking recently with my friends and family who accompanied and allegedly looked after me on a pub-crawl around Southam revealed few details. However, I do know that my best friend from school days, Helen Hayes (née King), made me a hat with the usual things hanging from it (Tampax, condoms, etc) and that I got terribly pissed.

Gully's stag night happened the week before mine and was along the same lines. I remember Gully telling me that he had asked my nephew Dan (just sixteen at the time) to keep an eye out to ensure that Gully's drinks were not being spiked with spirits. Dan assured Gully that if he thought they had been, he would knock the drinks over and pretend it was an accident. Dan was only sixteen but he had his plan all worked out. What a sensible lad. (Only joking Dan!)

The night before the wedding Helen stayed over with me at Mum and Derek's house in the nearby village of Stockton. I never slept a wink. I was far too excited about my big day and so Helen and I talked and talked. (Helen can talk for England!) She's a brill friend and knows more about me than anyone else does.

Deciding who to have as bridesmaids wasn't a problem. I couldn't decide between them all, so I had the lot. My sister Denise was maid of honour and my sister Jen, my nieces Zoë (my brother Steve's daughter) and Ellie (my brother Andy's daughter) and Helen were bridesmaids. Last, but by no means least, my nephew Luke (my sister Jen's son) was page boy. The bridesmaid's dresses were hired for the occasion while Denise made Zoë's and Ellie's dresses. Denise also made the cravats for the lads.

It was top hat and tails, too. Gully's best man was his best friend from school, Ted Collett. They've known each other most of their lives. The ushers were Gully's brother Andrew and my nephew Dan. He's Denise's lad, but, as I've said before, we've always been more like brother and sister.

I remember when Gully and I went to our families to tell them about our plans to be married. We both wanted top hat and tails and we knew that the majority of the men would be happy with that. However, the one person who we thought would object was Gully's dad, Ron, but we needn't have worried. When we told him, he was so pleased that we were getting married that he said he'd go dressed in a bin liner if that's what we wanted. He was chuffed to bits.

To my surprise, it was my dad, Geoff, who had the problem with wearing top hat and tails. He thought he would look silly in it. However, after convincing him that he would carry it off well – as he was tall – and with the veiled threat that if he didn't wear it, he wouldn't be giving me away, that seemed to do the trick. True enough, on the day, he looked great.

Sadly, a few weeks after our announcement, Gully's dad, Ron, died suddenly of a heart attack. The family was stunned. We could not believe it. I will never forget that phone call from Gully's mum, Rita. She and Louise, Gully's youngest sister (only sixteen), were there at the time Ron had collapsed in his armchair. Gully and I jumped into the car and drove the mile or so up the road to their house. We ran in and tried to resuscitate Ron, but try as we might we were unable to bring him round. That shook Gully big time. It affected him more than people realised. Afterwards, he questioned himself as to whether he did things right when trying to resuscitate his dad. I know that feeling, as the very same thing happened to me when Derek, my stepdad, died. When all your best efforts fail, you feel completely and utterly useless.

The organisation of our wedding day was very much a case of everyone chipping in in one way or another, whether it was financially or by giving their time. I know I drove my sister Denise absolutely potty with it all. Apparently, I talked about nothing else but 'the bloody wedding', as she put it, for week after week after week. I remember one evening when Helen, Denise, Jen and I were sitting in Denise's house with metres of a net material and what seemed like a ton of sugared almonds. We were wrapping a small number of almonds into little pieces of net and tying each one with burgundy ribbon, burgundy being the colour theme for the wedding. The sugared almonds were to be placed on the tables at the reception for the ladies. They were what I believe are called 'wedding favours'. Well, Denise, Jen and Helen were all well pissed off by the end of the evening. Denise said, 'If I ever see another bloody sugar almond ...!' Denise said it, but I'm certain both Jen and Helen were thinking it.

My mum paid for the reception, which was at the Stoneythorpe Hotel in Southam. Earlier in the year, Mum, Derek and Gully had gone to France for the day to buy the wine and champagne for the reception. Margaret Houghton, the manageress and owner of the hotel, had kindly suggested that we did that rather than pay the hotel's wine prices. She was also happy to charge corkage at just £1.50 a bottle, which was brilliant, as most other places were charging a corkage fee of at least £5 and that was if you bought their wine, too. Mum, Denise, Jen and I had worked on and off at the Stoneythorpe Hotel for years and had created a long-term friendship with Margaret and her husband, Bert. They were very good to us. Gully's mum Rita, paid for the wedding cake. It was a very hard day for Rita as Ron wasn't there with her to see their eldest son marry.

My brother Andy had offered to sort out my transport for the day. He had initially booked me a glass, horse-drawn, open carriage. Then he thought better of it after realising that I would be coming from Mum's house, which was actually in Stockton, the next village on. Andy didn't want to risk 'the most beautiful bride in the world' (my words, not his) falling foul of wet weather. It was also a fair distance to travel by carriage. I'd actually told Andy that I'd love to arrive at the church in a Jaguar car. I love Jags and I will have one, one day. (Mind you, I might have to nick it, but there you go!) Andy said he would do what he could, but I never found out what he had done until my special day.

On the day, I was dressed and ready to go. Andy came into the room and announced that the cars had arrived. He watched my face as I walked out of the house and saw not one but two white Rolls-Royces. Wow! Andy turned to me and said, 'Sorry, Bab, but I couldn't get you a Jag, so I thought, "Sod it! It's two Rolls-Royces instead!" They were fabulous and I think I actually enjoyed them more than I would have the Jag. Such luxury!

As the glorious white Rolls-Royce with Dad and me inside pulled up silently and gracefully outside the church, I thought, 'Oh shit!' There were loads of onlookers. Denise and Dad helped me out of the car. My dress was a little tangled as I recall, but they sorted it and then I stood up, took Dad's arm and we walked slowly up to the church door. It was at that point that I really started to feel nervous – and a little sick. I had some photos taken with Dad and with the bridesmaids and then, before I knew it, I was standing in the entrance of the church waiting for the music to start. When it did, Dad patted my hand and said, 'You ready then?' My heart was in my mouth. I turned around to my sister Denise and said, 'Oh 'Nise ...' She said, 'You'll be fine. Go on,' and then pushed me in the back. (Bloody charming, eh?)

It wasn't that I had any doubts about what I was doing. I wanted to marry Gully. I was just so nervous and overawed by the whole thing. Back then, I wasn't used to getting all the attention. I was quite shy in those days but, as you've probably gathered, I'm not quite so shy now!

The service, conducted by Reverend Worrall went without a fault. I remember the vicar saying during the ceremony that Gully and I had already been through so much together with Gully's serious illness that, in comparison, the rest of our lives together should be relatively easy. (Yes, of course.) On seeing the service on video afterwards, I noticed that I was actually rocking back and forth at the altar. I wasn't conscious that I was doing that at the time. It looked as though I was about to pass out but I can assure you that was not the case. I think it was just a 'comfort rock', but on the video it looks quite amusing.

After the service, we all went outside for the photographs in the church grounds. They seemed to take forever. The photographer was very demanding. After what seemed hours, my smile was wearing thin and my back was beginning to ache from all the positions he had me in. 'Ah,' I hear you say, 'I bet that was nothing compared to her wedding night!' How wrong could you be? Read on ...

Everything went well at the reception, too. The chicken meal was lovely and the speeches were very good. Gully was so nervous about doing his speech. He is quite a shy person, but nevertheless he delivered it very well and it was very touching. He thanked me for caring for him when he was seriously ill and, of course, mentioned how sad he was – and of course we all were – that his dad, Ron, never got to see us get married.

Before he delivered his speech, my dad Geoff took his false teeth out. He was so worried that he might spit them out while in mid flow. His speech was short and sweet and emotional. Ted's best man's speech was lovely, too, and he also got quite emotional. Earlier, Gully had asked Ted to retrieve some flowers that we were going to present to our mothers. In doing so, he managed to knock the fire extinguisher off the wall. Luckily for him (and us), it never went off.

The entertainment at the reception was a disco and all the guests seemed to enjoy themselves. It was a great day. Everything had gone according to plan. The weather had stayed fine, although at one point we did think it was going to rain. At the end of the day, after all the excitement, and the fact that I was drinking anything that was put in my hand (mainly wine or champagne), I was a little the worse for wear. I remember Gully not being too happy with me. Fortunately, we were staying that evening at the Stoneythorpe Hotel, so Gully didn't have too much trouble guiding me upstairs. When we finally got to our room, I crashed, fully clothed, on to the bed. Gully had to undress me.

Oh well!

The following day, the new Mr and Mrs Gulliver travelled to Billsley Manor near Stratford-upon-Avon, a very, very posh place where you had to pay a fiver to look at the menu in your room. (That's no joke.) The stay there was Ted's wedding present to us. It was absolutely lovely. The following Tuesday, Gully and I flew out to Malta for our honeymoon. Tina Metcalfe, my Warwickshire darts team mate, and her husband Chris had a three-bedroom flat there in a place called Pretty Bay. It was in a great position – just across the road from the beach. We had been out there before with Tina and Chris, but they had offered the flat to us for our honeymoon. It was their present to us. We were both so grateful to them and everyone who had helped make our wedding and honeymoon days to remember.

I had never been so happy.

Chapter Eleven

The Year of the Cat(rina)

I am certain that all key sportsmen and women can point to one particular year and say, 'During that period everything fell into place. That was when I *knew* I could be a world champion.' For me the 1996–97 darts season was that time.

I did not have my greatest victories on the oche during that period. However, it was the time during which I proved myself on the European darts circuit and began to climb the world rankings. It was also during this time I realised that I could make it as a darts professional and was determined to earn my living from the sport.

Although I was playing really well, there were no outward indications that 1996–97 was going to be a great year. If you looked at the final points table for the World Darts Federation Europe Grand Prix – where points were awarded for success in the numerous open tournaments played across Europe – published in October 1996, I was languishing in joint eleventh place with Pauline Dyer of England and Belgium's Vicky Pruim and was way off the money. Deta Hedman had won the top prize of £600 with a massive 72 points. I had most recently played in the Denmark Open and only made the last sixteen of the Ladies' Singles before losing 3–1 to the world number two, Holland's Francis Hoenselaar, and that was despite averaging 30 points per dart. I had also been a beaten quarter-finalist in the Denmark Ladies' Pairs. My partner was Belgium's Yvette Stevens who, at her own admittance, played absolute crap, so things didn't appear to be looking too good for the coming season.

However, having said that, I had qualified once again for the London play-offs of the WINMAU World Masters Women's World Singles as Warwickshire Ladies' county qualifier and had done reasonably well in the Embassy Gold Cup Ladies' Singles. The WINMAU play-offs and the Gold Cup were held at Trentham Gardens in Stoke. The Gold Cup saw the usual high calibre of lady darts players taking part and nothing could be taken for granted. There were no easy rides in this competition as all the ladies had qualified via the tough county play-offs. I made it to the last eight but then met an on-form Lisa Munt of Surrey who, after a well-balanced tussle of a game, beat me 3–2. I walked away with £250 for making the quarter-finals which, even compared to some ladies' competitions today, was good money.

Around this time, I scored another few points for the ladies by joining a very élite club. Following in the footsteps of two of the best lady players I have ever met – Deta Hedman and Mandy Solomons – I was granted membership of a men's Super League darts team. I had applied to the Warwickshire County Darts Organisation to play for Leamington St Patrick in the Men's Super League and, after due consideration, I was accepted, becoming the first woman ever to be allowed to register in that league. Needless to say, I was thrilled, but it wasn't perhaps the breakthrough that you might think. It certainly did not open the floodgates for all ladies to apply for registration – oh no. In order to prevent an influx of applications from ladies, the league imposed one major qualification; that any lady applying must be in the top twenty rankings in the UK. However, one small step ...

My first opportunity to show the lads what I could do came in a home game against Stratford Yard of Ale. I was drawn against a guy named Nigel Humphries. I scored a maximum 180 in the third leg and beat him 3–2. Shortly afterwards, against the Poldsworth Red Lion, I played Gary Podmore, hit a dozen scores of 100 or more and won by three games to two, achieving a creditable average of 24.22 per dart. Reporter Alan Towe wrote in *Darts World* magazine, 'It appears that Leamington St Patrick's have certainly signed up a winner.' How right you were, Alan. Without wanting to bore anyone, I won my next two matches 3–0 against Brian Nicholls (Birmingham Central) and 3–1 against Graham Fox (Rugby Ansells). Played four, won four. What an excellent start. After just four games, I had chalked up an average of 26.38, which placed me fifty-fifth in the Warwickshire Men's Super League averages, a list that consisted of over 140 male darts players – and me. Even the famous darts Master of Ceremonies, Martin Fitzmaurice, was sitting up and taking notice. He wrote in his column 'Martin's Madhouse' in *Darts World*, 'In a recent Madhouse I mentioned the excellent progress made by Warwickshire's Trina Gulliver in her first year on the European circuit. Warwickshire Men's Super League have now rewarded her by allowing her to play in their league and there is no doubt in my mind that this can only improve and benefit Trina in her future exploits.' Praise indeed and praise that I hoped would encourage me to do well in the WINMAU World Women's Masters in December 1996.

The venue for the World Masters was the Paragon Hotel, in west London. I felt confident and started off really well, beating Australia's Megan Rodgers 3–0 in the group semi-finals, then

103

taking out the USA's Julie Nicholl 3-2 in the group finals. That set me up with a quarter-final match against the brilliant Deta Hedman. I triumphed 3-2 and with Deta's scalp on my belt I felt sure that it would be my year to win the WINMAU for the first time, but it was not to be. I lost to Germany's Heike Ernst 3-1 in the semi-final. I would like to have said that I was beaten by that year's Women's Master but, unfortunately, Heike then went on to lose 3-1 in the final to Scotland's Sharon Douglas.

In addition to tournaments and the Men's Super League, I was also playing for Leamington Sureway Heating in the Ladies' Super League and with the season about half completed I was continuing to show improvement. I led the ranking list with five wins out of five outings with a running average score of 21.36 per dart, my best being a staggering 27.83. I also held the 'Least Dart' leg of fifteen darts. Things were genuinely looking up, yet that first major title eluded me.

Then in March 1997, to put everything into perspective, the final Men's and Ladies' Earnings Rankings for 1996 were published. These were based on the sums won in BDO and World Darts Federation (WDF) tournaments and did not include any income derived from exhibition work. The figures made me wonder what the future really held for me in terms of earning a living from the sport I loved. Essex's Deta Hedman topped the ladies' earnings list with £6,410. Not much you might think. Well, in the previous year Deta had earned only £3,775! Mandy Solomons was listed in second place with £3,900, down from £5,755 the previous year. In fact, only nine women had earned over £1,000. Me? Well, I was way down the table in joint fourteenth place with Sonia Duffy and Pauline Dyer each with massive earnings of £550. In total, only sixteen lady darts players were listed as collecting prize-money of £500 or more in the year compared with nineteen in 1995.

Meanwhile, in the men's listings, England and Warwickshire's

Steve Beaton (the 1996 Embassy World Professional Champion) was top with £37,460 (up from £4,550 in 1995) and Phil Taylor second with £21,425. Phil's earnings were only £1,600 more than the total earned by the top ten women players put together! I hope you might discern a pattern developing here! (I'll have much more to say about ladies' prize money later.)

In February 1997, I travelled to the Sporthal at Delden in The Netherlands to play in the Dutch Open. I was one of a large contingent of British players hoping to make their mark on this major European darts event. However, I knew that the key threat would come from Holland's Francis Hoenselaar, the World number one. She had won the Dutch Open Ladies' Singles for the previous two years. I gave of my best and made the final against Francis but even with an average of 26.39 per dart, Francis was simply too good for me. Her average of 27.60 made all the difference and I lost the final 3–0, while Francis completed a hat-trick of wins. This final place for me in the Dutch Open meant that I moved to the number four spot in the provisional Ladies' International Rankings; not bad considering I'd only started travelling the European circuit the previous summer.

In March 1997, the BDO selected its teams to represent England in the forthcoming British Internationals against Scotland and Wales to be contested in April at the Lakeside Country Club at Frimley Green in Surrey, the so-called Home of Darts. The women's team consisted of Deta Hedman (Essex), Toni Rundle (Cornwall), Mandy Solomons (London), Pauline Dyer (Middlesex), Sue Edwards (London) and me! This wasn't the first time I had played for England. The first time was back in April 1994 and as always I felt proud to put on the England shirt – it never fails to send a shiver down my spine! On the day, the team selected to play comprised Sue Edwards, Pauline Dyer, Mandy Solomons and me.

In the match against Wales, Leanne Maddock beat me. Even though my average was 23.15 per dart, Leanne pulled out all the stops and with an excellent average of 25.91 sent me away with a 3–0 defeat and my tail firmly between my legs. Despite losing my match, England managed to draw 2–2 with the Welsh Ladies.

Against Scotland it was a different story with the England Ladies running out 3–1 winners and me gaining my first international win. Even so, I wasn't playing at my absolute best against Scotland's Lesley Roberts, who I have to say produced an impressive scoring performance against me, averaging 24.33 against mine of 22.10. However, I was better at finishing and secured the match for England 3–0. Unfortunately, my win wasn't enough for the England Ladies to win the international as England's Men had done. We were pipped at the post by the ladies from Wales. Both teams had accrued three points, but Wales had won more 'legs' than us, so they won the title.

You will have noticed that the original team selection for the England Ladies included one of the greatest ever ladies' darts players, Deta Hedman, yet she did not actually play in the international. The reason for this, and it came as a shock not only to ladies darts but to the wider darts community, was that Deta had decided to call it a day and quit the sport. Apparently, Deta had become disillusioned by the poor financial rewards in women's darts. She told friends that she wanted her life to take a new direction away from the darts tournament circuit. Deta had been at the top of ladies darts for more than ten years and had won almost every title ladies darts had to offer. In reporting Deta's decision, *Darts World* said, 'Deta's decision to leave the sport will almost certainly add weight to the campaign to raise the profile and rewards for the top women in darts.'

Yeah, right.

Olly Croft, a Director of the British Darts Organisation (BDO), called Deta's retirement 'one of the biggest disappointments of recent times'. Olly wrote, 'She has been a true world-beater and a credit to women's darts and we shall miss her greatly.' Then he added, 'unless, of course, she can be tempted to return?' It was a great disappointment, Deta was missed and, no, she didn't come back to darts – well, not BDO darts anyway.

Clearly, I was disappointed that Deta had made this decision and I did try to change her mind; a lot of people did. It just didn't seem right to me. She'd been a good friend around the circuit and she'd taught me a great deal. Although she listened to everyone, she went ahead and retired. I remember thinking at the time that there was much more to her retiring than just a lack of decent prize money but I never found out what. Deta is a very private person but certainly spoke her mind and let you know if you ever pissed her off. I think, in addition to the lack of respectable prize money on the ladies' circuit, Deta got fed up with the continual back biting which always seems to accompany anyone who succeeds in darts, or any other sport, where others have failed, or are failing. Like many others, I did ask Deta why she was giving up the sport but I received the same answer as everyone else, 'I'm just fed up with it.' Not for one moment did I ever think of Deta's leaving being of potential benefit to me and my future place in ladies' darts. At the time, all I thought was that Deta was a great loss. However, I later found out, to my surprise, that Deta's premature departure would open a door for me which, if she had remained in the sport, might have remained closed to me for a good number of years.

Although the English men had triumphed in the Internationals it was left to me to fly the flag at the following German Open as one by one the lads fell by the wayside. I was full of confidence as I stepped up to the oche, one of 239 starters, and proceeded to storm through the field of ladies to meet fellow England international and former number one Sharon Colclough in the final. In my semi-final, I had beaten Germany's Tamara Fey who had done me a great favour in the quarter-finals by dispatching the favourite, Francis Hoenselaar. In the other semi-final, Sharon had won through in straight sets against Holland's Kitty van der Vliet, so the stage was set for an all-England showdown.

In the best-of-three-sets final, I went off to a flying start, taking the first set 2–0, but Sharon came back at me to take the second by the same margin. Game on! Sharon then took the first leg of the deciding set in seventeen darts and then, thankfully, missed a match-winning double in the second leg. Encouraged by Sharon's miss, I took the next three legs in 22, 17 and 19 darts to lift the title and over £500 in prize money. My average per dart was 24.20 compared to Sharon's 23.73. The win tasted so good, but more was to come. Wales' great ladies' darts ambassador, Sandra Greatbatch, partnered me in the German Open Ladies' Pairs, which we won in style beating the Belgian pairing of Vicky Pruim and Sandra Pollet 3–0 in the final. However, my greatest moment of the whole tournament, apart from actually winning my first major European title, was when I achieved a 170 game shot in our semi-final against Germany's Enid Fry and Gabi Kassel. (For the uninitiated, this is the highest checkout possible on a standard dartboard with three darts and can only be achieved by hitting two treble twenties and then the bull's-eye to finish; the bull representing double twenty-five, or fifty.)

The next challenge for me was the England National Singles at Hemsby in Norfolk in May. I had another good run in the Ladies' Singles making the final but coming up against my great friend, Cumbria's Crissy Howat. Crissy had won the event two years earlier and was hoping to repeat her success. She had been runner-up last time and really wanted her title back. I played the best I could on the day, averaging over 24 per dart but Crissy's 25.70 and her final three winning legs of 20, 18 and 20 darts outclassed me and I was beaten by three games to one. For all our hard work Crissy collected £350 for winning and I picked up £150 as runner-up, while the Men's winner, London's Andy Hayfield, banked £800 and the runner-up Steve Douglas of Kent received £300. Shortly afterwards, I won through at county level to ensure that I would represent Warwickshire in the Ladies' Singles of the Embassy Gold Cup later that year and I also secured my place with fellow Warwickshire lady Gail Marshall in the final of the Gold Cup Ladies' Pairs.

During June I received my 'call-up' for England duty as a member of the Ladies' team for the World Cup that was to take place in Perth in Australia in early October. In my heart of hearts, I always knew that I had a chance of securing a place in the World Cup team but was never absolutely sure, so when I received the phone call I was chuffed to bits. Gully was there when the call came through and he was over the moon as were the rest of my family whom I telephoned immediately after a celebratory hug with Gully. It was a great responsibility for me, especially as I realised that I had been chosen to replace the 'recently-retired' Deta Hedman. Olly Croft of the BDO wrote,

'Taking [Deta's] place in the England team alongside Mandy Solomons is the exciting Trina Gulliver, who set women's darts alight last season with a winning streak that included three European titles: Swiss Open, German Open and Welsh Open. Trina's success once again epitomises the growth and strength of women's darts and appropriately her first games for England will be in the WDF World Cup XI in Perth, Western Australia, this October. What a baptism into international darts for a player who was virtually unknown outside her county (Warwickshire) a year ago and is now getting ever closer to her ambition to be crowned Women's World No. 1!'

So, no pressure then!

I hadn't realised that Deta's decision to leave the sport would result in such an opportunity, but now I was in the England short squad. No, that has nothing to do with how tall the players are! In the British Internationals, which take place annually around April, the team consists of twelve men and six ladies, but for the World and European cups the squad is reduced to four men and two ladies; thus 'short squad'. I had every intention of holding on to my place, which meant that I would have to impress from day one. My England Ladies' team colleague was London's Mandy Solomons, whom I knew very well from the circuit. I also knew that she would guide me through the World Cup experience.

Being selected to represent my country in Australia gave me an amazing boost and within days of being selected I had won two more major titles, as far as I know a unique double in ladies' darts at that time and one that perhaps still stands to this day. I flew out of England at the beginning of the weekend to Basle to compete in the Ladies' Singles of the Swiss Open. Even though I say it myself, I dominated the ladies' tournament with averages that matched the men's event. I met the Swiss number one, Lisa Huber, in the semi-finals and hit a 29.52 average, which Lisa just couldn't reply to, and I ran out a 4–1 winner. In the final, I met Finland's Tarja Salminen and although my average slipped a little to 27.03 it was still good enough for me to take the match 5–1 and collect the £450 first prize.

There was little time for celebrations, as I had to catch the 6.00 a.m. flight back to Heathrow the following morning and then drive down to Camber Sands in East Sussex in time for the start of the England Open Ladies' Singles. Despite the fact that I had had little sleep, the form I had produced in Switzerland stayed with me as I sailed through the opposition and found myself in the semi-final against Middlesex's Maggie Sutton whom I beat 3–0. My good friend Crissy Howat beat Mandy Solomons 3–2 in her semi so we were on for a repeat of the National Singles final.

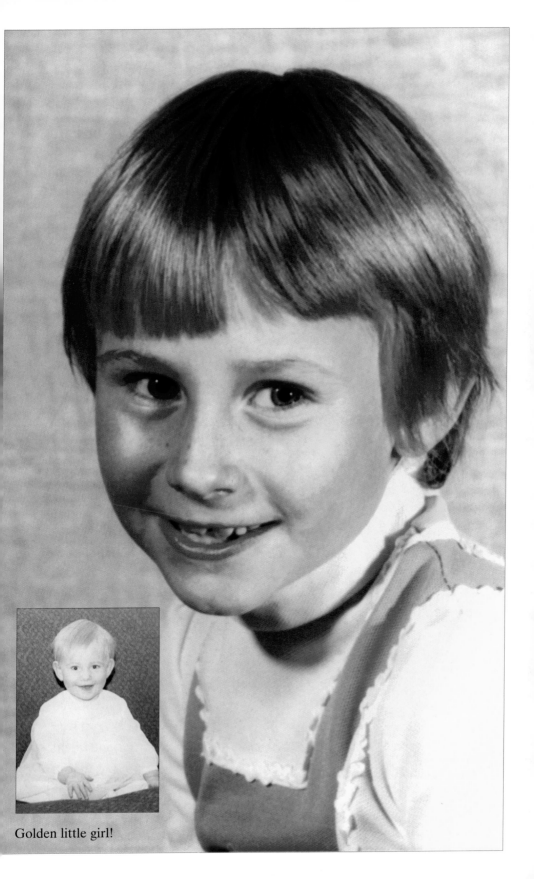

Golden little girl!

Top left: Me and Debbie Jones (*right*), my best friend from Linley Road.

Top right: I *hated* school!

Bottom: My college class – I'd certainly have to get used to being the only girl!

Top: My hero and my rock: my mother Muriel.

Bottom: Rene and Dad.

Top: Julie and Graham Reeves of Reeves Boatbuilders – they have made it possible for me to succeed in darts.

I have proudly represented my country on a number of occasions. Here I am with the team at the 1999 World Cup XII in South Africa (*middle*) and preparing to set off for the 2005 World Cup in Australia (*bottom*).

Top: *Still* the only woman in the picture! I was the first woman ever to compete in the British Pentathlon and finished a respectable twelfth. There's Martin Adams on the end with his winner's trophy.

Bottom: Looks like I'm playing catch-up with the girls at the Norway Open in 2005 – (*from left to right*) Crissy, Clare and Fran.

Top: Receiving my 2002 WINMAU World Masters title from Ian Flack in Bridlington.

Bottom left: The best shot in the west?

Bottom right: Keeping it in the family. I've always enjoyed sharing my success with the people that matter most to me – here are (*from right to left*) my mum, my two great-nieces, Leah and Erin, and my sister Denise.

Although I was showing no signs of fatigue, Crissy went into a two legs to nil lead in next to no time. I was really on the rack and then Crissy missed a double for the match and I sneaked in and took the leg. I took the next two legs as well, maintaining my Swiss Open average of 27-plus per dart to run out the 3–2 winner. Revenge certainly tasted sweet as I picked up the £450 winner's cheque, £750 less than the Men's champion Worcestershire's Andy Smith received, while Crissy picked up £175 as runner-up.

Apart from the unique double win in one weekend, these victories placed me provisionally in number one position in the Ladies' World Rankings for the first time, but could I hold on to that position until the placings were published? It was certainly a rewarding weekend, hectic, but well worth it. In the July *Darts World*, the banner headline read, 'GULLIVER'S TRAVELS – TRINA WINS TWO MAJOR TITLES IN ONE WEEKEND.' Predictably perhaps it would be 'Gulliver's Travels' that I would use as the title of my column in that magazine once I had become World Champion for the first time.

That incredible weekend of darts was followed shortly afterwards by a victory for me in the Ladies' Singles of the Welsh Open at Pontins, in Prestatyn. In the semi-final I beat the previous year's winner, Scotland's Anne Kirk. Mandy Solomons had registered a staggering 31.98 average when beating Cheshire's Jane Stubbs 3–0 in the second semi-final. The scene was set for a tough final. However, I was still in good form and beat Jane by three games to two. I took home a cheque for £500. That was exactly the same amount as Lancashire's Ian Roe won for being runner-up in the men's event, which had been won by Pembrokeshire publican Marshall James who had netted £1,200.

When the inter-county averages were published in July 1997, the top lady was Deta Hedman. This list shows two averages: the average score per dart thrown and the ADAVE (or ADjusted

AVErage) which is the average score plus a bonus point per set won and it dictates your position on the list. I was third in the averages with an average per dart of 22.66 and an ADAVE of 30.66, up from twelfth position the previous year. London's Sue Edwards had an average per dart that was higher than mine (23.15) but she had won fewer sets than I had and so her adjusted average was 29.15 putting her in twelfth place, down from sixth the previous year. Deta had retained her position with an astonishing record of played nine, won nine, an average score per dart thrown of 24.52 and an adjusted average of 33.52. Hampshire's Annie Armour, who had not been placed the previous year, was second having played nine, won eight (Average 23.59; ADAVE 31.59) and I was just behind her having played nine, won eight but with an average per dart of 22.66 and an ADAVE of 30.66. I had improved on last year by nine places, so I was pleased with my progress. However, if the men's and ladies' lists had been combined, only Deta's county average would have qualified her for a place in the men's top 150; in sixtieth place. The top men at that time were, at number one, Hertfordshire's Denis Ovens (Average 29.71; ADAVE 38.71) with Mervyn King (Norfolk) second (Average 30.47; ADAVE 38.47) and Worcestershire's Andy Smith in third place with an average of 28.98 and an ADAVE of 37.98. My average per dart was nearly eight points less than Mervyn's, but I knew I was capable of taking on the men and hitting better averages and was determined to raise my game to their level. Overall, I realised I had done OK and Peter Prestidge, who reported on Warwickshire County darts and Super League matches for *Darts World* magazine seemed to agree.

In the August 1997 issue Peter wrote, 'Individual achievements this year in Warwickshire have been eclipsed by Trina Gulliver who in twelve months has raised her game more than anybody would have thought possible. She set her heart on the 'top spot' in ladies' darts and has worked hard to reach her goal.'

I had indeed worked hard, but then you only ever get out of something what you put in and I was putting in a lot. However, I knew I could do better. That same month the Women's International Rankings were published and I was in third place with 41 points, Deta second on 48 points and Francis top with 53. There was my next target, to become number one and stay there.

Then, strangely, the wins stopped – but only for a while.

During August, I played in the British Classic Darts Championships at the Norbreck Castle Hotel in Blackpool. I lost in the quarter-finals, I forget who to, and picked up a bank-balance busting £35. Then it was on to the Belgium Open where the World's number one lady, Holland's Francis Hoenselaar, showed us all why she was the top lady darts player by winning the Ladies' Singles title with a standard of play and averages that eclipsed most players in the men's section. I came close though. One hundred and eighteen starters were whittled down to two and Francis and I met in the final. Francis had beaten Belgium's Sandra Pollet 3–0 in her semi-final with a 28.90 average per dart and I had won my semi-final 3–0 against Germany's Heike Ernst with a very respectable average of 30.06.

In the final, I played really well and opened up a 3–1 lead in the best-of-seven games with winning legs of 18, 15 and 15 darts. Then Francis went up a gear and clawed her way back to level the match 3–3. In the deciding leg, after five visits to the oche, I only needed 14 to win the game, while Francis required only 20. I should have hit the double seven, but I didn't. I scored too many and 'busted' and then could only stand by and hope that Francis missed her double with three darts. Dream on! Francis hit the winning double ten with her first dart and that was it: game, set and match. But what a game! At one stage, Francis was averaging 36.66 per dart! Her overall average was 30.05, while mine was 26.76. The MC, Martin Fitzmaurice, was really impressed with my performance and I was thrilled when he wrote,

> 'When Deta Hedman retired from playing earlier this year many thought that the great battles between her and Francis Hoenselaar would be a thing of the past. How wrong they were; along comes the lovely Trina Gulliver and the epic matches reappear. A seven-leg thriller with Francis registering 30.05 and the English lady 26.76 in a match that saw Francis finish with 11 tons, 7 x 140s and 1 x 180 and Trina 14 tons, 1 x 140 and two maximums. Absolute class!'

Now there's a man who knows his darts!

Shortly afterwards, I played in the Norway Open. Eurosport televised the event; the first time in darts history that a European Open tournament had been televised across the whole of Europe. The atmosphere was great and was enhanced by the teams of cameramen and lighting crews as they busied themselves round the stage area. I had to be at my best for the cameras but, in the end, I didn't even make the semis, being knocked out in the quarter-finals by Crissy Howat. Francis Hoenselaar had dominated and eventually won that match. She was the one woman I knew I had to beat, and beat consistently, if I was to relieve her of her number one position. In the Norway Open Ladies' Pairs, Sandra Greatbatch and I went one better than I had in the singles making the semi-finals only to be beaten by England's Carol Halden and that ever-present threat, Crissy Howat.

September saw England take on both Northern Ireland and the Republic of Ireland in international matches over one weekend at the Belgrave Sports & Social Club in Tamworth, Staffordshire. Despite being in Staffordshire this lovely venue was in fact the Warwickshire County team's home venue and so I felt that I already had home advantage over my opponents and so it proved. In the first match against Northern Ireland, I played Denise Cassidy. It was a terrific game of darts. Denise and I shared 18 tons. Denise hit a 16-dart leg and I hit 17-darter. I eventually ran out the winner by three games to one. My average was 25.37 compared to Denise's 24.41. The England Ladies won the overall match 5–1.

The following day, against the Republic of Ireland, I was drawn against Catherine Smith who played way below her capabilities. Catherine averaged a poor 14.87 per dart while I achieved 25.47 (for which I won the 'Lady of the Match Award') and eased through the match to win 3–0 and contribute to the England Ladies' team's 6–0 whitewash of the girls from the Republic.

In October 1997, the final World Darts Federation Grand Prix table, based on success around the European darts circuit over the season, was published and showed Francis to be the winner with 60 points, receiving £600, me second on 50 points (£400) and Deta – even though she didn't complete the season – third with 40 points (£200). I was very pleased with my progress, but knew I could do better.

Next up was the Danish Open and, once again, I didn't do as well as I expected, losing in the semi-final to England's Sharon Colclough. Once again, Francis took the spoils, this time denying Sharon another title. I didn't fare much better in the Ladies' Pairs with Carol Halden; in fact, it was worse, as we were knocked out in the quarter-finals. I was really on a low at this time; so close and yet so far and with the World Cup in Australia looming I was afraid that these recent results would affect my form.

Gully, my sister Denise, her partner Ian and my mum all accompanied me to Australia for the World Cup. On the way out, we decided to stop off in Singapore for a couple of days and although we managed to get out and about, visiting, among other places, a crocodile farm – there were some big buggers there I can tell you – two days wasn't enough to do the place justice. We all suffered from jet lag anyway and spent most of the first day asleep.

Most of the players added a week on to their trip to Australia so they could take in the sights while they were there. After all, it's a long way to go for just five days, two of those travelling. Although other players decided to have their week after the World Cup, my family and I decided we would go the previous week. I'd never travelled that far in my life before and knowing what I was like with the journeys for short European routes, I thought it only wise, thinking that it would allow me time both to acclimatise and prepare myself better for the competition.

The venue was a huge sports arena in a massive complex in Perth called The Burslem that included a hotel and casino. To be honest it was too large, swallowed up the players and diluted the atmosphere. However, I'm not saying I didn't enjoy it – well at least the first competition. I started very well in Perth by winning the Ladies' Pacific Masters, beating my England team-mate Mandy Solomons 4–2 in the final. I thought that boded well for both of us in the forthcoming World Cup, but how wrong could I be? Whether it was nerves or not, I couldn't say, but both Mandy and I lost in the quarter-finals.

Wales' Sandra Greatbatch defeated me, but not before a controversial moment that I suppose revealed my inexperience at such auspicious occasions. It was three all in the deciding set and it was – I thought – my turn to throw, so I stepped up to the oche and threw. I didn't realise that on the last leg you had to bull up; that is, both Sandra and I had to throw one dart for nearest the bull to decide who throws first in the deciding leg. However, not realising the proper procedure, I'd gone for treble twenty. It was obvious to everyone that I had, but a Welsh BDO official insisted that that was to be considered my throw for the bullseye. I thought, 'You're joking.' England officials tried to persuade the tournament officials otherwise, pointing out that I didn't realise that I had to throw for the bull's-eye, but all to no avail. Rules were rules and, OK, I was a little green. It was my mistake so I could do no more than go with the official decision. One thing upset me more than the official's unwillingness to concede that I had made an error and let me throw again. Despite Sandra and I having been playing pairs together on a few occasions, she didn't turn round and insist I throw again and ask the officials to give me the benefit of the doubt. I certainly would have done if the boot had been on the other foot, regardless of what the Welsh officials might insist.

I was so upset by the incident that I just couldn't concentrate on the last leg and lost. But I won't take anything away from Sandra. She played some great darts. Sandra came up to me after the match to talk to me but I simply couldn't face her at that point. Anyway, we have since talked about it and she appreciated how hurt I was and how annoyed I was with myself. She was in a difficult situation with the officials insisting that I'd thrown for bull so I had to put the whole thing down to experience. Apart from that incident, Sandra and I get along fine. She won't mind my saying that she's been around for years, is always very competitive and a threat in competitions. Sandra is still an international player and continues to win top tournaments.

After our defeats, Mandy and I could do nothing but sit back and watch New Zealand's Noeline Gear win the Women's Singles with a decisive 4–0 win over Northern Ireland's Denise Cassidy. The Women's World Cup went to America who beat New Zealand by a solitary point. The England Ladies ended up a very disappointing *eighth* in the table. Even the Philippines did better than we did. They came third. Also ahead of us were Northern Ireland, Wales, Australia and Germany. The only consolation for me was that my tournament average of 23.89 topped the women's list. My concern was, once again, whether I could keep my place in the England World Cup squad.

The other consolation was that the Australian people were so friendly. On arrival, we had met a couple called Don and Pat King who were involved with the running of the darts. They really welcomed my family and the England team with open arms. They were great. They even took my family and me to a wildlife park where we were able to see kangaroos, koalas and emus which were absolutely amazing.

At the end of the tournament they invited the England team to their 'shack', a hut next to the sea, for a 'barbie'. They arranged for a bus to pick us up from the hotel. I'd been looking forward to it but wasn't very well on the day. I was really ill. I had drunk too much the night before and had what can only be described as a mighty hangover. The night before had been the farewell banquet, which, up to a point, I had enjoyed immensely. Afterwards, my family, Mandy Solomons and Leanne Maddock decided to go to the casino next door.

I don't think any of us had a gamble but we did go to the bar and watch everything going on around us. Mandy, Leanne and I decided to try a few cocktails. We chose one called an Orgasm, which was made up of Cointreau, Tia Maria and Bailey's – later to be described by Martin Fitzmaurice as a 'Gully Buster'. It was a lovely drink but we accidentally went a little overboard and had far too many. I felt tipsy and Leanne could barely speak a word. We knew that Mandy had had too many when she started speaking in a very squeaky voice. It was hilarious trying to get Leanne into the cab. She was the worst out the three of us by far. She had told us that she was supposed to be going bungee jumping the next morning. What? We all thought – NO CHANCE! Next day, the morning of the BBQ had arrived. I was feeling as sick as a dog but made the BBQ, while Mandy stayed in bed all day and – yes, you've guessed it! – Leanne was up at first light and did her bungee jump. We couldn't bloody believe it.

Even though I reckoned I was the most sober of the three of

us when we left the casino, I seemed to be suffering most in the morning. When the bus picked us up for the BBQ we stopped half way for a drink. Just the thought of it made me feel ill. I thought I was going to pass out so I got off the bus and squatted down on the ground. My theory was that if I did pass out then it wouldn't hurt as much from that height. Martin has a photograph that really tells the story. At the BBQ I topped up. You know – 'hair of the dog'! By the time the bus arrived to take us all back to the hotel, I was feeling OK. That was just as well really as the bus ran out of petrol on the way and we had to wait for someone to go and commandeer enough fuel for us to travel to a petrol station to fill up. However, the good news was that there was enough beer on board to keep us all occupied and amused while we waited.

Eleven days after returning to Britain, I was again back to winning form. I won the Women's British Matchplay at the Haven Seashore holiday village at Great Yarmouth, beating Sandra Greatbatch 3–1 in the final. It was sweet revenge for my defeat at her hands in the quarter-finals of the World Cup. According to the darts press, my victory in the British Matchplay 'rubber-stamped a tremendous season for the lady from Warwickshire', but as you have seen, 1997 had been by no means an easy ride. It had been one hectic and steep learning curve. The Matchplay title was my sixth major tournament win during that year, the others being the German, English, Welsh and Swiss Opens plus the Pacific Masters. I had also been runner-up in the Dutch and Belgian Opens and that put me only two points away from the place I desperately wanted to be: number one in the international ranking tables. The Men's winner had been Essex's Kevin Painter (beating Warwickshire's Steve Beaton in the final 3–0) and it was at this point that Kevin and I joined forces with Martin Fitzmaurice and Kevin's manager

Mel Simpson to feature in a new Darts Roadshow called 'The Beauties and the Beast'.

But as the year drew to a close I gave a couple of performances that I would rather forget but, of course, need to be recorded. In November, the inaugural Lowenbrau International Darts Weekend at the Moat House, in Bournemouth, might have generally been a great success, but not for me. I could and should have done better, but had to be satisfied with being a beaten semi-finalist as England team-mate Mandy Solomons took the glory. Then I was dumped out of the Embassy Gold Cup Ladies' Singles at the Trentham Gardens in Stoke-on-Trent at the quarter-finals stage again, this time by Surrey's Kerry Simmons. I had come so far and done so well in a little over twelve months. Worse was to come. At the WINMAU World Masters in London, I was the number two seed, had made the semis in the previous year and was expecting to do well. *Darts World* described me in the build up as 'England's very own scoring sensation', but I was anything but a 'sensation' that day. I took an early bath, losing in my group final to London's Apylee Jones. I was out of the contest and out of the money. My England colleague Mandy Solomons won the title (beating Wales' Sandra Greatbatch 3–1 in the final) and banked the £1,400 cheque.

The year had been a whirlwind for me. I had achieved so much and won more major tournaments than I could have ever thought possible in such a relatively short space of time. To start with, there was that Ladies number one position. I'd held it provisionally during the year but never permanently. That was my *real* goal for 1998 to achieve that position and keep it. Also, despite the poor prize-money the ladies' game seemed to be on the up with averages continuing to improve, yet little media attention was being given to our game. I wanted to do something about that, too. Of the two I guess I knew which would be the most difficult to achieve.

Throughout 1997 I had maintained a professional attitude to darts and commanded respect from my fellow darts players and vice-versa. I was enjoying life on the oche and, despite being described in *Darts Player 98* magazine as 'a modest, happy-go-lucky character', my opponents knew that whenever I played, I played to win.

Despite a number of setbacks towards the end of 1997, I knew that year had been a turning point in my career. My overall performance convinced me that I should stay with the darts. In any case, I was committed and contracted to the 'Beauties and the Beast' tour.

What *was* I letting myself in for?

Chapter Twelve

Beauties and the Beast

Exhibition work is the life-blood of the professional darts player. Apart from participating in tournaments and chasing ranking points across the world there is the exhibition circuit. When I say 'circuit', it's really a question of going where the bookings take you; one week you might be in Scotland, the next on the south coast of England and the week after that somewhere in the middle.

Unlike other sportsmen and women, all top darts players are accessible. I don't know of any other sport where the fans can get so close to the top names. In fact, I can't think of a sport where one night members of a pub or club darts team are playing a league match and the next a world champion walks through the door, takes on their best players for up to twenty games and afterwards sits down and chats to the fans about anything and everything for as long as they like. Darts has always been the sport of the people and I'm certain that the top professionals want to keep it that way. I certainly do. I love meeting people. I love talking to the fans and, most of all, I like taking on the lads.

The first exhibition I ever did was at Leamington Spa in 1994, the same year in which I was picked to play for England. I was twenty-four. My Warwickshire team-mate, Leamington-based Nick Gedney, was already playing for England's national team. The BDO selectors had picked Nick the previous season and as a spin-off of that he was already doing some exhibitions locally. Nick was a fantastic darts player who threw his darts very straight and at a steady pace. He was about 5 feet 8 inches tall, with dark hair and a moustache and it was Nick who started me on the exhibition trail. When I was selected to play for my country, Nick invited me along to one of his exhibition nights just to see – I thought – what it was all about. I was excited by the prospect and said, 'Oh, all right. That'll be great.' Nick then said, 'You can join in on the night. When I have a break, you can take on a few.' I was temporarily speechless and then said, 'Aw ...' Nick smiled and added, 'I'll bung you a few quid.' 'No, no, no, no,' I replied, 'I don't want anything.' I then agreed and went along to the Warwick Arms in Leamington for my first public exhibition.

Would I enjoy it, or would I make a public exhibition of myself?

When I told Gully he was fine about it. He'd met Nick before and liked him. In fact, he commented how nice it was of Nick to invite me along. Gully came with me as I think he was uncertain as to how these types of event might turn out. We were both as nervous as each other as to how the evening might go. Gully was also a bit wary. He had this special gift of sniffing out trouble five minutes before it was due to start. I swear he had eyes in the back of his head on occasions. If we were out somewhere, he could sense a fight about to start, even though everything seemed normal to me. He would say to me 'It's time to go', or something like that, and we'd go and hear perhaps a day or two afterwards that there'd been a fight shortly after we'd left. But it's very rare indeed to witness fighting at darts events. With all the alcohol around and the media image of darts players being loud, beer-guzzling, fat slobs, you'd think that fights would be the hallmark of darts matches, but no, quite the opposite. The crowds are loud, yes, but rarely disorderly. I think it's because the crowds are self-policing. They love their darts and the last thing they want is to be thrown out of the venue with the risk of being banned for the rest of the season and even told never to return. At the World Championships, for example, if anyone heckles the players on stage while they're throwing and the heckler persists after being warned a couple of times by the MC to keep quiet, it has been known for the whole table to be ejected from the venue and told not to return even if they've tickets for the entire week! Thus the responsibility is on the group to behave.

Graham Sanders was landlord of the Warwick Arms at the time of my first exhibition. I hadn't met Graham before but I found him to be a typical landlord with a great personality and the gift of the gab. Graham was fair haired, about 5 feet 10 inches, a very confident bloke, always smiling. He was a keen darts player and was selected for Warwickshire. He later moved to Kent and played for that county, too. Graham gave me a warm welcome and then Nick briefed me about the format of the night as the customers came in and the crowd grew. In the end, I had nothing to fear. There was no baptism of fire. The atmosphere was great from the start and I had a really good laugh and thoroughly enjoyed the evening. It was like nothing I had experienced before. Of course, I was used to playing Super League, county and tournament darts but this exhibition was something else. I did well, playing four games (two ladies and two men) and won every one. Afterwards Nick tried to pay me for taking part but I refused to take any money from him. One thing I'll say about Nick is that he always encouraged me and this chance to play in an exhibition was just one of the ways he helped me in my career in darts. I'll always be grateful to him because he's always put himself out to help me. Thanks Nick.

Later, I met Mel Simpson, who is the manager of darts professional Kevin Painter. Kev played Essex county darts at the time. Mel was talking to Kevin and me about an idea he had come up with of putting a show together: a road show featuring the two of us playing the darts and the self-styled 'Number One Darts Master of Ceremonies' Martin Fitzmaurice keeping it all together with jokes and banter. It seemed a great idea and an even greater opportunity for me to make my name known to a much wider public. Mel came up with the name for the show, 'Beauties and the Beast'. Kevin is a very attractive man and, in all modesty, I'm not at all bad looking, so we were the 'beauties' and Martin ... well ... Martin's just Martin. It was billed as 'An Evening of Darts and Comedy' and God did we have some laughs – and we played some great darts, too.

I made all the staging for the show, a full stage set-up. At the time, I had a BMW tourer, the car provided for me by Car Consultants, which was like an estate car so I designed the set-up so that it would fit in the back. It all interlocked. Gully drove me to venues and I must admit he was brilliant at packing and unpacking the car. He'd got it off to a fine art: putting everything in, the way it was packed, the way it was put up. It took him less than half an hour to erect the entire set-up. Sometimes, I'd be able to help Gully with the construction, while on other occasions Kev's driver, Fred, would assist.

The show consisted of Kevin and me playing eight players each while Martin kept the whole thing going, mainly by telling his outrageous stories and taking the mick out of Kev and me and our opponents. We had no choice about whom we played as that was all left to the landlord or landlady of the pub or club hosting the show. The names were sometimes picked out of the hat full of selected players, while other pubs had special play-offs before the night to decide who qualified to play us. In other cases, volunteers were asked for on the night. Sometimes, I played against women and Kev played the men, but, again, it was up to the host or hostess. It didn't matter to us.

Every opponent had to fill in a form. It was basically a short biography of each player including their name, age, occupation, claim to fame, favourite sports personality and ambitions. Not only did it help Martin introduce them but it also provided fuel for his sense of humour and most of the time he'd find something to embarrass them with or wind them up about. If he couldn't, then he'd make something up.

Kev and I would play each of our eight opponents one leg of 701, straight in, double finish. The longer game of 701, rather than 301 or 501, always favours the professional darts player as it helps eliminate the odd flash of genius that an opponent might produce in a shorter format. It also guarantees that each opponent spends at least a while up on stage to be cheered on by his or her friends. As these were fun shows, Kev and I used to try and finish our games with trick shots such as finishing a game on two doubles. For example, if I needed 40 points to win, instead of going for double twenty (double top), which is the usual way to go, I'd shoot for double fifteen, double five. The longer format of 701 usually afforded us the time to do this.

I learnt a lot from Kev about how to perform at exhibitions and how to work the crowds. It's not about the professional darts players turning up and hammering people out of sight. It's about entertainment and having a laugh. Mind you, with Martin Fitzmaurice on the mic no one had much choice really. In between games Martin kept the punters entertained, often taking the mick out of someone in the audience, keeping everyone laughing. It wasn't a serious night at all. It was billed as a darts and comedy evening and that's exactly what it was. During the matches, if an opponent were playing badly and, say, scored 26, Martin would call a hundred or even 180. It was all good fun. It really didn't matter if Kev or I won or lost. Entertainment was the key.

At the end of the evening, we'd have a question-and-answer session that was always entertaining. Martin introduced the session and stipulated that Kev and I would answer anything. Ask the question and they would get an honest answer – and they did. I've lost track of the number of times during these sessions when blokes have said, 'I think you're gorgeous. Will you marry me?' Another favourite of the lads is 'Can I have your phone number?' The answer is always a smile and a firm 'No'. Another question that came up regularly on the 'Beauties and the Beast' tour was 'Are you and Kev an item or just good friends?' That was really quite funny, as Martin would have already introduced Gully during the evening as my husband; Martin commenting what an unlucky bugger Gully was, having to put up with me. So you realised that the guy asking the question had either been out in the toilet when this part was mentioned or just saw his question as a wind-up, just to try and cause us a bit of embarrassment. Whatever the question, they all got an answer. It's just knowing how to deal with them; that's the thing. You can either go really red and blush and get embarrassed or give them a real good answer – which we did. On one occasion, someone asked us both, 'How much do you earn?' and, quick as a flash, we both replied, 'Not as much as you' and Martin said, 'Next question.'

Once the questions had dried up, we'd finish the night by thanking people, especially Martin, and then we'd spend some time signing autographs and selling merchandise. Although Martin can be very difficult to work with at times – and that's not just me saying that as Martin will tell you that himself – in my opinion he is the best MC in the business. He can be as miserable as hell all day but put a mic in his hand at an exhibition and his attitude changes. He warms the crowd up before major tournaments, settles them down and makes them laugh. But he's always going on about people, especially top darts players as being 'pop stars'. He'll be talking to a player who holds a strong view about something, which Martin disagrees with, and Martin will say 'Oh you think you're a pop star'. It's his way of saying 'You're getting a little bit above yourself. Don't forget your roots and who helped put you where you are today' – by which he means the BDO. He's always saying it and always, always uses that phrase and yet he can be the biggest pop star ever!

In addition to 'The Beauties and the Beast' show, Mel Simpson tried to arrange it so that both Kev and I had work over and above the show. As soon as the shows' schedule was set, Mel not only promoted it but he also sought bookings for Kev and me, individual exhibition work within the same vicinity. Mel also ensured that Kevin and I did separate exhibitions on different nights so that Martin Fitzmaurice could accompany us both as MC. Actually, until that time, I'd never really done an exhibition on my own but I soon got into it. I remember an exhibition night down at Shepton Mallet in Somerset. I played sixteen lads and I walloped them all. I played really well. I hit *thirteen* maximum 180s and the lads seemed pretty impressed. At the end of the evening, they said to Martin, 'Bring her back sometime because we're gonna get her back.' That was how my solo exhibitions really kicked off. I play lads, girls, whatever. It doesn't bother me who I take on. I was asked recently if there would ever be a chance of my taking on the men's multi-world champion Phil 'The Power' Taylor. My answer was simply 'Bring him on!' I'm ready and, unlike a lot of the male professionals, I won't be phased by him or his incredible record and reputation.

I love playing against the lads. When players waiting to take part against me in an exhibition see me beat their friends with relative ease they sometimes get a little bit embarrassed and some even back out, saying 'I'm not playing *her*'. A few of them try to retrieve their biography sheets, telling Martin 'No. I've changed my mind. I've watched her play. I want my sheet back. I'm not playing'. Because they knew I was a woman, they thought I'd be easy to beat, but once I've proved my point ...

We had so many laughs on the road with 'The Beauties and the Beast' show that it's so difficult to select one favourite incident. However, one specific evening springs to mind. It had little to do with darts but probably more to do with alcohol. 'The Beauties and the Beast' were booked to appear at the Wheatsheaf in Leamington Spa, a pub run by the England Ladies International, Yorkshire's Tammy Montgomery. We'd had a really good night. The fans had been great. Kev and I came out of the pub and were walking across the car park, saying goodbye to everyone. Kev was engaged in a bit of banter with Doreen, Martin's wife, who always drove Martin as he can't drive. Eventually, Kev and I moved away from the vehicle chatting and laughing and then we decided, just like that, to drop our trousers in front of Doreen's car. As the car moved towards the car park entrance with Martin in the passenger seat, Kev and I stepped in front of the car. I turned and dropped my trousers (keeping my thong on) but Kev decided to drop the whole lot. So there we were, bare-arsed, caught in Doreen's car headlights. Doreen swerved round us, sped out of the car park and off down the road. Martin later told us that Doreen had nearly crashed the car because she was crying so much that her eyes had filled with tears of laughter and she could hardly see the road.

Mel continued to find bookings for Kev and me all over the country and I managed to obtain local bookings for myself round the Warwickshire area. Mel also had brewery contacts and we did a number of shows for Punch Taverns. The company sponsored our exhibitions, paying us a fee, so that the cost to the landlord or landlady of the pub was low. That kind of financial backing from organisations like Punch Taverns meant that Mel could book a good number of exhibitions, which kept Kev and me in work for some time.

I learnt so much from being on the road with 'The Beauties and the Beast' show and, if it hadn't been for Mel Simpson and Kevin Painter, I wouldn't have been able to go full time with the darts. However, Mel was setting me up with so many exhibitions that it came to the point where I was burning the candle at both ends. I was earning good money; in fact, enough seriously to consider going professional. In the first year of 'The Beauties and the Beast' we did eighty shows and the money was good. Compared to being on the road, the carpentry was becoming a little tedious and, despite the pressures of exhibition work, throwing a few arrows was a lot easier than throwing timber about so I thought, 'Why not?' If things didn't work out, then I'd always have a trade behind me and could go back to it. So that was another decision made – to do the darts full time. I was determined to make a living out of the sport I loved. The darts work was coming in and was taking over my life. I was on the exhibition circuit and, slowly but surely, establishing my reputation nationally. Alongside the darts, my carpentry business was going really well but between the two there was no contest.

I was determined to make it as a full-time professional darts player.

Chapter Thirteen

Where Would I be Without Them?

There have been a few catty letters appearing in the pages of *Darts World* about how only a handful of professional lady darts players are winning all the major titles and how things should be changed to allow more women a chance of taking some of the spoils. I have more to say about this, but let me first get something absolutely straight.

It has taken me a long, long time and I've worked very, *very* hard to be where I am today – the number one lady darts player on the planet and seven-times Lakeside World Professional Ladies' Darts Champion. Without the loving support of Gully and my family and friends I would never have made it; never achieved my dream of winning the World Women's Professional Darts Championship and then winning it again and again and again and ...

There is nothing easy about the world of professional darts, especially the ladies' game, as there is far less prize money and fewer major competitions for us compared with the men. Like all my fellow professionals, I have to pursue ranking points over many hundreds – no, thousands – of miles, by car, by plane and by boat from my home in Oxfordshire to anywhere in the world. It is very tiring work, moving from place to place, country to country; living out of a suitcase and playing darts in venues that range from dingy smoked-filled club rooms in dingy cities to the luxury of the Lakeside Complex nestled in the green Surrey countryside. It can also be extremely expensive. I found out something very quickly ...

You cannot succeed in this business without sponsors.

I want to tell you about all those people who have helped my career and the time and effort I initially had to put in to secure their sponsorship and the good fortune I had along the way. It was never going to be easy. I knew that. I prepared myself for out-and-out failure and, to begin with, I experienced just that. However, I was determined to find them and find them I did. Before I succeeded, though, I first went on the circuit and tried to afford it on my own ... well with my mum in tow.

I first decided to do the European darts circuit in 1995 and travel out to where the ranking points were to be fought for. My first major event was the Swiss Open in Basle. My mum had not long lost her third husband Derek and she needed something to occupy her mind, so I invited her to travel to Switzerland to support me. To be truthful, I needed somebody for company because it was a new experience and I didn't want to travel alone. I didn't know what to expect.

The venue was huge; like a huge concert hall and it all felt a bit strange. I think I was overwhelmed by the whole idea of competing on the international circuit but, fortunately for me, Deta Hedman was there, too. I had admired Deta for a long time and so was thrilled when she took me under her wing and guided this nervous 'new girl' through the procedures and processes.

They seemed to vary from competition to competition, even something simple, such as whether or not you had to be at a certain place at a certain time or just wait for your name to be called. It can all seem a bit confusing and it was, but Deta helped sort me out. I'd say 'What do I do now? Do we wait for our names to be called out because that's how we usually do it in England?' and Deta would say 'No, you're in so-and-so group, so go and watch your board'. Then she'd come up with some finer points of detail, such as 'Watch out for the sevens and the fours. When they write them up here they look very similar'. She made me feel at my ease and I will always be grateful to her for seeing me through my first international competition.

I didn't do too badly for my initial outing. I fought through to the quarter-finals in the Women's Singles so I was pleased with myself. For the Women's Pairs I was looking for a partner, so the MC, Martin Fitzmaurice, paired me with a Danish player, Gerda Stoddard, and we ended up winning the event! I was gob-smacked – and what a great start to my career in world darts! Despite my success at the first attempt, I returned from Basle out of pocket. It had been a very expensive trip. I had paid for myself to go to that event and the prize money didn't even cover my expenses. If I was to progress professionally at all, I needed to travel to accrue the ranking points, but I couldn't do it if every trip was going to cost me money. I desperately needed a sponsor.

Although the money was a bit tight, I continued to win competitions – or come close – and it was during this time that I began writing to potential sponsors. What a job that was! I sent out hundreds of letters, received few responses and all of those said 'No'. What was it with those people who didn't even bother to reply? Surely it's only common courtesy to respond? But then I suppose they receive loads of requests for this or that and, being busy folks, just consigned my letter to the bin. I was really frustrated. There I was with enough talent, I reckoned, to make it to the top in ladies' darts, yet no one was interested in investing in me. For weeks on end I kept writing the letters and still nothing. The weeks turned into months and I became disheartened with the whole thing. I was very despondent and I felt that I couldn't write another letter. Luckily, my heart was still in my darts and I continued to play well but I was desperate for someone to come on board and back me.

In what wasn't even quite a year I'd gone from nowhere in the world of ladies' darts to number ten in the rankings. It had been very hard and expensive work picking up points here and there, but I was using up all mine and Gully's savings to do it. As usual, Gully was very, very supportive and then the crunch point came. I was unsure whether or not I would be able to do the circuit for the following year. Expenses were rising and our funds were depleted. OK, so we had about a couple of grand in an 'emergency fund' but we didn't want to break into that. My mum, who had travelled with me, had also spent most of her savings helping me pursue my dream. There seemed no alternative but to give up my quest and go back to joinery and restrict my darts to playing for my county. My dream, it seemed, would not be achieved.

However, just as I was reaching the end of my tether and on the brink of giving up on a career in international darts, fate took a hand.

I had known Graham Reeves by sight for a number of years. He ran a local company called Reeves Boatbuilders and had a passing interest in local darts. One Friday evening, by chance, we were both attending a darts presentation in Southam and we got talking generally about the game and then he asked me how I was doing. Of course, I went right into it, telling him how well I was doing, where I'd been playing, where I was in the rankings and so on and he appeared to be quite impressed. He said, 'Hey. That's really good.' But I then said, 'Yeah, but it looks as though I might have to jack it in. It's becoming too expensive and I've used all my savings up and ...' He came right back at me and said, 'Trina, you can't do that. You're doing so well.' I said, 'But I can't really afford to do it anymore. If only I—'

Graham interrupted me by touching my arm. 'Hold on,' he said and excused himself for a moment. He walked across the room and chatted with a friend of his, Johnny King, who had a paint-spraying business in the town.

Before I knew it Graham was back at my side. 'Sorry about that,' he said, 'Right then. What's your next tournament?' I replied, 'The Swiss Open, I think.' 'So how much will that cost you?' he asked. From off the top of my head I replied, 'Rough guess: about three hundred and fifty quid for flight and accommodation.' As quick as a flash, Graham said, 'Right. Me and Johnny'll do it.' I was flabbergasted. My jaw nearly dropped to the floor but I managed to say 'What do you mean?' Graham said, 'I've just had a word with Johnny King and he and I have agreed to pay for you to go to the Swiss Open.' I said, 'You're joking!' He smiled broadly and replied, 'No we're not. We'll do it. We'll cover your costs.' I went 'That's brilliant! Thanks.' 'Come to the office on Monday,' said Graham, and we'll have a chat.' Still in a state of euphoria, I simply murmured, 'OK. Thanks.'

Needless to say, I was really chuffed that someone had faith in me. We met briefly on the Monday and Graham agreed to cover my expenses and I agreed to meet with him again upon my return from Switzerland.

When I came back from Switzerland I met Graham at his yard to update him and to thank him for his support. He asked me how I'd done. I told him and he invited me into his office. I sat down not knowing what was coming next. 'So,' said Graham, 'How much did it cost you to do the circuit last year?' The question took me a little by surprise. I thought about it for a short while and replied, 'I suppose you're talking about three thousand pounds really for the amount of tournaments that I did. I could obviously do more if I went further afield but mainly the European tour, just doing Europe around three thousand and then spending money on top of that.' 'Right,' said Graham, 'If you had sponsorship that covered your expenses, how do you think you'll do in the next year? Do you think you could be number one in the world?' I smiled and said confidently, 'Yeah, without a doubt.' He seemed a bit surprised and perhaps even a little unsettled by my reply and asked, 'Do you really?' and I said, 'Yeah. I do. I've gone from nowhere to number ten in the world in one season. I can be number one and I'll do it within the next year.' Graham leant forward and said, 'Trina, I like your style.'

Unbeknown to me Graham had spoken with his wife Julie and his brothers David and Trevor and what he said next was to change my life. 'Right,' said Graham, 'Julie, David, Trevor and I have had a word and we're going to pay for you to do the circuit for a year.' I was ... Well, I was ... I put my hands to my mouth in disbelief and exclaimed, 'You're joking!' 'No,' said Graham, 'we'll sponsor you to cover your expenses for the next season.' I could hardly believe what I was hearing. 'Well, what do you want me to do? Do you want me to put your name on my shirt?' Graham laughed and replied, 'You can if you want but—'

I went on, 'Well you've got to get something out of it. I mean you can't back me and expect nothing in return. I mean, surely it doesn't work that way. Do you want a percentage of my winnings?' He simply said, 'No.' I said, 'You're joking!' He said, 'No. I'm serious. We want to back you.' I said, 'Wicked! That's brilliant. I'll be number one, I guarantee!' Graham smiled again and said, 'It doesn't matter if you don't. Just go out there and do your best.' All I could do was repeat, 'That's brilliant,' adding 'absolutely brilliant.'

That was a real life-changing moment.

Working with Graham and Julie was so relaxed. As far as I can recall, it's all been done on trust, nothing formally in writing. We've never had a written schedule detailing where I'm going or what I'm going to do. I say to them 'Is it OK if I go to so-and-so?' and they reply 'Yeah. Fine. How much is that? Do you want a cheque?' and I say 'Yes please'. They've really never wanted anything from me in return. However, I have occasionally said to them that I'd go along to boat shows with them and they've said, 'OK, that'd be great', only for me to ask, 'When is it?' and find out that, time and time again, the shows are on a bank holiday, when I'm playing a major tournament either at home or abroad. For example, the August Bank Holiday always clashes with the Denmark Open. I'll say 'Oh that's OK. I'll miss the Denmark Open', and they'll say 'Oh no you won't. You go to that'. They've always put my needs first and have been really, really good ... superb.

What more can I say about Reeves Boatbuilders? Graham and Julie gave me the opportunity to fulfil a dream and I wasn't going to let them down. Less than one year later I was number one. To celebrate being on top of the world, I had a party at the Stoneythorpe Hotel in Southam. Graham and Julie were so chuffed for me. They've been absolutely brilliant – just fantastic – and they're still with me today and remain my key sponsors. I really do find it very difficult to put into words what their sponsorship has meant to me. I owe them so much. I remember Graham saying to me, 'You don't sell me any boats, but we like our name associated with you. We enjoy doing it. We love being part of your success'. My 'thank-you' to Graham and Julie for supporting me and my career in top-flight darts is that every year I treat them and a couple of guests to the World Finals at Lakeside and fortunately for me – and for them – I've produced the goods seven years out of seven – so far. If it weren't for them, I'd probably ...

It just doesn't bear thinking about.

Although Graham and Julie are my main sponsors, I have managed over the years to secure backing from other companies.

As soon as Reeves Boatbuilders began to sponsor me I seemed to attract interest from others. I'll talk about them all here and hope that I don't miss anyone out! They have all helped me on my way at different times and, if it weren't for them, things would have been very different.

Obviously, travelling takes up a great deal of my time and so anyone who is on the road for so long must have a decent car otherwise you can arrive at venues tired and out of sorts. Fortunately, in 1998, roughly two years after Reeves decided to back me, Car Consultants, new and used car dealers of Ufton (just outside Southam), came up trumps and provided me with a BMW 318 tourer. I was absolutely thrilled with it and I even had a photo of me with the car featured in *Darts World* magazine.

I was put in touch with the company by Gully's uncle, Jeff Jenkins, and he said to me, 'Why don't you have a word with the boss of Car Consultants, Richard Wright? He might be interested.' I said, 'OK. I'll do that.' And a few days later I met with Richard, told him what I was all about and how well I was doing in the sport of darts and then said, 'I'm looking for a car because I'm doing so many miles travelling to and from tournaments and exhibitions and things like that. It would be nice to have a sponsored car.' After what was a fairly short conversation, Richard said, 'Yes. We can do something for you.' There and then, Richard decided to back me by providing me with a car. Like Reeves Boatbuilders, Car Consultants is another local company that has supported me for many years. My second car from them was a Mitsubishi Carisma. When Car Consultants gave me that car, I treated myself to a personalised number plate G5 GUL. Today, I'm on my third car from them, a very nice Nissan Primera 1.8.

As a result of my working with the top darts player Kevin Painter and his manager, Mel Simpson, I received further sponsorship from McCourt Meats, a butchery company based in March in Cambridgeshire. The deal was that I would receive a fee per year plus bonuses depending on how well I did in tournaments from the semi-finals onwards. Mel had secured sponsorship for Kevin and when we went on the road together with Martin Fitzmaurice on the 'Beauties and the Beast' exhibition tour, Mel gained some sponsorship from the company for me, too. All I had to do was wear the McCourt Meats name on my shirt during exhibitions and tournaments. So my shirt was becoming a little cluttered with all the sponsors, Reeves having agreed that Car Consultants could be on my shirt – where I was allowed more than one sponsor to be shown – provided that Car Consultants allowed Reeves Boatbuilders to be on the car. It sounds complicated, but it wasn't really. I am really grateful to Mel and Kevin for the help they have given me in my career. Mel produced lots of exhibition work for both Kevin and me and, as for Kevin, well I learnt a lot from him about how to perform at exhibitions. As you might imagine, it's so very different to playing in serious tournaments.

Until 1998 I had had to find my own sponsors with little or no help from anyone else, but now with sponsors on board I was feeling great and a lot of financial worries had been lifted from my shoulders. Imagine my surprise then when I received an approach from the world famous WINMAU Dartboard Company which, at that time, was based in Haverhill, in Suffolk. The approach came directly from the top man, Frank Bilotta, the managing director. I met Frank and we deliberated over a number of issues and came up with an agreement that we were both happy with: a one-year contract in the first instance to see how things went. The basis of the contract was that I received a set amount of money in sponsorship per year, plus royalties on my 'Trina Gulliver' darts. In addition, if I reached the final of any tournament that was listed on our agreed schedule of events, I would receive a bonus.

The following year (1999), as my initial contract came to an end, Gary Cartwright came on board as marketing manager of WINMAU. He and the company had been pleased with my progress, the way I had represented the company and the way I had conducted myself and they wanted to extend my contract for another year. However, the company was about to release a three-year catalogue that included the Trina Gulliver darts and I thought it was only fair that, if they wanted the rights to my darts for three years, they should sponsor me for three years. Gary agreed and WINMAU and I have had three-year contracts ever since which have worked really, really well. Eight years on, and WINMAU and I are still together. It's a great working relationship that has gone from strength to strength. My winning the World Masters, which the company sponsors, five times and of course my seven world titles has helped cement our professional relationship. WINMAU has been very good to me over the years and I feel very comfortable with them. There's a very relaxed atmosphere about it all and, when Ian Flack took over from Gary as marketing manager, things just got even better. Ian and I have become great friends. After the move of WINMAU to Bridgend, in Mid Glamorgan, and with people like Steph Klinkenbergh, who used to work at the former head office at Haverhill, and subsequently other super staff to help and support me, it's become a fabulous working experience.

Another sponsor I have is Westpoint Shirts, a company based in Bolton in Lancashire that is run by Vera and Peter Lingard. They've been sponsoring my shirts for well over five years. When I was working with Kevin Painter, they used to supply his shirts and so they began providing mine, which initially meant just a black one and a red one with my name printed on them. Vera and Peter are great and for a while now Vera has gone out and looked for material especially for me. She knows I love my shirts and she always finds really nice stuff. She seems to know by instinct what I like. In fact, thanks to Vera and Peter, I've built up a bit of a reputation for my shirts. This is partly due to the fact that they are exclusive to me. Whatever material Vera finds and uses for me, she won't use to make shirts for anybody else. Since 2000–01, Vera and Peter have provided my shirts as part of a sponsorship deal. They do a great job for me and I feel comfortable and confident when I wear their shirts in competitions – and that's so important.

Another of my sponsors is The Sign Depot run by Tom Doyle which is based in Leamington Spa. Tom provides the artwork for my car and I have to say it looks very impressive. In return, he puts his company's name on the car, too. So that costs me nothing, my car looks great and they have a free advert that travels thousands of miles a year all over the country advertising their business.

One short-term sponsor I had was Britannia Kitchen Supplies of Southam. Before I approached them, I bought a display unit off an old friend in the carpentry trade, a bloke named Billy Moulding who was a right character. He was involved with the company SDL Displays who made display boards. I needed a couple for my exhibitions, so I went down to see him, grovelled a bit and smiled a lot and asked if he had a couple to spare and – bless him – he gave me them. In return for his providing them, I did a bit of advertising for his company on the stage set-up.

A little later, because the edges of the boards were very lightweight and needed altering, I took them to Britannia Kitchen Suppliers and said to the bloke there: 'I want these alterations done to the edges. Your work is all aluminium. Would you be able to do it for me?' The smile must have worked because he said, 'No problem. Just tell us what you want.' Of course, I then asked, 'How much is that going to cost?' and, strange for a kitchen supplier, he was stuck for an answer. All he said was 'I don't know', so I jumped in with 'How about in return for you doing the work for me for nothing, I'll advertise your company wherever I go with my stage set-up for a year', and he said, 'Yeah. OK' – and that was that sorted out.

I also had a number of temporary sponsors for one year, all of which were found for me by one very kind man. His name is Paul Varney, an accountant who drank at my sister's pub, the Boat Inn at Stockton in Warwickshire. Paul sorted out no less than *five* sponsors for me: Wright, Hassall & Co, Solicitors (no, that name is not a wind-up and, no, it shouldn't be 'Right Hassle'!); Daffern & Co (Chartered Accountants); Coventry Chemicals; R. C. & N. Finance Company and Carwood Motor Units. Paul negotiated with each of the companies and came up with sponsorship totalling £2,000, which was brilliant.

My most recent and current sponsor is a company based in Leamington Spa called A New Body. As the name suggests, they provide gym equipment and they were good enough to supply me with a very good quality treadmill to keep me nice and trim. I know darts has the image of 'all beer bellies and fags', but in the professional game it's not like that anymore. Darts is a recognised sport now and the standards are much higher. And believe me when I say that you have to be fit to be a professional darts player. In order to win highly competitive matches, you cannot afford to have a sluggish lifestyle. I like to stay fit and A New Body is helping me do that. In return, I agreed to have the company name featured on my stage set-up.

So, after what was a tough start, I managed to secure a good number of sponsors, many of whom still remain loyal to me today and I to them. It's nice to have people around you who you know you can rely on. Thanks to them, I've achieved every goal I've set for myself so far and I sincerely hope that I will continue to reward them with success after success. It seems to have gone very well so far but I simply wouldn't have been able to do it without their help and support.

Not a chance.

Chapter Fourteen

I Aim to be Master of the World

Throughout the late 1990s, I continued to practise hard and travel the circuit in search of those valuable ranking points that would consolidate my position as the Women's number one. In August 1999, I was still in winning form when I beat Yorkshire's Karen Smith in the final to win the Belgium Open and pocket a cheque for £500.

Earlier that summer I had failed to make the final of the England Open at Camber Sands in Sussex, but I was still a winner when the BDO chairman presented me with the BDO Personality of the Year Award which I won jointly with my great friend Crissy Howat and Scotland's Anne Kirk. I also came close to becoming British Inter-County Lady Player of the Season for the second year running, being edged out of the title in a very tight contest. It went right down to the last match but Cambridgeshire's Sandra Greatbatch won all nine of her games, whereas I won eight. That single defeat wrested my title away from me but, as usual, I prepared to fight back.

The three-way award of the BDO Personality of the Year Award reflected the extent of progress in women's darts over the previous year. Morale among the ladies was very high indeed and even Olly Croft – the top man at the BDO – made reference to it in his preview of the forthcoming season. He wrote in *Darts World* that 'the standards in women's darts have reached an all-time high'. He added that there was an extra incentive for top women players to do well in the Embassy World Championship play-offs. We were approaching the new millennium and what a start it would be to that historic year if a woman made it through to the Embassy finals and on to the stage at Lakeside. There was certainly an air of anticipation across the darts world that a woman *could* do it and I for one was determined to be that woman. However, before that, there was more work to do and more points to accrue.

That campaign didn't start very well as I failed to make the Embassy Gold Cup National Finals. However, I went over to Denmark in September and won the Open there, beating Sharon Colclough in the final. The following month, I was proudly representing my country in the World Cup XII in Durban in South Africa. London's Apylee Jones and I took the Women's World Cup with a points total of 51, almost double that of our nearest rivals, The Netherlands, who had 28 points. Reigning champions America finished way down the field in ninth position with only 12 points. There was simply no stopping Apylee and me. I won the Ladies' Singles, beating Francis Hoenselaar in the final 4–3. Then Apylee and I took the Ladies' Pairs title with a relatively easy 4–1 victory over Sweden's Kristina Korpi and Carina Ekberg. Mind you, we did have a few problems in the Pairs semi-final against Francis and Kitty van der Vliet, but we won eventually with a tight 4–3 score line. After the World Cup victory, in which the England lads also won the Men's World team title, I felt I was ready to take another title and set my sights on December and the WINMAU World Masters. I wanted to impress my new sponsor and what better way to do that than by winning their major trophy, the World Masters? I had something to prove to them. I was feeling confident and was ready. Also, there was the little matter of the richest prize in women's darts at the time – £3,000. In those days that was a great deal of money.

Seventy-two top lady darts players from around the world descended on the Lakeside Country Club at Frimley Green in December to take part in the WINMAU Ladies' World Masters. While the main focus of the media, as always, was on the men's tournament – which was won by England's Andy 'The Viking' Fordham – the ladies put on a show of darts that was the envy of many men. Francis and I were the top seeds and the two favourites to reach the final.

While Francis and I progressed through the field with relative ease, other top ladies were falling by the wayside. Apylee Jones, my World-Cup-Pairs-winning partner, crashed out to Finland's Tarja Salminem, while another Finnish player, Sari Saylova, ended the dreams of the four-time Masters champion Mandy Solomons, winning 3–2. England's Tricia Wright, the number eight seed, went out to Stacy Bromberg from the USA.

I then met the gritty Tarja Salminem in the quarter-finals. I survived a tough five-leg tussle to go through to the semis where I met the previous year's winner, England's Karen Smith. In that semi-final, I soon found myself 1–0 down, but fought back to take a 2–1 lead, only to find that Karen had another gear. She brought the match back to level at 2–2. Only my determination, and a timely maximum 180, saw me to victory on double twenty. I was certainly relieved to get that match over and waited to see whom I would meet in the final.

Guess who?

My old adversary Francis Hoenselaar had been battling away in her half of the draw and had disposed clinically of Belgium's

Vicky Pruim 3–0 in her quarter-final. Francis's semi-final opponent was Scotland's Anne Kirk, who had ended Stacy Bromberg's run by beating her 3–2 in the quarters. Unfortunately, on this occasion, Anne lacked the firepower to deal with Francis and was crushed 3–0, thereby setting up the predicted final, or as a *Darts World* correspondent wrote, an 'eagerly awaited clash of the Titans [which] did not disappoint'.

It was one hell of a game. We both knew each other's game so well. We were evenly matched and so I guessed it would be the first one to make a mistake who would pick up the cheque for the runner-up. That person turned out to be me. I missed double nineteen in the opening leg and found myself 1–0 down. I came back at Francis in the second leg and levelled the match. In the third leg, I was progressing well until Francis hit a spectacular out-shot of 117 checking out on double top. In the vital fourth, which I simply had to win to stay in the match, I hit a maximum 180 and two tons and, after only twelve darts, left myself needing double top. I thought I had a chance, but Francis had other ideas. She had reduced her score to 81 in nine darts and stepped confidently up to the oche. She then shot single 15, single 16 and a bull's-eye (50 points or double 25) for a magnificent finish to win the leg, take the match and the title. I warmly congratulated Francis and walked off-stage with my dreams in tatters.

While a joyous and tearful Francis was telling journalists how happy she was to have won the title at last (she had been trying to win the Masters since 1991), I commiserated with my friends and then sat reflecting on the match and what I had done wrong. Missing that double nineteen at the start of the match was a mistake, but I'd fought back. After that I didn't do anything wrong – except lose! I had played well and achieved the higher average per dart, but those two quality finishes by Francis nailed me. It might have taken Francis eight years to win the Masters, but I wasn't prepared to wait that long! I was determined to return the following year and make that title my own.

During our final, Francis and I both averaged over 31 points per dart: Francis 31.68 and me 32.52. These were important statistics because our averages were higher than those achieved by Andy Fordham and Wayne Jones in the Men's final! Surely now people in the darts world would pay attention and give the ladies' game more exposure and raise our profile in the sport. Surely this was a great example of 'girl power' – a very popular phrase at that time – and there was general anticipation that it would not be very long before a woman – or even women – would be standing alongside the men on the World Championship stage at Lakeside. Despite the disappointment of losing in the World Masters final, I was still up for it. I wanted to be the first woman to take on the men in the Embassy. However, the play-offs came and went – and so did I. I made it through the first couple of rounds but that was it. I was bitterly disappointed. I desperately wanted to make a point to the men but, on this occasion, I failed.

So, regrettably, as the new millennium dawned, there was no super start for the ladies' game. No woman had made it through the play-offs of the Embassy so it was an all-male affair yet again. I sat in the audience at Lakeside and watched Ted 'The Count' Hankey thrash Ronnie Baxter 6–0 in the shortest Embassy World Darts Championship final ever – a mere forty-seven minutes. As the final score line suggests, Ted was unstoppable and amazingly won the title with a 170 out-shot to take home £2,000 for the highest finish to add to his £44,000 for winning the contest. I thought, 'Wouldn't it be great if one day there was prize money like that in the ladies' game – or even half that!'

As for the Embassy World Championship title, I knew that I'd be up for another go in the play-offs later in the year, believing that this would be the only route open to me to become a real world-beater. I still believed that women's darts needed its own world championship but any noises I had made at those in authority had fallen on deaf ears. Despite praise for the ladies' game coming from the very highest office of the BDO, there was no immediate sign after the 2000 Embassy finals of any major change in our sport from the women's point of view. However, a few days later a number of other top lady dart players and I were approached by Tommy Cox, Tournament Director of the Professional Darts Corporation (PDC), with an interesting proposition.

The Professional Darts Corporation (or rather the 'World Darts Council' as it was originally called) was formed in 1992 when a group of professional players, their managers and some members of the darts industry decided to move away from the British Darts Organisation (BDO), the latter having controlled world darts since the mid 1970s. The reasons for the split were many but, in essence, the sixteen top professionals simply wanted their own organisation and so detached themselves from the BDO. What then followed was a dreadful period of claim and counter-claim by both parties that eventually resulted in the whole matter going to the High Court in 1997, the judgement finding in favour of the PDC. There was to be no restriction of trade and every darts player could play in any competition he or she wanted. However, this outcome continued to present problems and it appeared to me as a relative newcomer to the sport that there was a lot to answer for on both sides. Personally, I prefer to stay neutral in such affairs. I'm not a political animal but what happened next led to me to become embroiled in a matter that put me on the spot, challenged my loyalties and led to my making a decision that would change the course of my life.

A little while after the Embassy finals, Tommy Cox informed me that the Board of the PDC had considered and approved the proposal to include a top woman darts player in the line-up for the next Skol World Darts Championship. This was the major tournament in the PDC calendar. The venue was the Circus Tavern in Purfleet, Essex and the championship was featured on Sky Sports. Previously the PDC World Championship had only been open to men and, naturally, I was very pleased about being given the chance to play. I thought, 'At last! Here's the opportunity the top ladies had been waiting for. A guaranteed place in a world championship darts final against the men.' At last, someone was prepared to stop paying lip service to the ladies' game and actually do something about it. At last, it was time for us to show the men what we were made of. I was very pleased with the proposal and was quoted in the press as saying 'Darts is a sport that women and men can play at the same standard and I know that all of the top female players will be looking forward to the opportunity to prove it'.

Honestly, that's what I felt at the time.

It had not been an easy process for the PDC to decide to invite a woman to participate. The World Professional Darts Players' Association (WPDPA), which had a place on the PDC Board, had to agree. After all, the acceptance of a lady player directly into the finals meant that one male WPDPA member would be denied a place.

Surprisingly, and refreshingly, after due consideration, the WPDPA agreed to the proposal for a one-year trial period in the first instance. Following this approval, the PDC had drawn up a schedule of a number of worldwide women's darts tournaments for the coming year. According to *Darts World* magazine, the PDC's proposal was that the top eight women on that list on 1 October 2000 would be invited to take part in a straight knockout tournament, the winner being awarded the thirty-second place in the line-up of the Skol World Darts Championship. The knockout would take place at the end of October at the Crosbie Cedars Hotel in Rosslare in the Republic of Ireland and would be a featured part of the PDC's annual

World Grand Prix darts competition. As far as I was concerned, this PDC proposal was opening a crack in the door for women's darts and I and others were ready to step through it. Tommy Cox contacted me directly and invited me, as the number-one-ranked woman in the world, to play. I didn't accept straightaway. I felt that, because of my loyalty to the BDO, I ought to let them know. I phoned a friend and asked for his advice. He was certain that the BDO would not take kindly to the approach, so off he went and told Olly Croft what Tommy had offered me. In the meantime, I provisionally accepted Tommy's offer. It seemed to me that, at last, the ladies' game was being recognised but at the back of my mind, nagging away, was a fear that the BDO would do something. I suppose I should have realised how the news would be received.

The BDO were not happy.

By the summer of 2000 rumours started around the darts circuit and in the darts press that any British women accepting a place in the PDC's knockout tournament in Ireland would lose all their ranking points and, without beating about the bush, that's exactly what happened. According to Tommy Cox, the Chairman of the PDC, Mike Titmus, confronted the BDO's General Manager, Olly Croft, about the situation and Olly confirmed that any player who competed in Rosslare would be 'stripped of BDO/WDF ranking points'. It all seemed to me to be totally contrary to what had been agreed in the High Court about no restriction of trade. What a dilemma to be faced with! As the world number one, I simply could not afford to argue with the powers-that-be at the BDO and take the risk of losing those precious points and my position. I argued that it was unfair of the BDO to give lady players such an ultimatum, deducting points when the BDO themselves had nothing to offer us. I had fought so hard to achieve my number-one status and simply was not prepared to give it up. There was no other course open to me.

I had no choice. I really had no choice.

I contacted Tommy Cox and told him that, regrettably, I was no longer able to compete in the PDC knockout. He was furious, not at me but at the BDO. He later wrote, 'Have some people learned absolutely nothing? Do they actually want to return to the strife which tortured our game for so long and ultimately to the costly and traumatic return to the law courts?' He added, 'For an organisation to turn on its own, with only vindictiveness as a justification, is criminal', and concluded with a plea to 'end this lunacy now'.

Under similar pressure, all the other British lady darters either failed to accept the PDC's initial invitation or withdrew from the PDC event. Thus our best ever chance of participating in a world darts championship, other than trying to reach the Embassy final via the play-offs, was gone. Within a few short months, Tommy Cox's brilliant idea had been reduced to rubble with no small amount of embarrassment on the part of the PDC, in particular in connection with Sky Television, whom the corporation were in negotiations with to televise the knockout.

What happened next took the darts community by surprise. In September 2000, the British Darts Organisation announced in a blaze of publicity that 'WOMEN GET THEIR OWN WORLD CHAMPIONSHIPS'. The BDO would be staging the first-ever Women's World Darts Championship in January as an integral part of the 2001 Embassy World Darts Championship at Lakeside.

Chuffin' hell! Coincidence or what?

Now I can reveal that when I had spoken to the BDO at the time of their threat to deduct points if the ladies participated in the Skol World Championships, the question was put to me, 'How do you think the ladies would respond to having their very own world championships at Lakeside at the same time as the men's?' That was a silly question really. I, of course, replied, 'We would love it.' After all, that was what we'd been asking for – fighting for – for ages: separate recognition for the ladies' game at the very highest level. For ages the BDO didn't appear to have listened to us at all, yet as soon as the PDC proposal hit the headlines, they clearly had a swift rethink.

I was so pleased at the BDO's decision and by the fact that I had played a small part in establishing the Women's World Darts Championship. It was now up to me to reinforce my world number one position by securing for myself that first world crown.

Chapter Fifteen

Champion of the World

Coincidence or not, needless to say the BDO's announcement was welcomed by all those connected with ladies' darts. The Women's World Darts Championship, with a prize fund of £8,000 (with £4,000 going to the eventual winner), would be competed for during the same week as the 2001 Embassy World Darts Championship, Saturday 6 to Sunday 14 January

The BDO commented at the time of the announcement that the championship had been created 'to rightly acknowledge and reward the outstanding progress made in women's darts during the last decade'. And rightly so. They added, 'Their very presence guarantees that the 2001 Women's World Championship will have the strongest possible line-up to launch women's world darts into the next millennium.' I was obviously proud to be part of the line-up and, indeed, was quoted in *Darts World* as saying 'The announcement of the Women's World Darts Championship from the BDO is wonderful news and illustrates that they have not only listened but also done something positive to make it happen. I am really looking forward to creating darts history at Lakeside, and I have no doubt that Crissy and Francis feel exactly the same'.

The proposed line-up for the World Championship would consist of only four players: the three top-ranked ladies and a fourth to be determined via a ladies' play-off as part of the Embassy International Play-Offs which were to take place at Lakeside on 30 November 2000. At the time of the BDO announcement, I had slipped to number two with Crissy Howat ranked number one and Francis number three and thus we automatically qualified. From that point, quite rightly, women were excluded from what had now become the men's tournament. We were happy with that because we now had our very own world championship.

With so few players taking part in the new Ladies' World Championship final, there was bound to be some grumbling in the ranks and indeed that surfaced on the circuit with some venom. There were those who felt that it simply couldn't be a world championship event, that it was a farce and that it was laughable and meant nothing. Martin Fitzmaurice wrote that the BDO announcement had 'been greeted by some ladies with disdain and a totally negative attitude', adding that 'these, thankfully, [are] only a small minority'. He defended the short format and the limited field arguing that the main aim had been to 'get this long overdue championship into the darting calendar'. That, he said, had been achieved and it was now up to everyone involved to make it work, to 'make it a resounding success', so that in the following year more ladies would be afforded the opportunity of taking part. Predictably, Martin also enthusiastically congratulated all those for bringing 'this much-deserved tournament' into the ladies' darts calendar. 'Gone are the days', said Martin, 'when the ladies had to play in the qualifying rounds with the men to reach the stage of the

Lakeside and of course there is the little matter of £8,000 new prize money on offer.' There were those, like me, who were simply grateful that the ladies' game was being recognised in this way and who felt this was a real breakthrough – and that wasn't just because I automatically qualified.

I don't know how many times I have to say it, but it is extremely hard work travelling around Britain and the rest of Europe accumulating ranking points with only the World Darts Federation (WDF) ranking tables acting as an indicator of who is the world's best. But here, at last, something was being done. Yes, of course, I would have loved to have seen a bigger competition between the top eight or even the top sixteen ladies, but, for whatever reasons, the BDO did not go down that route: not to begin with, anyway. No matter how unfair the 'top three plus one qualifier' set-up was, there was no doubt that the introduction of a separate ladies' world championship was the shot in the arm women's darts needed. But it wasn't totally clear if this was to be a 'one-off'. There were those cynics who predicted that it would be for only one year and that the powers-that-be were only trying to embarrass the PDC, which they had succeeded in doing. In my head, I was clear that, if the ladies put up a good show the first time, then the BDO would have no choice but to continue the Women's World Championship in the years to come.

Meanwhile, I was still travelling and accumulating points. I won the Norway Open, beating Francis 4–3. It was a very tight match and only a momentary loss of concentration on Francis' part allowed me in to take the match on double eighteen. Francis and I also picked up the Ladies' Pairs title, whitewashing the Swedish partnership of Kristina Korpi and Carina Ekberg 4–0 in the final. But Francis had her revenge on me in the Denmark Open shortly afterwards when, in another closely fought contest, it was my turn to be edged out 4–3.

In the Europe Cup held in Holland in October 2000, I was

victorious in the Ladies' Singles against Denmark's Anne Louise Anderson. I was unstoppable as I cruised to a 4–0 win. Days later, I was in Liverpool for the Elkadart British Open and won the Ladies' Singles title for the third successive year, overhauling Scotland's Anne Kirk 3–0 in the final to pick up the trophy and a cheque for £800. Francis and I took the Ladies' Pairs title, too, beating Tricia Wright and Crissy Howat, which added another £100 to the bank balance.

I was on a roll.

At this point, the PDC's plans for a female darter to play in the Skol World Championship seemed in tatters. With almost all of the top ladies – under threat of losing ranking points or simply out of personal preference – siding with the BDO, the tournament's organiser Tommy Cox admitted that this had caused acute embarrassment to the PDC, who had to '[s]heepishly ... retract every single word it had said to Sky Sports about the merits of covering the ladies' final'. Tommy pointed out that since the legal ruling, the Tomlin Order, there was no reason why women could not play in both world championships. He added, 'I can't for the life of me see why all women can't play in all events open to them, without any threats or sanctions.' I understood where he was coming from, but he wasn't standing where I was. I wasn't prepared to gamble all I had achieved by participating in the PDC World Championship and lose out on a crack at the Embassy World title. Perhaps I felt that eventually some good would come of all the commotion, but I was wrong.

While some people might have believed that the PDC plans to have a lady player in the Skol World Championships were scuppered, they were very, very wrong. By the autumn there were only two ladies left, Gayl King (Canadian Open Champion) and the US star player Stacy Bromberg, but then Stacy withdrew, too. Gayl stood firm and earned her right to play, the PDC later confirming that she had been given automatic entry into the

Rubbing shoulders with the stars: putting the rock 'n' roll back into darts with the Kaiser Chiefs (*top*); and with *A Question of Sport* and *I'm a Celebrity Get Me Out of Here* star Phil Tufnell (*bottom*). I think he wasn't a bad cricket player for England too!

Top: The legendary Scottish goalkeeper Andy Goram.

Bottom: 'Take your time, nice and easy…' Tony Green from *Bullseye* and Mike Gregory.

'Let's play daaaarts!' With the one
and only Martin Fitzmaurice.

Top left: Showing off my 2003 World Championship trophy in the players' lounge at Lakeside.

Top right: With my 'big brother', Andy 'The Viking' Fordham (*left*) and Martin Adams.

Below: Winning the Lorna Croft Memorial Trophy as IDPA Women's Player of the Year brought tears to my eyes!

Putting the family on hold… I couldn't give up my world championship without a fight, and I took my fourth consecutive title against Francis (*below, right*) at Lakeside.

Winning the Desert Classic (*top left*) was a good enough reason to fly to Las Vegas –
but being maid of honour at the wedding of my good friends Crissy Howart and
Peter 'One Dart' Manley was a better one!

Top: Clare and I were named 'Team of the Year' in the 2005 BBC TV *South Today* Sports Awards for our outstanding achievements in the World Cup in Perth.

Bottom left: I was thrilled and delighted to be awarded the 'Sportswoman of the Year Award' in the inaugural Coventry, Solihull and Warwickshire Sports Awards.

Bottom right: With my friend and legend, the 'Crafty Cockney' Eric Bristow.

Top: Spot the difference? My Lakeside victories in 2006 and 2007 – I haven't aged a bit!

Bottom: Top of the world once more, comparing trophies with the men's 2007 World Champion, Martin 'Wolfie' Adams. 'Awooooo!'

Skol and would take up that thirty-second place at the Circus Tavern on 28 December.

What I felt about the situation did not appear to affect my play at all: indeed, quite the contrary. In November, at the Jersey Festival of Darts, I met Francis in the final and beat her 3–2. Francis actually had three chances to save the match but let me in to secure the win on double one. What a confidence-booster that was for the forthcoming World Championship, but then again, as I often say, you are only as good as your last dart.

At the end of the final, the organisers could not find the trophy. They asked me if I knew where it was because I had won the title the previous year. I was absolutely sure that, in order to save me the trouble of transporting it back again the following year, I had left the trophy in Jersey. I was insistent – as insistent as the men from the BDO were that the trophy was not on the island or indeed in their possession – but the trophy did not come to light, so I received the winner's cheque for £1,500, but no trophy. On the way home, I wondered what could possibly have happened to it. Had it been stolen? Had the organisers stored it away somewhere safe and forgotten where? Can you imagine, then, how embarrassed I felt when I arrived home and discovered the trophy was there? I'd had it all the time.

'Embarrassed' is not the word!

Two days after my Jersey triumph, I played at the Trentham Gardens in Stoke, where I won my first Embassy Gold Cup Ladies' Singles title with a 3–0 win over my great friend and rival, Crissy Howat. I was really chuffed. I desperately needed that title because it is one of the most difficult ones to win, since in every round you play a county champion so there are no easy games. Surprisingly, though, I managed it without dropping a single leg.

On 30 November, London's Mandy Solomons, one of the very best lady darts players in the country and a former number one, fought her way through a strong field of sixty top ladies from all over the world to secure that coveted fourth World Championship place, beating Belgium's Vicky Pruim 3–0 in the play-off final. So the line-up, but not the draw, was known. All was set for the inaugural Embassy Women's World Championship. I was immediately installed as the bookies' favourite, but before that there was the little matter of the WINMAU World Masters.

Francis had triumphed over me in the previous year's WINMAU final and I was determined not to let that happen again. Francis and I were in different halves of the draw so it seemed inevitable that we would meet in the final. That was what everyone seemed to expect and Francis and I didn't let them down. In the last sixteen I convincingly beat England's Natalie Jones 3–0, while in her half of the draw Francis beat Sue Talbot 3–1. In the quarter-finals I was up against Oxford's Clare Bywaters, always a tricky opponent, but I won 3–2. As I beat Northern Ireland's Denise Cassidy 3–0 in my semi-final, Francis was also whitewashing Staffordshire's Sherrie Dodd 3–0 in hers.

In the final, I took the opening leg against the throw, but that was only after we had both missed winning doubles. In the second leg I shot out on double eighteen with Francis a long way back but, as usual, Francis found a second gear and hit a maximum 180 and two tons to pull one leg back. However, I was in no mood to let the Masters slip away from me and with a couple of 140s in the fourth leg I shot out on double sixteen to lift the trophy. Revenge really tasted *very* sweet!

Outside, away from the action, Gully sat in the car.

On this occasion *Darts World* reporter Wayne Baker interviewed Gully (in the car) and he told Wayne, 'I just don't watch her play. It's nothing to do with nerves.' Gully explained that his non-appearance during tournaments was as a result of him attending a county game and was actually encouraged, by whom I do not know, *not* to watch me. He went outside and I won. Ever since then, wrote Wayne, whenever I played, Gully always found an excuse 'to go to the toilet, recover something from the car ... or simply pop outside of the venue for a breath of fresh air'. Although I could never see the funny side of Gully's actions, he obviously could, as he told Wayne, 'I've lost count of the number of car parks I have studied meticulously. I really could write a guide about them.'

Yeah. Right ...

On 28 December 2000, at the Circus Tavern, Canada's Gayl King stepped up to the oche in the Skol World Championship and made darts history as the first woman ever to play in the finals of a world championship tournament previously only open to male competitors. Her opponent was the Geordie darter, and PDC-ranked twenty-ninth in the world, Graeme Stoddart. Gayl wasn't expected to do much good against Graeme, but, cheered on by the capacity crowd, she took the first set after being two legs down. A major upset seemed possible, but then Graeme regained his form and came out the winner 3–1. Afterwards, Graeme told reporters, 'After losing the first set, I tried to phone International Rescue, but they were engaged.' Gayl said, 'It was great, awesome – different to anything I've played in before.' She had successfully overcome all the hype. I thought Gayl had put in a good performance and had done the ladies' game proud. Graeme was also quoted as saying 'Women deserve their own world championship. Let the men have the men's and the women have the women's'. Perhaps he didn't relish the thought of having to go through all that again against another top lady!

On Sunday 7 January 2001, Crissy Howat and I stepped on to the stage at the Lakeside for the opening semi-final of the inaugural Women's World Darts Championship. This was history in the making. The format was the first to two sets and best of five legs to each set. Crissy and I threw our six practice darts and were then called to order by the referee. The crowd was hushed and Crissy threw those historic first three darts. Her nerves showed as she struck 41, and I fared little better with 55. But after that I was away. I hit two maximum 180s in the opening set to take it 3–0. In the second set, I hit two more maximums and then secured the third leg with a 118 finish.

My main rival, Francis Hoenselaar, wasn't having it quite so easy in her semi-final. She was up against the former world number one and four-time WINMAU Ladies' World Master, Mandy Solomons, and Mandy was in vintage form. Although she hit a maximum in the first set, Francis missed doubles and gifted the set to Mandy. Francis then staged a fight back and won the second set. The deciding third set went all the way to five legs and, after both Francis and Mandy missed doubles, it was Mandy who secured her place in the final by shooting out on double nine. So the much-predicted Gulliver-Hoenselaar final wasn't to be.

The final took place on Thursday, 11 January. I was unusually nervous, unlike Mandy who, as-cool-as-you-like, took the first set 3–1. Even though I missed seven doubles in the second set, I scored much higher than Mandy and managed to draw level by winning the set 3–0. But Mandy wasn't finished. Throwing first in the first leg of the deciding set, she hit a magnificent thirteen-darter. I had to defend my throw in the second leg or that was the end of my dream. Not only did I do that, but I also broke Mandy's throw in the third leg to win it against the darts. I threw first in the final leg. I hit two maximums, while Mandy's scoring was erratic, and I clinched victory with double top.

I can't describe how I felt when that winning dart went in. I had really thought that Mandy had the beating of me until the final leg. She had played so well and I knew that if she had levelled the match at 2–2 she would have won the tournament. It was so very close but I wasn't to be denied. I'd done it. I'd fulfilled my dream. I had made darts history. I was the first-ever Embassy Women's World Darts Champion. I was on top of the world ...

... and Gully was out in the car park!

Chapter Sixteen

The Aftermath

After my victory, Gully told the *Darts World* reporter Wayne Baker that during the coming year he planned to continue his trend of seeking refuge in the car park every time I made a final.

He was certainly very pleased for me and recognised how hard I had worked to become World Champion but, for now, Gully was content to sit down and 'savour ... the match on video in comfort with a nice long drink'! Looking back, I suppose the chances are that that was where we both seriously began to lose the plot.

As for ladies' darts in general, I was clearly hoping that our inaugural World Championship at Lakeside would make the national daily newspapers. Certainly Gayl King's participation in the PDC had received considerable coverage in the UK, including articles in *The Times* ('Woman with guts shakes up the beer bellies') and the *Guardian* ('Gayl force hits the bull's-eye'). Back in Canada, the *Ottawa Sun* featured an article: 'King aims to be queen of darts'. After her match the *Daily Express* headline read,

'King rocks oche but Stoddart squeezes through.' Given all this excellent publicity from not only the tabloids but also the quality press, I was confident that the Lakeside Ladies' would receive its fair share of publicity, too.

As usual, the men's game was extensively reported and John 'Boy' Walton played out of his skin all week to lift the trophy. John became only the third male player ever to win the Embassy after winning the World Masters title (the others were Eric Bristow and Wales' Ritchie Burnett). Now I had done it for the first time for the ladies and so where were the reporters? Only Mel Webb of *The Times* seemed to have appreciated what I had achieved. He produced a superb article about my victory and summed up my feelings when he wrote, 'She had won five important titles in the previous ten weeks, including the World Masters, but none of those victories was remotely as sweet as this.'

I was really disappointed that reports on my victory were few and far between and that television coverage had been scant. I think the only woman to make news on the oche that week was Emma Hughes and, as far as I know, she wasn't even a darts player! Emma, a twenty-four-year old hairdresser from Wolvercote in Oxfordshire, caused chaos during one of the men's matches when she stripped naked and streaked across the Lakeside stage. It was the first time anything like that had happened in twenty-four years of televised Embassy darts. The BBC2 coverage was halted while Lakeside bouncers pursued the naked girl round the venue. Emma later told reporters, 'I'm a huge darts fan and I've always wanted to streak. I was going to do it at a snooker match but I heard no one had done it at darts.' I think she (or rather her bare arse) received more column inches than the entire Ladies' Championship. Perhaps that's the only way the ladies' will be noticed, by taking all our clothes off. However, that wouldn't get us anywhere and, in any case, topless darts had already been tried on L!ve TV.

Seriously, though, I was upset about the lack of national coverage, not just for my sake but also for women's darts as a whole. It was such an opportunity to promote our sport, yet no one seemed interested. Mandy, Crissy, Francis and I had put ladies' darts firmly on the world map, we had played some marvellous darts and put on a great show and I was hopeful that we could build on what we had achieved.

By comparison, the reception I received when I arrived home in Southam was something else. It was *brilliant.* All the local newspapers carried stories about my success. The *Coventry Evening Telegraph* produced a special two-page feature with several photographs, while the local *Courier, Advertiser* and *Observer* all carried stories with pictures. I also received a very nice letter from the local council congratulating me on becoming World Champion and for putting Southam on the map.

There were numerous phone calls, from what seemed like everyone in darts, who called to say well done and many more from women telling me that my win had inspired them to take up the game. I was overwhelmed with all the messages I received and it would have taken me until the next world championship to reply to them all, but, fortunately, I was able to do this through *Darts World* magazine. Immediately after my victory I was approached by Tony Wood, the Editor of *Darts World*, and contributor Wayne Baker to write a regular monthly column for the magazine, which would include news of my darts tournaments and exhibitions and any other items I felt like writing about. Not surprisingly, perhaps, the column was (and still is) called 'Gulliver's Travels'. One of the first articles I wrote included a big thank-you to all those who had supported me and congratulated me on my success.

It was two weeks after Lakeside before I could hold a celebration party for family and friends. We all met at my house and awaited the minibus to take us to the venue, the

Stoneythorpe Hotel in Southam. Imagine my surprise when a stretch limousine pulled up outside the house! I had to pinch myself to make sure I wasn't dreaming. I found out soon afterwards that the limousine had been provided by one of my main sponsors, Reeves Boatbuilders. But the surprises didn't end there. One of my other sponsors, Car Consultants, agreed to replace my existing car with a new one.

At that time, Bert Houghton owned the Stoneythorpe Hotel and the manageress was his wife Margaret. My mum had worked there behind the bar or as a cook and my sisters were head waitresses for major functions, like weddings. Me? I washed up. Working Christmas Day at the Stoneythorpe was good fun. Once the customers had all gone, Bert and Margaret would invite all the staff to sit down with them afterwards and have Christmas dinner. We all had a great rapport with them.

So when I approached them about a party to celebrate my success they were very accommodating indeed. Food was laid on and a disco: nothing too complicated. I invited everyone whom I felt had supported me and helped me in my career, including family, friends and sponsors. I gave a short speech thanking everyone. Beforehand, I was a little nervous, so I wrote a few things down to make certain I didn't miss anyone, or anything, out. It was a great night. Sadly, Margaret and Bert are no longer with us, but the hotel is still family owned and they continue to be most accommodating and still avoid taking bookings for any dates a few weeks after Lakeside just in case I win the title again and call them.

Two months after my world title win, I was still on cloud nine. The phone was ringing continuously and my diary was full for months ahead. One of the outcomes from one of the phone calls was that I had appointed a European manager, Ad Schoofs, to help promote me on the continent, particularly in Holland where the game had grown out of all proportion since Raymond van

Barneveld (popularly known as 'Barney') won consecutive Embassy World Championships in 1998 and 1999. The country had quite literally gone 'darts mad' – and it remains so to this day. Ad was also Barney's manager at that time and plans were made for Barney and me to team up for a series of roadshows but, unfortunately, these didn't materialise.

Bugger!

But I was teamed up with the Men's World Champion, John 'Boy' Walton, for a number of Embassy Roadshows and those went extremely well. We covered most of the country and had a great time. I was hardly ever home.

By March, I was feeling battle weary. I was like 'a girl in a suitcase'. My life was a permanent whirl and, with exhibition work three or four days a week and other darting commitments, I could be away from home for anything up to six days at a time. I'd arrive home, unpack, wash, iron and pack again and get back on the road. Weary, yes, but I loved every minute. This is what I had worked hard to achieve. I was World Champion and was now reaping the benefits of that success. Most of my work at that time was UK based. However, I was hopeful of some work in Holland later in the year and was looking forward to going over there but, like the Barney–Trina Roadshow idea, those plans never came to anything.

One part of my body suffered more than any other when I was on the road: my back. The thing that really bothered me was sleeping in strange beds. Like most folk, I feel there's nothing quite like your own bed – and I couldn't wait to get home to mine. One of the reasons for this is that I have an orthopaedic bed. I have arthritis in my back and need to sleep on a firm mattress: one that gives me the necessary support. I see an osteopath once a year for what I term my MOT. I always feel so much better after seeing him. He does such a good job that I feel six inches taller when he's finished with me!

Also in March the Embassy Roadshows with John kicked off in Sheffield. It was a great start with a superb atmosphere and I'm sure we gave the fans a great evening of darts entertainment. Next was Scotland, not famed for its good weather. The conditions were so bad that the car slid all over the place. Again, the fans were great but we were both very glad to return to the Midlands and less ice and snow.

Although the phone had gone a little quieter by the beginning of April, I was extremely pleased the way things were going. My diary was bulging. I had a new car, which was just as well as I was travelling over 25,000 miles a year, and the roadshows were proving very popular indeed.

In addition, Ian Waller, a tireless charity worker, who set up the Heart of Darts charity a short time before, had approached me. The charity raised funds primarily for disadvantaged children and adults who were unable to obtain funding elsewhere. Ian asked if I would accept the post of president of the organisation, to help promote the Heart of Darts and raise its profile. I was proud and honoured to become the figurehead. My good friend, the darts champion Andy 'The Viking' Fordham, was already an ambassador for the Heart of Darts, so I was doubly pleased to offer up my time to such a good cause.

Of course, I continued on the circuit, playing to win and playing for those crucial ranking points that would keep me in the number one position. One of the major trophies I had failed to win to date was the Isle of Man Open. I maintained that record when, having cruised through to the last eight, I crashed out 3-2 to London's Apylee Jones who, I have to say, was in blistering form. Apylee went on to win the title beating an out-of-form Francis 3-0. Then Francis and I teamed up for the Ladies' Doubles. We made the final, where we met England team-mates Tricia Wright and Crissy Howat. The match went to a deciding fifth set which, as a *Darts World* reporter recorded, 'went to the delighted underdogs'. I pocketed £100 for making the last eight of the singles and shared £200 with Francis for reaching the final of the doubles. I returned to my practice dartboard, determined to improve on those performances.

Early on, I hadn't been doing very well to be honest but, after a slow start, that all changed – or so I thought. In Helsinki, in May, I won the Ladies' Singles title in the Finland Open. I had won it two years previously in 1999, beating Crissy in the final and this year I did it again, 4–2. That had been Crissy's third runners-up spot in that competition in four years, although Crissy had won the title in 2000. Francis and I thought we were the strongest possible combination to win the Ladies' Doubles but failed to make the final, being beaten by the relatively unknown Finnish pair, Carina Sahlberg and Hannel Varis in the semis.

I then packed my bags and travelled to Canada for the Golden Harvest North American Cup in Saskatoon. Although things didn't go well for me – I only made the last eight – I enjoyed playing in the tournament, so much so that before I left I paid my entry fee for the next year's event.

After the experience of defeat in Canada, I was keen to make amends and was soon heading into North Wales for the Welsh Open. I was disappointed to have to settle for a last-eight place but I have to admit it was a very difficult tournament to win, as there was such a strong field. It was marvellous to see Sweden's Carina Ekberg take the title 3–0 against Wales' Sandra Greatbatch as she had played brilliantly all day. The last eight was becoming a bit of a habit. I entered the Swiss Open and, again, failed in the quarter-finals. The final was fought out between two Dutch stars, Mieke de Boer and my friend Francis, Francis taking the title 2–0.

It was at times like these that I was so pleased to have secured my sponsors. Eighth place money is always low, whatever the competition, but you needed to enter these tournaments to pick up the ranking points. Without Reeves Boatbuilders, Car Consultants and others, I would never have sustained my career in darts.

It was June 2001, nearly halfway through the year and there had been no word about a second Ladies' World Championship. The euphoria that had washed over me for several months after my World Championship win had abated and I was becoming increasingly concerned that, as the sceptics had predicted, it had been a 'one-off'. Was my world crown going to be the first and last of its kind? Was the real aftermath for me to be consigned to history as the only woman to be crowned Embassy Ladies World Champion? In my heart I knew there would be a 2002 contest – and of course the WINMAU World Masters was definitely on – but no confirmation of a second world championship had yet been received from the powers that be at BDO headquarters.

Surely it wouldn't be too long before an announcement was made?

Chapter Seventeen

The Defence of My Titles

Towards the end of the summer of 2001, the British Darts Organisation finally announced that the second Embassy Women's World Championship would take place at Lakeside in January 2002 as an integral part of the of the Twenty-fifth Anniversary Embassy World Professional Darts Championships.

I must admit to having been a bit worried as time was moving on. However, to their credit, Imperial Tobacco, BBC Sport and the BDO had considered the position, were pleased with how it all went in January and how successful it was and so decided to keep their promise to us – by which I mean women dart players as a whole. Despite my concerns, Olly Croft of the BDO, stated that 'the commitment of the BDO to women's darts has never been in any doubt'. He added, 'Prior to the millennium no one would have even dreamed of women's darts staging its own World Championship, but the BDO, having listened to the players and recognised the strength of the women's game, has made the dream a reality.'

Me? I'd been dreaming about a women's world championship long before the end of the old millennium and at the back of my mind was the Gayl King business ...

Despite such thoughts, I was obviously thrilled at the announcement. I would now be able to defend my title against the best women darts players in the world and prove to everyone that I could retain my title. However, I took particular pleasure from the kind words Olly wrote about me in *Darts World*. He said, 'All of the players who took part were a credit to our sport – none more so than Trina Gulliver, who has let everyone know just how proud she is to have made history as the very first Embassy Women's World Champion. She is a wonderful ambassador who is a credit not only to women's darts, but also to the sport worldwide. Her success is a credit to the women's game at the very top level ...'

What a reference from the top man at the BDO!

Apart from this heap of praise, there were two other surprises from the men at BDO headquarters at Muswell Hill. Firstly, the starting line-up for the championship was to be increased from four in 2001 to eight. I saw this as due reward for the way women's darts had progressed over the past few years. Secondly, the BDO announced that the prize money was being increased from £8,000 in 2001 to £10,000 in 2002. This was not as big a surprise as you might first imagine, as the prize money for the first four places stayed the same; the additional £2,000 was to cover the award of £500 to each of the four players who would take positions five to eight in the extended competition. However, overall, lady darts players were pleased and I looked forward to defending my title.

In July, I began my campaign in earnest with a 3–2 win over Francis in the England Open held at Pontins Brean Sands, picking up £500. It was good to see Avon's Chris Mason back on the circuit and winning the men's event 2–0 against Scotland's Mike

Veitch. I also wanted to do something for the Heart of Darts charity while I was there and, with a lot of help from my friends, the folks at Pontins and the BDO, the ladies took on the men in a game of football. I wondered if the lads could actually play football as well as they talked about it. I have to admit they were not bad. However, the ladies put up a great performance and with assistance from the referee, the linesmen and our 'secret weapon' (having about ten people in goal) the ladies won. MC Martin Fitzmaurice had earlier agreed to referee the match but didn't in the end, claiming injury. There didn't appear to be that much wrong with him, though, as he stood on the touchline bellowing out support for my team. A good number of players from both teams sustained injuries on the field, bruised arms and legs (and of course a little bruised pride for the lads) but, thankfully, nothing too serious. I received a groin strain. The England Open was the following day and it was quite amusing watching so many people, including myself, limping into the venue.

Also during July, Gully and I were really proud to be Godparents to Georgia, the daughter of my former Warwickshire County colleague Gail Marshall. It was a brilliant day, and two-year-old Georgina behaved very well until someone poured water all over her head. She looked about as if asking 'What's all this about then?' It was a very proud moment for Gully and me.

A few days later I was bound for the Portland Club in Inverness to take part in a brand new tournament, the first ever International Dart Players Association (IDPA) Masters. Sixteen top players had been invited to participate, including Francis and me. The organisers asked Francis and me to do the draw. Francis was drawn against Colin Monk, a darts player with a wealth of experience, who had appeared in numerous Embassy World Championships and won many titles at home and on the continent. It was a draw that none of the men wanted and there was an audible sigh of relief around the room as Colin's name came out – well, apart from Colin. Francis then pulled my name out of the hat and then it was up to me to pull the name of the player I would play. I looked at the card and smiled. That wasn't because I thought it was a good draw for me. No, it was probably the worst. I announced the name 'Andy Fordham'. I heard Andy cry out, 'Oh no!'

Colin played very well against Francis and beat her 4–1. Then came the Gulliver versus Fordham match. After only a few minutes I found myself 2–0 down but I went up a gear and levelled it at 3–3. I had taken Andy to the final leg. Had I the beating of him? No, I hadn't. With Andy throwing first he was soon down to 102 while I was waiting for him to miss that out-shot to give me the opportunity to go out on 136. He never gave me the chance as he took out the finish and won the match. I had enjoyed the match immensely but in the end just had to be happy that I had made 'The Viking' sweat a bit!

At last, Gully and I were able to find time for a holiday. We went to Crete for a week and had a lovely, relaxing time. When I came back everyone asked, 'Where's your tan?' What people don't realise is that I'm not one for lying out in the sun all day and burning. I'm your typical English rose really.

The day after we returned from holiday, I took part in the British Pentathlon at the Rainham Mark Social Club in Kent. A week of total relaxation was not perhaps the best preparation for the most demanding darts tournament on the circuit. However, I was determined to make my mark as I was the first woman player ever to compete in it. Fortunately, England's Martin Adams gave me lots of advice and encouragement before and during the event. It was a very, very, long day and I came a creditable twelfth out of a field of twenty with 305 points: not bad for my first attempt. Martin actually won the tournament with 432 points, a mere seven points ahead of Lancashire's Ronnie 'The Rocket' Baxter.

I was chuffed to bits to have been given the opportunity to

play in the Pentathlon and was pleased with my performance. Most of all, I was hoping that my performance might lead to the ladies having a pentathlon of their own the following year. The problem though was finding a sponsor. The Pentathlon was not televised which made it doubly difficult to secure sponsors for a ladies' version. Although I hoped a sponsor could be secured, my fallback position was (fingers crossed) that I would be invited back to contest the men's event next year.

I'd also recently taken delivery of my new sponsored car from Car Consultants, a Mitsubishi Carisma. I decided to give the car a good road test by driving over to the continent for the Belgium Open, which was held at the Old Exchange Market in the centre of Antwerp. It turned out to be a great Embassy double act with John 'Boy' Walton taking the men's title and me winning the ladies' with a 3–0 victory over Crissy. I also travelled to the Norway Open, a title I had won twice before, but I was denied a third win, as an on-form Crissy gained revenge for losing the Belgian Open by beating me 4–1 in the final.

In September, the England team flew off to Kuala Lumpur for the thirteenth World Cup. The four-man team consisted of Martin Adams, Andy Fordham, Mervyn King and John 'Boy' Walton; the ladies team comprising of Mandy Solomons and me. The England youth team consisted of two up-and-coming young players, Stephen Bunting from Merseyside and Hampshire's Laura Power. England was hot favourite to take all three events.

As it turned out, the men stormed through to take the title with a clean sweep. No one could touch them. They scored a record total of 202 points with Finland second, way back on 110 points. In the Boys' Singles, Stephen Bunting swept all before him and took the title with a 3–1 victory over Sweden's Markus Korhonen. Laura played well and made the semi-final where she met South Africa's Melody Unger. Unfortunately, Laura just couldn't hit that winning double and Melody went through.

When it came to totting up the points at the end, the Swedish team took the youth title by a single point.

I really don't know what to say about the women's performance. I remember writing in my *Gulliver's Travels* column, 'Unfortunately, Mandy and I couldn't quite get it together ...' That was a bit of an understatement! The reporter in *Darts World* wrote sympathetically, 'A disappointing World Cup befell England's Trina Gulliver and Mandy Solomons who have both won the World Cup Singles in previous tournaments.' What 'befell' us was that we failed to make the latter stages of the Women's Singles and only managed a quarter-final place in the Women's Pairs. I was thoroughly beaten by Scotland's Anne Kirk in the singles, but then I think I was due that from Anne, as in our previous few meetings I had always come out on top. At the end of the competition we found ourselves in a lowly fifth position with a mere thirteen points: two points behind Japan and a massive fifty-three points behind the winners, The Netherlands.

What can I say? Let's move on ...

Once home from Malaysia, I was keen to put that disastrous World Cup performance behind me. I practised hard and focused on the next big challenge: defending my Embassy Gold Cup Ladies title, which was being held at Trentham Gardens in Stoke-on-Trent, at the beginning of November. But, sadly, my form deserted me and I failed to make the final sixteen. The winner was Cornwall's Nicola Furze who beat Cambridgeshire's Sandra Greatbatch (winner of the title in 1989) 3–2 to take my title and £2,000 in prize money. I didn't fare much better in the Ladies' Pairs, as my Warwickshire colleague Cheryl Jackson and I went out in the last sixteen, sharing prize money of £50. But soon it would be time to travel down to Frimley Green for the WINMAU World Masters to defend my title. That title is so precious to me and, as the tournament is organised under the name of one of my main sponsors, I owned it to them to do well again.

Well ...

The WINMAU World Masters opened on my thirty-second birthday on 30 November. The BDO had even managed to attract the BBC TV cameras there and the finals were to be shown on *Sunday Grandstand*. I was having a lovely day until I came up against Switzerland's Lisa Huber in the last sixteen and lost 3–0. Lisa played extremely well, the result reflecting the fact that I kept missing those little bits round the outside of the dartboard: they call it 'double trouble'. Lisa lost in the next round and the victory deservedly went to Scotland's Anne Kirk who beat America's Marilyn Popp in the final 3–1.

Even though I wasn't happy with my performance that weekend, I was absolutely thrilled to be asked to do the draw for the Embassy World Championships, due to be held in January 2002 live on BBC TV. What made it even more special was that I shared the responsibility with the legendary Leighton Rees, one of Wales' most famous darts players and, of course, the very first Embassy World Champion, a feat he achieved in 1978. I had met Leighton before, but what a privilege it was for me to be on stage with him. He was such a gentleman. It was a very sad day for the sport of darts when he died in 2003.

The draw proved to be very interesting. Before I had stepped up on stage some of the lads had come up to me and said, 'Be nice to me.' So what pairing did we pull out first – John 'Boy' Walton versus Andy 'The Viking' Fordham. Next came Raymond Van Barneveld against Bobby George. With the draw completed, I tried to sneak back to my seat quietly, but a voice boomed out 'GULLIVER, CAN I HAVE A WORD!' It was 'The Viking'. I thought I was in deep trouble, but following a long, meaningful and grovelling apology, I lived to tell the tale.

Once I returned home, I reviewed the high and low points of the weekend. Obviously, I was disappointed with yet another unsuccessful title defence and that didn't augur well for the

World Championship. Something had to be done. Through the gloom came a ray of light: in fact, a whole load of lights! Imagine my surprise and pride when the Mayor of Southam – my hometown – contacted me and said, 'Would you do us the pleasure of switching on the town's Christmas lights?' Well, the mayor didn't have to ask me twice! I'd lived in Southam all my life and was proud of the town and, whenever possible, I still do what I can to promote it. This was also a brilliant opportunity for me to mention and thank my locally based sponsors. So that was the Southam lights turned on. I'd lost my Gold Cup and Masters titles. Would I be able to turn on a bright performance at Frimley Green in the World Championships?

Or was this going to be third time *un*lucky?

Chapter Eighteen

World Champion Again ... but Only Just!

I ended the year 2001 on a low. Even the final Embassy Roadshow at Newhaven on the south coast of England, with John 'Boy' Walton and MC Tony Green and the rest of the crew, had been difficult. That wasn't because it was the last one. The problem was that we were all taken ill with what we believed was food poisoning. Needless to say, it could have been very embarrassing for us all but, following some treatment with over-the-counter cure-alls, everything went well in the end and, fortunately, there was no call on the heavy-duty Pampers.

As the New Year began, I reflected on losing those two titles. (I lost sight of the fact that, during 2001, I had won the British Open (for the fourth time), the Jersey Open (for the third time in a row), the England Open, the Finland Open, the British Classic, the Irish Masters *and* the Belgium Open! I was annoyed with myself when I failed to retain the Embassy Gold Cup, so you can imagine how I felt when I flopped in the World Masters event.

Next up was the BIG ONE, the Embassy World Championships. I had to stay focused. I had everything to lose (again). I had something to prove to my supporters, my sponsors and myself, but I knew, too, that the other finalists would see me as particularly vulnerable and might just seize the opportunity to take my title. I was determined not to let that happen.

What a battle it was!

In the qualifiers played earlier, America's Stacy Bromberg, who apart from being a great darts player was a private investigator, had taken care of two strong contenders, Denise Cassidy of Northern Ireland and the Dutch sharpshooter Mieke de Boer. Another potential threat, Scotland's Anne Kirk, failed to make the finals when she was beaten 3–2 by Mandy Solomons in a gripping encounter. London's Apylee Jones, always in there or thereabouts, reached her board final in the qualifiers only to see her dreams turn to ashes as Gwent's Jan Robbins took her place at Frimley Green 3–0. The final player to qualify was the Welsh ladies' captain and Cambridgeshire County player, Sandra Greatbatch. Sandra came from 2–0 behind in her board final against Lancashire's Debbie Baxter to claim her place. Those four players would join the four seeded players, Francis Hoenselaar (Holland), Belgium's Vicky Pruim, England's Crissy Howat and me in what turned out to be a very exciting Embassy Ladies final. It was an impressive field.

And it didn't go all my own way ...

I played out of my skin in the quarter-final against my England team-mate Mandy Solomons, whom I had met and beaten in the previous year's final. I felt in control all of the time and took the match 2–0 with an average of 86.70 per three darts compared to Mandy's average of 70.02.

Vicky Pruim, whom I met in the semis, had kept a clean slate in her win over Jan Robbins. For whatever reason, my darts became a bit wayward and I found myself skilfully planting darts in the one and five segments of the dartboard when they should, of course, have been in the twenties. Despite this inexplicable drop in form, I managed to scrape through to my second world final 2–1.

Meanwhile, the second finalist had been determined. Francis was desperate to make up for her disappointing performance in the championship in 2001, when she lost in the semi-final to Mandy, and began her campaign by beating Stacy Bromberg 2–0 and then defeating Sandra Greatbatch 2–1 in the semis. (Sandra had earlier caused the upset of the championships when beating the heavily fancied Crissy Howat 2–0 in the quarter-finals.) So the scene was set for a 'clash of the Titans', Holland against England, me against my good friend and adversary, Francis.

In the final, Francis went off like a rocket. She stormed into the lead by taking the first set 3–1. Once again, in the second set, my darts seemed to have a mind of their own and I experienced a bit of 'double trouble'. However, with a maximum score of 180 plus an 86 out-shot, finishing on the bull's-eye, I managed to pull things back level in sets with a 3–1 win.

The third and final set was unbelievable. Despite some errant darts, with the help of my second maximum of the match, I went into a 2–0 lead, only to see Francis claw it back with finishes of 99 and 61 to level it up. Scores of 121 and 140 helped me to take the lead in the fifth and deciding set. I eventually left myself 114 and knew it was a crucial shot, with Francis hard on my heels. I kept thinking how I had missed doubles during the earlier rounds of the championship and that thought unnerved me a little. I may have looked cool as my first dart went into the treble twenty segment. I may have looked composed when a single fourteen with the second dart set me up for victory on double top, but I still had to hit it. It was a real pressure shot.

Relief – sheer relief – washed over me as the third dart found double twenty. It was a brilliant feeling. I'd won! More importantly, I had defended and retained my title successfully. I turned and shook hands with Francis and then we embraced. Francis had certainly made up for her disappointing performance the previous year. She was so pleased to have made the final, but of course was disappointed that she did not win the title for Holland. Francis and I are good friends off stage but, once we are on the oche, there is no love lost between us. Then we are up there to do a job and be professional about it. We had certainly put on a great show and that could only have been good for the ladies' game. It had also confirmed my status as the top lady darts player in the world.

But there was another reason why I was desperate to retain my title. In the first year that I had become world champion, one of the driving forces, over and above my family, who urged me on and continued to encourage me, no matter what, was my good friend Julia Raggett. Julia should have been supporting me as she had the previous year but she was too ill to attend. Instead, my friend was in Myton Hospice, sadly very poorly suffering the final throes of terminal cancer. She was only thirty-five. I had known her for eight years and we were good friends. She had supported me throughout my career but had been particularly enthusiastic during my Embassy World Championship campaign. Julia had played Super League and local darts in Southam and her warmth and beautiful smile were disarming. If you ever watch a video re-run of my 2002 world championship 114 out-shot to win you will actually see me mouthing the words, 'Come on. This is for Julia.' Julia died soon afterwards, in late February. In lasting memory to her name, the Southam Darts team set up the Julia Raggett Memorial Fund, which raises money for cancer-associated charities through darts.

During my speech at the reception later, I dedicated my World Championship win to Julia. She was the kind of person we all hope we can meet during our lifetime. I couldn't have wished for a nicer friend.

I still miss her.

While I was going through an emotional upheaval on the world championship stage, Gully, as usual, wasn't there to witness the defence of my title. He spent the time pacing the car park or sitting in the car. He was still waiting to watch the video of my match twenty-four hours later!

The winner of the Men's Embassy World Championship in 2002 was thirty-five-year-old Tony David, the first Australian ever to lift the coveted trophy. Tony's battle had not only been against some of the finest dart players ever gathered together in one place but also against a condition that would have seen many people simply giving up the idea of playing darts. Tony is an arthritic haemophiliac and as a result is unable to fully extend his darts-throwing arm. His condition was diagnosed when he was a child and doctors once told his parents that he had a limited time to live, but thankfully, Tony proved the medical profession wrong.

Starting out as a 50–1 outsider to win the title, Tony's journey through to the final featured victories over Wales' Ritchie Davies, Marko Pusa (Finland), Scotland's Bob Taylor and the England Captain, Martin Adams. He met England's Mervyn King in the final and, in an exciting match, Tony ran out the winner 6–4. Mervyn King, who has yet to win the World Championship, but is always there or thereabouts, told *Darts World* at the time, 'I played like a plonker and he just bashed me up.' Thus it was Tony who joined Tony Green and me on the Embassy Roadshows. They were due to start almost immediately at York, ending later in the year in Dumfries. I had thoroughly enjoyed the Roadshows with John 'Boy' Walton and now was very much looking forward to life on the road with the two Tonys.

During the men's final of the Dutch Open in February, Shaun Greatbatch caused a sensation. Shaun achieved the first 'live' televised nine-dart game of 501 against Lancashire's Steve

Coote. Veteran darter, John Lowe had hit a nine-darter on television back in 1984, but his was recorded and transmitted later, as was American Paul Lim's perfect game in the Embassy in 1990, whereas Shaun's was broadcast live by the Dutch television company SBS6. For those who are not sure, that's the same thing as scoring 147 in snooker – it's the perfect game. But, unlike snookers' 147, the nine-darter can be achieved any number of ways. On this historic occasion, Shaun went out hitting seven consecutive treble twenties, followed by treble fifteen and finishing on double eighteen. The 5,000-strong crowd went mad and the game had to be halted for a while. All credit to Shaun, he kept his cool and eventually won the final 4–2. I've hit nine-darters in the past, but never in front of the cameras. I've come close a few times but it is one of my unfulfilled ambitions to achieve that live on the Lakeside stage in the World Championship finals.

At the Dutch Open, I went out of the Ladies' Singles in the last eight, beaten by Surrey's Tricia Wright. Francis took the title, beating Tricia 3–2 in the final. It was her sixth Dutch Open title and, of course, the home crowd loved it. The only compensation for me was victory with Francis in the Ladies' Pairs event. Francis is a formidable player and I often wonder if I hadn't appeared just how much she would have ruled the ladies' game. I honestly believe she would have become the Phil Taylor of women's darts, sweeping all before her. In a way, it's a good job I came on the scene!

However, there was more news from our friends in Holland. A brand new darts competition was to be introduced in that country in September called the World Darts Trophy with television coverage by SBS6. Not only was this great news for darts, but it was also even greater news for us ladies. We were to have our own competition with £9,000 for the winner: the biggest ever winner's cheque in the women's game. The top six women in the BDO international rankings would be joined in the event by two 'wild card' entries selected by the promoters. That was another great step forwards for women's darts and the game in general – and another target for me for 2002!

The other good news was that my friend Clare Bywaters, an impressive Oxfordshire County player (later to move over to Warwickshire 'A') had been amongst those selected to represent England in the forthcoming Internationals. In the end, the place went to Yorkshire's Karen Smith, but Clare's time would come and she and I would also meet on the oche many, many times in the future. However, little did I know at the time, that the relationship between Clare and I would develop into a very close friendship that would later result in us buying a house together when both of our existing relationships collapsed.

During March 2002, I competed in the Isle of Man Open, bidding to win the only major that had so far eluded me. It eluded me again. I was full of confidence and had been optimistic of a good run. Francis and I were confident of winning the Ladies' Pairs. We were hot favourites to take the title but we received a rude awakening when Apylee Jones and Sue Edwards dumped us out at the quarter-final stage. I fared little better in the Ladies' Singles.

Sure, I started well, but my Manx jinx struck again. I didn't even make the last sixteen, falling to an on-form Mandy Solomons in an earlier round. Mandy went on to reach the final. In the meantime, Crissy Howat swept through the field in her half of the draw and then defeated Mandy in the final. The new 'slim line' Crissy, who had previously won the Isle of Man Open in 1998, put her success down to the strict diet plan that she and her partner, the professional darts player Peter 'One Dart' Manley, had been on. Crissy's daughter, Michelle Jackson, had also joined them on the diet although she didn't need to lose weight. She was just keeping fit and keeping Crissy and Peter company.

In April, I started out on a new exhibition/roadshow tour, this time with Andy 'The Viking' Fordham and MC Martin Fitzmaurice. It was called The Big, Big and Beautiful Roadshow and it kicked off on St George's Day, 23 April. I was hoping that, as both Andy and I were involved closely with the Heart of Darts charity, we could raise a few pounds for that cause during our time on the road.

By May, the Embassy Roadshows with Tony David were also underway and were going really well. Our first show had been at York, followed by Billingham and then Pontefract. Tony had asked me to help administer his injections! He told me, 'There's nothing to it.' Of course not, Tony! I do this sort of thing all the time.

I'm not squeamish but ...

Immediately after the Pontefract Roadshow, I was off again to the continent for the German Open. Well, when I say 'off again' I actually mean I set off twice. Twenty-five minutes into my journey to Birmingham airport, I was driving along and going over in my mind – as you do – whether or not I had remembered everything. Had I remembered my passport? I knew that I had removed one from the drawer at home. But was it mine? I stopped the car, checked my bag – and NO it wasn't! I'd picked up Gully's passport by mistake. I thought, 'Chuffin' hell!' I turned the car around, headed back home, collected the right passport and made it to the airport just as check-in was closing with only seconds to spare.

After that I did OK, although Francis beat me 2–1 in the final after another of our tough battles on the oche. Francis and I then took the Ladies' Pairs title, beating Crissy Howat and Tricia Wright 2–1. On the plane home from Germany, I did some thinking. I was so busy that I reckoned that I'd be lucky if I got one day a week off over the forthcoming three months. As a professional darts player, travelling takes up so much time, and then of course there's time spent at tournaments and in practice honing your skills, plus time that has to be set aside for media interviews and meeting and chatting with the fans, the paying public. I also had to fit in time to work at home, to wash and iron and to prepare myself (and pack my cases) in readiness for the next stop on my hectic schedule. Among all of that I tried desperately hard to fit in some quality time with Gully.

Back on the road, Tony David and I received a fabulous welcome at the Embassy Roadshow at Wrexham. They had put up a huge banner congratulating us on our Embassy victories. It was marvellous. Tony had taken to the Roadshows like a duck to water and was handling the hectic pace very well, although I did have to take him to hospital on one occasion. Don't panic! It was no problem. Tony had simply run out of his medication.

There was also something to celebrate in the Inter County Competition during April as my county team, Warwickshire Ladies 'A', became champions of the Premier Division for the first time ever. The crucial winning points had been achieved during the penultimate match of the season, against Lancashire. The Warwickshire ladies beat the Lancashire ladies 5–1, which took them seven points clear and gave us an unassailable lead in the table. The successful team on that day consisted of Debbie McPherson, Vicki Byrne, Clare Bywaters, Lesley Newcombe, Pat Thornton and me. Pat was the only one to lose her match, but we didn't hold that against her. Well done, girls! Well done each and every one of you.

As the summer approached, I finally found a little time to reflect on the first half of 2002. All in all, it had been a difficult time for me. Losing my friend Julia to cancer had been an almighty blow, not only to me but to all those who knew and loved her, but I was thinking of her, wishing she were there. I thought to myself, 'What would Julia say to me if she was to walk through that door now and see me like this, in sad but reflective mood?'

Julia would have smiled in my face, put her arms around me, and said, 'Cheer up mate. It might never happen.'

Chapter Nineteen

Hat-trick

Despite feeling down at the end of May, I had seen some degree of success. I had won the BDO May Day 2002 Darts Festival at Hemsby Holiday Camp in Norfolk. I'd met Crissy in the final, taken the title with a 3–1 score line, and won £400. It was my first win in that event. Tony David and I played in the Mixed Pairs, a formidable double Embassy partnership, and ran out winners, beating Dorset's Simon and Claire Whatley 3–1 to share the £400 prize.

The England National Singles were played at the same venue and I was successful in winning the Ladies' title for the first time, overcoming Somerset's Karen Littler in the final and receiving – yes – £400 for my troubles. Not a bad few days considering. It was good news all round for Warwickshire, as my county colleague, Tony Brown, won the Men's National Singles title.

I had also won my third Finnish Open during May, beating Crissy 4–1 in the final. The England captain, Martin Adams, took the men's title with a victory over the home favourite, Jarko Komula. In the British International Championships at Bridlington both the ladies' and the men's teams were victorious. I played a blinder against Wales' Sandra Greatbatch, averaging 33.40 per dart and beating her 3–0. I hit six scores of 100 or more plus two maximum 180s and picked up the 'Lady of the Match Award'. The England Ladies won the match against the Welsh girls overall 5–1.

I had another clean sheet (3–0) against Scotland in my game with Donna Robertson, hitting a lower average (28.90) and picking up my second 'Lady of the Match Award' of the competition. In fact, the whole team won. We whitewashed the Scots 6–0 and thus took the ladies' title and celebrated in good style. The full England team that won the championship was Crissy (Cumbria), Clare Bywaters (Warwickshire), Debra Royal (Lincolnshire), Sue Talbot (Suffolk), Karen Smith (Yorkshire), Marie Geaney (Somerset) and, of course, me.

After all that, I couldn't really see why I was so down come the summer, but I was. Perhaps I didn't realise it at the time but, looking back, I should have noticed. My life was in disarray. I just couldn't fit everything in. I had to step down as President of the Heart of Darts charity. I was working such long hours now that I just couldn't do the job justice. As you will have gathered, I never like to go about anything in a half-hearted way. Such a post demands a good deal of one's time and I just couldn't put the time in, so I reluctantly decided to hand the position over to someone who could. Someone else I had to consider, of course, was Gully.

He supported me in everything I did and there I was coming home from exhibitions and tournaments and then having to spend time on charity business when I should have been spending time with him. I had to get my priorities right. While the charity was important, Gully was more so. Of course, I still intended to support Heart of Darts in whatever way I could.

And I had so much to look forward to ...

Apart from the defence of my world title, I was targeting those other two titles I wanted back, the Gold Cup and the World Masters, plus there was the new World Trophy. Dates for that had been announced and the tournament was to take place in Utrecht between 7 and 15 September.

In June, I took the long flight to Canada to play in the Golden Harvest Cup in Saskatoon and it was well worth it. Surprisingly, I found that Deta Hedman, who had retired from the sport a few years earlier, playing. She had taken a holiday out there and decided to have a go. I met her in the semi-final and she played as if she had never been away. It was a great match, which I won – and guess who was waiting for me in the final? Francis. I had waited three years to take the title and not even Francis was to stop me this time. I won and pocketed a cheque for a massive $25,000. Well worth the trip!

In July, I successfully defended my England Open title against Holland's Karin Krappen – these Dutch girls get *everywhere*! – and came runner-up with Hampshire's James Wade in the Mixed Pairs. The day before, after a long day of preliminary rounds, Gully, Crissy, her daughter, Michelle Jackson, plus a few others and I took up Francis' invitation to attend her barbecue on the camp site. Fran's a really good cook and we ate, drank and were merry. At the end of the evening someone suggested that we had a 'Who can stand on their heads the longest?' competition. What a laugh. Eventually, Lincolnshire's Debbie Royal wiped the floor with the rest of us. By the time she was announced the winner, and after all the eating and drinking we'd done, it was more like a 'Who can stand on their head *at all?*' competition. I felt sick, but what a night!

Despite the best efforts of the BDO, a separate Pentathlon for the ladies had not materialised. Obtaining sponsorship for the men's tournaments was difficult enough and there was simply no one prepared to back a women's version. So I took on the lads again at the Rainham Mark Social Club in Kent. Unfortunately, I'd forgotten what a long, hard day it was and so performed poorly by my standards. I finished way down the field of twenty at a lowly seventeenth place and way, way off the money.

One of the highlights of the summer for me was being invited to open the fête at the Southam Primary School, the school I used to attend. It was lovely to be asked and the visit brought back lots of fond memories for me. The theme of the fête was sport and included not only a football tournament, netball and golf, but also darts. I had a great time and the cherry on the cake was seeing my nine-year-old nephew Jake, who plays in goal, and his team win the football tournament.

In August, I had entered both the Belgium Open and the British Classic. The Open was on a Saturday and the Classic on the Sunday. I chose to go by car as I thought there'd be problems getting flights back at the right times. So the four of us, Clare Bywaters, Crissy, Gully (navigating) and I piled into the car and off we went. I was wrong. Many players went by plane and had no difficulties whatsoever.

In the final of the Belgium Open, I was defeated 4–1 by Francis. To be honest, the way I had played that day, I was surprised to have made it past the third round. From Belgium we drove back to England and arrived at our hotel in Kettering at about 1.30 in the morning. The 2002 Red Dragon British Classic was held at the nearby Kettering Leisure Village later that day. I wondered what the day might bring. I had won the event for the past two years and was looking for a hat-trick. I felt more confident than I had done the previous day and played a lot better, although I rode my luck at times. I played Debbie Royal in the semi-final and she should have beaten me 3–0 but my game picked up and I pulled it back to 2–2 and then took the final set to come out the winner 3–2. I met London's Tricia Wright in the final, but I missed doubles and Tricia took the title 3–0. I was comprehensively beaten by Tricia.

Next up were the Denmark and Norway Opens. Again, I didn't fair as well as I had expected. I was knocked out of the Denmark Open in the last sixteen by Holland's Karin Krappen and then Francis beat me in the final of the Norway Open. But there was still the Embassy Gold Cup, one of the major titles I was expected to retain this year; one of my prime targets on my way, hopefully, to a third world championship success.

I don't really know what happened. I never even made the last sixteen of the Gold Cup. That was a disaster. However, Clare made it through to the final but was beaten by an on-form Marie Geaney (Somerset) 3–1. Cheryl Jackson and I managed runner-up position in the Ladies' Pairs, so that was some consolation, although not much.

Next up was the new tournament, the World Darts Trophy in Holland. With €15,000 (about £10,000) up for grabs for the ladies (the men's top prize was €45,000, about £30,000), I was expecting to perform well, and I didn't. Held at the vast Vechtsebanen Complex in Utrecht, the tournament promised much and it delivered in style. The whole atmosphere was breathtaking and the camaraderie between the players was second to none with everyone looking after one another.

The line-up for the ladies' quarter-final was exceptional and consisted of Crissy, Anne Kirk, Vicky Pruim, Carina Ekberg, Francis and me. Unfortunately, things didn't go as planned. The story of the match was that I missed my doubles and Anne hit them. It was as simple as that. Anne sent me packing two sets to one. That was my tournament over, so I decided to spend some time at Utrecht hospital.

Not deliberately you understand.

A couple of days after I'd played the quarter-final, I (and a number of others) had been bitten by mosquitoes. The little bugger that bit me had punctured the palm of my left hand –

fortunately, not my throwing hand. Silvia van Barneveld, wife of the World Champion Raymond van Barneveld, saw the wound. She looked very worried and pointed out that it seemed to be tracking up my arm. I asked her what that meant and she replied, 'If it gets to your heart, you've had it. You'd better get to hospital.' So, off I went to hospital for treatment. There I was given some antibiotics and assumed that my condition was no longer life threatening. As if being bitten by a bloody mosquito wasn't enough, I soon found that the antibiotics didn't agree with me. I won't go into any details, but, put it this way, for the rest of the week I would have appreciated sponsorship from Andrex, the makers of that extra soft toilet tissue.

Bloody mosquitoes!

The on-form Mieke de Boer pleased her home crowd by taking the Ladies' title in the World Darts Trophy beating Crissy 3–1 in the final. Everyone had expected the final to be an England–Holland affair fought out between Francis and me, but – well you know what happened to me – Francis was beaten in the semi-final 2–0 by Mieke.

In October's Europe Cup, which was held in Mechelen, in Belgium, Clare, playing in her first major, played some brilliant darts and won the Ladies' Singles, beating Francis 4–2 in the final. Clare's win helped secure runner-up position for the England ladies. The Dutch ladies ran out winners by a clear 20 points. I had earlier crashed out in the first round to Russia's up-and-coming star, Anastasia Dobromyslova.

The following day, Clare and I took an early flight back to London's Stansted airport to try and make our Warwickshire County fixture in Surrey. To make the flight we had to set our alarm clocks for 2.30 a.m.! When we left the hotel shortly afterwards, the celebration party was still going on! Apparently, the last revellers didn't go to bed until 6.30 a.m. That's Francis for you. A party animal!

Clare and I landed at Stansted at seven o'clock, which gave us plenty of time to drive down to Epsom, the venue of the county match. We had planned the route. It was simple: M11, then M25 and we were there. So there I was driving along the M11 with Clare in the passenger seat trying hard to stay awake. Suddenly I realised something. 'Clare.' I said. 'What?' replied my half-asleep friend. I paused and then said, 'I think we're going the wrong way.' Clare started and sat up in her seat. '*We?*' she said, repeating, '*We?*'

Clare was wide awake now.

I said, 'We're going towards Cambridge and we should be going towards London!'

'You're joking!' came the reply.

'I wish I was', I said. 'We'll come off at the next junction and turn around.'

Amid laughter and a few choice, unladylike words we turned off at junction 11 and headed back in the direction we had come from. By the time we had returned to the place where we had originally joined the M11 we had travelled about fifty miles out of our way. The good thing was though, that we still had plenty of time to make it to Epsom. 'Right' I said to Clare, 'M25 next, mate.' Clare pointed at the junction we were just passing and said, 'What? That turning there? The one we've just passed?' I couldn't believe it. I'd done it again! It was miles until the next opportunity to turn back presented itself. I think we travelled near enough right to the end of the M11.

It was not quite so funny second time around. Any trust Clare had in my driving had been dashed. At one point, she even offered to take over the driving. I often wonder what would have happened if she had. Would we have ended up in Cambridge? (Sorry, Clare. Only joking!) We managed to make the county game, but the Warwickshire Ladies' A were beaten 4–2, although I did win my game. Clare didn't, but then perhaps she was still getting over the experience of my driving! But Clare didn't have to face the trauma of my driving on the way back. Gully and Clare's boyfriend Ian had travelled down together to the match, as they both figured we would be too knackered to drive home. So Ian drove Clare home while Gully took control of my sponsored car and chauffeured me back to Warwickshire.

After that, my focus was all on the WINMAU World Masters. I had won it last year and needed to retain my title; not just for me but also for my sponsors, WINMAU. As it turned out, it was an all-England final. I had come up against the highly talented Dutch girl, Karin Krappen, in the semi-final and I had to fight hard to win through. Meanwhile, in the other semi-final, England's Karen Smith beat my key adversary Francis 4–1, winning her place in the final with a 116 check-out. To be honest it was a sloppy final. *Darts World* described my performance as 'lacklustre' and I have to agree with that. However, don't let that detract from the fact that I beat Karen 4–1.

Neither Karen (who had won the WINMAU title in 1998) nor I could reproduce the form we had shown in the earlier rounds and our averages were poor by comparison: 21.46 per dart for Karen and 22.70 for me. But there I was, posing for photographs with WINMAU'S Marketing Director, Ian Flack, holding the World Masters trophy and a cheque for £3,000.

In November, the Julia Raggett Memorial Cup was launched in memory of my good friend who had died earlier in the year. A four-person team event was held at the Harbury Club just outside Southam and the England Captain Martin Adams and MC Martin Fitzmaurice both gave their time free to help run the tournament that was organised by the Stoneythorpe Ladies B team. Other darts stars, including Phil 'The Power' Taylor, Steve Beaton, Francis, Crissy, Wayne Mardle, Peter Manley and Andy Fordham gave darts, shirts, caps and other items to auction or raffle. It was a great success with £3,000 being raised, which was split between Cancer Research UK and the local Myton Hospice, where Julia spent her last days.

My next darts success was in the Swedish Open, where I beat Francis in the final 4–1. It all boded well for the World Championships ... or did it? The line-up was known and the first-round draw had been done. The field consisted of Francis, Karin Krappen and Mieke de Boer (all from The Netherlands), Wales' Gaynor Williams and Linda Rogers-Pickett, Anne Kirk (Scotland) together with two English girls, Norwich's Dawn Standley and me. The ladies' matches were scheduled for Saturday 4 January and Sunday 5 January, and I had been drawn against Dawn and was due to play at 4.00 p.m. on the Sunday. Most pundits fancied another final between Francis and me, but Anne Kirk put an end to that by beating Francis 2–0 in the semi-finals.

Dawn made me work for my semi-final place. It was Dawn's first appearance in the World Championship finals, but you wouldn't have thought so. She forced a deciding set, but I triumphed with the top average of the first round, 25.81. In the semi, I met Mieke and soon wrapped up the first set 3–1 with a 100 checkout. The dreaded 'double trouble' returned to my game in the second set but I recovered the situation and hit a maximum and then a double eight to secure the match.

In the final against Anne, I was quickly in front, taking the first set 3–0. But in the second, I found myself trailing 2–0 but battled back to level. I hit a maximum 180 in the deciding fifth leg and then produced a 97 checkout (single 19, treble 18, double 12) to lift the title for the third time. My title-winning average was 28.31 and was the best in all the ladies' matches. Someone then pointed out to me that that average would not have been out of place in the men's championships. Wales' Ritchie Davies, who was runner-up in the men's event, only had an average of 23.40 per dart! He picked up £25,000 for being runner-up to Raymond van Barneveld, while I was rewarded with £4,000 for winning the ladies'! Is there any justice? Barney had won the Embassy for the third time, too, but his wins were not consecutive. Mine were.

To win one world title was something. To win a second was special, but to win three on the trot was absolutely unreal! I was in an utter daze for days. I kept saying to myself 'My God! I really did it!' I'd achieved it against the odds. I hadn't played consistently well during the year and the pre-tournament publicity really piled on the pressure. I had had high expectations of myself and desperately wanted to win a third time. Now I had succeeded in defending *my* title it was beholden on me to defend it again in 2004. It was, wasn't it?

Although I didn't see it at the time, what I decided to do next was to cause lasting damage to my relationship with Gully and eventually lead to divorce.

Chapter Twenty

Putting a Family
on Hold

I was on top of the world again and, as usual, I celebrated in style, but there was something else that needed to be said and I said it rather publicly in my 'Gulliver's Travels' column in *Darts World*.

I announced that winning the Embassy World Championship for the third time had made me revise my plans for the future, well, certainly in the short term. During 2002 Gully and I had discussed starting a family and there was certainly a suggestion that I would pack my darts away after my title defence and spend more time concentrating on expanding the Gulliver family.

But clearly there was now a nagging doubt in my mind.

I felt an obligation to come back and defend my title in 2004 and said as much in a television interview immediately after my third success. If I gave up the darts in favour of starting a family, the sport would never have seen me again. That would have pleased a few people, but only people who didn't matter to me anyway. Surely it was only right that I go down with all guns blazing rather than just hand over the title without a fight? That sounded more than reasonable to me. The more I thought about it, the more I felt determined to shelve the baby plans for a while at least. I just couldn't do both, although the thought of nursing a bump on the Lakeside stage the following January did make me smile.

I took a week's break and caught up with domestic chores, and then it was back to practise and preparations for a short series of exhibitions with MC Martin Fitzmaurice for the Welsh brewery, Brains.

On the wider darts front, there were fears for the future of the Embassy World Championships. The government had announced the total ban of sponsorship by tobacco companies and the British Darts Organisation had been fighting for the Embassy to be considered an 'exceptional global event' so that the ban on darts could be delayed, the same as had already been agreed for Formula One motor racing. As 2003 began, the BDO was still waiting to hear whether or not exceptional status had been granted. However, the good news was that the BDO had contingency plans in place but preferred not to announce these until the final government decision was forthcoming. Surely there was no way the premier darts championship would be lost to the sport?

February was an exceptionally busy month for me. I entered the first-ever International Dart Players Association (IDPA) Ladies Masters at the Portland Club, in Inverness. The ladies were treated very well by the hosts, to the extent that limousines, with bottles of champagne inside, picked us up from the hotel and took us to the venue. I made the final but was beaten 4–3 by Cumbria's Barbara Lee. Barbara had beaten Anne Kirk and Tricia Wright on her way to meeting me in the final. What a match it was! I took a 3–0 lead, but Barbara pulled it back to 3–3. We were so well matched that we had to throw twice for bull to see who started the deciding leg. Barbara won the darts and we exchanged tons and ton-plusses and headed towards a nail-biting finish. I was waiting on 66 when Barbara shot out on 64 and lifted the title. What a game! Well done, Barbara!

We had major problems getting home after that tournament. It had snowed so hard that some of the ladies' flights were cancelled and the news was that the conditions were unlikely to improve. So I decided to hire a car and drove Sally Smith, who played county darts for Somerset, and Clare home. Mad? Absolutely. I thought so from the start and I'm certain Sally and Clare felt so, too, but off we went. It took me ten hours to get us home. When I pulled up outside the house, I fell out of the car on to the ground, arms outstretched and unable to move.

Two days later, the three of us played in the Dutch Open. I only made the last sixteen in the Ladies' Singles, the victory going to Belgium's Sandra Pollet. Clare and Sally joined forces in the Ladies' Pairs but met Francis and me in the final and we beat them 2–0 to retain the title that we had won the previous year.

February also brought news of an honour that I had never expected to receive. You will remember how the mayor of my home town of Southam had previously asked me to switch on the Christmas lights, well, this time the mayor's office contacted me and said that a civic reception was being held in my honour in recognition of my achievement in winning three world titles. I couldn't believe it. The reception was held at the Southam Community Centre on Sunday 19 February 2003. I wore a smart suit for the occasion. Gully came with me but he didn't say very much.

I really didn't know what to expect. There were several of my former schoolteachers there, including Mrs Clarke, my former head of house, and Mr Savage, who, although he was the boys' physical education teacher when I was at school, had always followed my darts career through talking to my nieces and nephews as they went through school. They talked about my school days and referred to my 'steely determination to succeed'. (Yeah, right. Are you thinking what I'm thinking?) Was this really their opinion of the same Trina Jones who *hated* school? I was very nervous when each speaker stood up and quite apprehensive about what they might say. I found the whole experience a little uncomfortable, but it was also nice to hear so many people saying such nice things about me. It was a big honour for me and very special; something I shall never, ever forget.

The council presented me with an engraved crystal plate and I was told that there were plans to mark my darting success in another way. Ideas under discussion at that time were a young person's sporting achiever's fund and even a *statue*! (If that ever happens, I hope Martin Fitzmaurice is never reincarnated as a pigeon!) Nearly five years on, nothing much has happened. I did hear that there were plans to have a sculpture in steel erected on one of the traffic islands as you come into the town. The design was to be a crown with my name around it with three darts appearing from the centre. However, I understand that the highway authority put a stop to that, saying it would be too much of a distraction, but that doesn't mean that the proposal is dead and buried. No. The last I heard, off the record, was that plans are still afoot to do something. Whatever it is, and whenever it happens, I'll still be chuffed to bits.

As if the civic reception wasn't enough, that very same month Pete Murray, the Chairman of the England selectors, contacted me and informed me that I had been selected to captain the England Ladies' team. Paddy Reeson, the current non-playing captain had decided to retire and the job was now mine if I wanted it. My reaction? Something like 'My God! Yes! Yes! Yes!' which is usually a phrase I use in another recreational activity! To say I was delighted would be an understatement. I just hoped I'd carry out my duties as well as Paddy had.

That same month I missed my annual pilgrimage to the Isle of Man Open, but for a very good reason. I attended Mervyn King's wedding. Mervyn is a great, and sometimes temperamental, player and he has won most major darts titles, yet the Embassy always eluded him. Any hope of Mervyn securing that coveted title evaporated when he transferred his allegiance from the BDO to the Professional Darts Corporation (PDC) in 2007.

Never had I seen a man so proud and happy as Mervyn looked on his wedding day and his wife Tracey looked stunning. Martin Adams was best man and, as I expected, he did a great job. It was a superb day and the Isle of Man Open would have to be a target for me for the following year, provided I was still playing.

Any arguments about whether or not I would still be playing darts next year or whether Gully and I were going to start a family in 2003 disappeared a few days later when I signed a new three-year contract with the WINMAU Dartboard Company. The company had sponsored me for four years and had clearly been pleased with the results. Ian Flack, Marketing Director for WINMAU said of me in a press release: 'Trina is everything we look for in a darts professional. She is a supremely talented darts player, is very well spoken, highly presentable and well respected on the darts circuit for her honesty, integrity and phenomenal ability. She has become one of the WINMAU family, and we are thrilled that we can continue our superb relationship with Trina over the next three years.'

Needless to say, with praise like that, I wanted to do my utmost to deliver the goods again, not only for WINMAU but also for my other sponsors.

In April, I nervously stepped up on stage at the British International Championships in Merthyr Tydfil as Captain of the England Ladies' team. Both teams – men and women –

maintained a one hundred per cent record and so lifted both titles. I averaged 27.11 against Scotland's Anne Kirk, who I beat 3–1, and increased this to 28.90 when I whitewashed Wales' Julie Gore 3–0. I was awarded the 'Woman of the Match Award' for both games. The England Ladies beat Scotland overall 4–2 and Wales by a similar scoreline. My winning team consisted of Clare, Crissy, Marie Geaney, Debra Royal, Karen Smith and Apylee Jones. The girls were so supportive and they certainly helped me lead them to victory over our old adversaries.

Another 'old adversary' is my friend and MC Martin Fitzmaurice. He and I had some great laughs during the Brains exhibitions but I was so often on the receiving end of his jokes. When I was over in Bochum for the German Open, I decided it was time for a bit of revenge. It was time to cool off 'the Fat Man'. With a little time to spare for shopping before the matches kicked off, some of the girls and I rediscovered a toy and joke shop that we had visited on a previous visit to the town and looked round for an appropriate practical joke. We spent half an hour in the shop laughing about the stuff on display and I finally decided on a 'booster water pistol'.

I carefully worked out my plan of attack. I would find out which bar Martin was in (and I was *pretty* certain he would be in a bar) and then I'd walk in wearing shades and a long leather coat that concealed my weapon. You get the picture? Well, that's what I *thought* of doing. As it turned out, I wore a short blue denim jacket, concealing the water pistol and my driving glasses.

I walked into the bar and, sure enough, there was Martin sitting in the corner, chatting away to friends and fans, totally absorbed in conversation and oblivious to everything else that was happening around him. I was able to approach him without being noticed. I got closer and closer until he was within my sights. I took the water pistol out of my jacket, aimed and fired! The water hit him square on the top of his bald head and ricocheted off it, soaking an innocent bystander! (Sorry, whoever you were!)

I'd never seen Martin move so quickly in my life! It took him some minutes to work out where the water had come from and who the culprit was. When he realised it was me, he stopped swearing and told me he loved me dearly. No, to be honest, he carried on swearing. I was eventually disarmed and received a soaking in return.

Soon it was down to the serious business of earning those all-important ranking points. Francis and I won the Ladies' Pairs title and I took the Ladies' Singles title by beating Sweden's Carina Ekberg. I was very pleased, as I hadn't won the German Open title since 1997. This return to form seemed to bode well for the future, but ...

I only made it as far as the last eight at the England National Singles tournament in May, which was eventually won by Staffordshire's Sarah Hall who beat Debra Royal (Lincolnshire) 3–0 in the final. Disappointingly, due to other darting commitments, I was unable to travel to Finland to defend my Finnish Open title. I always like to return to defend my titles but on this occasion I was so busy. That, I suppose, is one of the problems of being a world champion and in demand. However, I did find time to respond to yet another request from the Mayor of Southam. This time it was to launch the Southam website which told you all you needed to know about my home town. The mayor invited me to make the first 'hit' on the site.

During May, I struggled to find time to be at home. It was a tortuous life in a way, but I loved being busy and I loved my trade. I was going out on the road, coming home, spending a couple of days with Gully and then I was packing the suitcases again and going off to Birmingham airport en route to my next tournament or exhibition. I treasured those few moments that Gully and I managed to spend together but more often than not they were restricted to brief conversations as I was tied to the washing machine, the tumble dryer or the ironing board – or practising – when perhaps we should have been sat down together working out our future plans. But the job was calling me ...

I spent a busy month in Lloret de Mar on Spain's Costa Brava playing exhibitions and promoting a new tournament called Fun in the Sun. I was accompanied by Mervyn King, Francis, Barney, Holland's John Paul van Aker, John 'Boy' Walton, Martin Adams, Martin Fitzmaurice and Belgium's Erik Clarys. Gully came along, too, as did Martin Adams' wife, Sharon, Tracey King, Silvia Barneveld and Sally Walton. After competing in an exhibition, we all went to a nearby fairground. Now, I'm not a great fan of theme parks or fairground rides – the most dangerous I ever get is a go on the dodgems. My delicate stomach can't take waltzers or roller coasters and so I always avoid the ones that spin you round, throw you about or turn you upside down.

Merv tried to convince me to go on a particular ride. It was shaped like a metal ball. Two people sat in it and then they were catapulted about 300 feet or more into the air on ropes, the ball spinning as it hurtled heavenwards – 'No, thanks. I'm not interested.' I was eventually convinced by Silvia van Barneveld that it would be fun, so she and I tried it – and I'm glad I did. It was brilliant and I was so pleased that I wasn't sick all over Silvia – and I'm sure she was, too! Most of our group had a go and I have to admit that there were some who looked a lot greener than me when they came off it.

No sooner had I returned home from Spain than I was off to Canada with Clare to the Golden Harvest Open to defend my title. We stopped off on the way to take in Niagara Falls. What an awesome sight! I played well at Saskatoon but Francis played better and took my title. However, the $10,000 runner's-up prize money helped to console me!

The month of June was a time of great sadness for the world

of darts. Leighton Rees, the 'Gentleman of Darts', first Embassy World Champion and one of the greatest Welsh darts players of all time, died. Hours earlier, during the same weekend, Lorna Croft, wife of the BDO Director Olly Croft also passed away. Lorna had played a vital, behind-the-scenes role for many years. Whenever I met her, Lorna would always ask how I was and was always willing to help anyone before giving any thought about herself or her own personal battles with life.

I attended Lorna's funeral. Floral tributes completely covered the front lawn of her home in Muswell Hill. About 400 mourners followed the horse-drawn, glass hearse from the family home to the nearby Methodist church where she and Olly had been married fifty years earlier. The service was beautiful, with endearing tributes from her children and grandchildren. She was a truly wonderful person.

I still miss her.

For dear Leighton, the Glyntaff crematorium chapel at Pontypridd was packed with family, friends and many representatives of the Welsh darts community. On his passing I was reminded of when we did the 'live' Embassy draw together. He was so nervous that he actually thanked me afterwards for helping him through it. There was the first ever Embassy World Professional Darts Champion thanking little old *me* for helping *him*! He obviously didn't realise what a pleasure and honour it was for me to be up there on stage with one of my heroes. He was a great man and a great player and did an awful lot for darts. In fact, if it weren't for dedicated people like Leighton and Lorna, people like me would not be where we are today.

No, that's right. If it hadn't been for them, I'd probably have been at home with Gully and ...

Chapter Twenty-one

Four Up!

The summer of 2003 was so busy for me. I'd missed the Swiss Open in 2002 but had decided to enter the following year. The weather out there was blazing hot. It was 34 degrees Centigrade outside and inside the venue we roasted. The hall had huge glass windows. Although the blinds were drawn, the heat was intense. Francis and I won the Ladies' Doubles but Francis beat me in the final of the Ladies' Singles. She was really beginning to annoy me! (Only joking, Francis!)

After some exhibition work on the Isle of Wight, I went to the England Open at Brean Sands where I had my revenge on Francis for beating me in the Swiss Open by winning the Ladies' Singles. As expected, she and I met in the final and it was classic stuff. Francis hit form quickly and was soon in a 2–0 lead in a best-of-five-game final. Francis was cruising and I was heading for another bruising. In the all-important third game, after only fifteen darts, Francis was waiting to hit double top to take the title. But I was having none of it and raised my game, winning with a 103 out-shot.

I then won the next game to level the score at 2–2, but again Francis accelerated away and was poised after nineteen darts to take the match with double ten. However, she had to wait for me to see if I could hit a 76 finish. I did it and was crowned England Open Ladies' Singles Champion for the third year running – another hat-trick!

Then it was barbecue time again. In the previous year, Francis had played host but this year it was my turn. Luckily, there were no fatalities, but then that was probably because Gully did most of the cooking. Have you noticed how lads take over the running of a barbecue but few of them actually transfer those skills to the kitchen? Gully was very good at barbecues and made the meanest salads but that's as far as it went really. Me? I consider myself a very good cook, but my lifestyle means that I rarely have the opportunity to shine in that department. It's sad when the 'Friends and Family' numbers on your phone consists mainly of the local takeaways!

The next Pentathlon came and went and I finished up in fifteenth place, way behind the winner, my 'big brother', Andy Fordham. That's a standing joke between us. I do have a real brother called Andy, who watches over me. Before I went to any tournament my brother Andy used to say 'Is Gully going with you?' If I said, 'No', he'd then ask, 'Is Fordy going?' to which the reply was usually 'Yes'. Then he would say 'That's OK then. You'll be all right. He'll look after you', and of course my 'big brother' always did. It's really good to have people you can rely on, especially in the hectic world of professional darts.

August saw me right back on form as I won the IDPA Ladies' Masters at the Portland Club. I met Barbara Lee in the final, which was a repeat of the previous year, except this time I exacted my revenge on Barbara in a very close match. I thought

I was on top of it all as I went 2–0 up, but Barbara staged a comeback and levelled at 3–3, but I managed to win the deciding leg to take the title.

The Embassy Gold Cup followed at the Lakeside in Frimley Green. Unfortunately, this contest, which was in its twenty-sixth year, had fallen foul of the government's clampdown on tobacco sponsorship in sport. The government had decided not to treat darts as an exception and so it was to be the last Embassy Gold Cup and I was determined to leave my permanent mark on that championship. I beat Avon's Sue Edwards 3–0 in the Ladies' Singles final with an average per dart of 25.91 compared to Sue's 20.00. I then teamed up with Clare and we took the Ladies' Pairs with a 3–1 victory over Norfolk's Dawn Standley and Janice Butters. I certainly left my mark that day! For the record, the last winner of the men's Embassy Gold Cup was Cheshire's Brian Derbyshire who beat the 2001 champion – Wales' Ritchie Burnett – two games to nil. The Men's Pairs winners were Pembrokeshire's Mark Lewis and Lee Drummond, who beat the 'two Gary's' – Stirlingshire's Gary Robson and Gary Anderson – 4–3.

I didn't fare quite so well in Belgium. Switzerland's Lisa Huber was on form, threw excellent darts against me in the semi-final and sent me packing. Lisa went on to take the title against Francis. Soon afterwards, I was back home and competing in the Red Dragon British Classic at the Kettering Leisure Village. I had been on a potential hat-trick in the previous year but Tricia Wright had denied me that third victory in a row. This year, I made no mistake. I met Belgium's Sandra Pollet in the final and, although Sandra's average per dart was higher than mine (25.47 compared to my 24.45), I hit my doubles, won the final 3–1 and collected £500.

Around about this time of year, I would normally have travelled to the Norway Open but this year I had a more important task to perform. I was to be a bridesmaid at the wedding of my nephew Dan. I know that may seem a bit strange that I should accept such a role from my nephew but there is only eight years between us and, as I've said many times before, we're more like brother and sister than nephew and aunt. (He calls me 'Sis' and I call him 'Bro' – among other things!)

Dan's ceremony was a bit different to other church weddings. His wife-to-be, Teresa, was so nervous on the day that, instead of walking down the aisle to meet her husband-to-be, it was Dan who walked down the aisle to where Teresa was waiting. I'm sure it was nerves rather than shyness. (Teresa certainly wasn't shy on her hen night!) Dan walked down the aisle to the song 'The Boys are Back in Town'. The vicar thought it was hilarious. It was a brilliant day and everything went without a hitch. I was so proud to have been a part of Dan and Teresa's special day.

In September, I secured my first victory in the Bavaria World Darts Trophy and picked up the winner's cheque of €15,000. I met Scotland's Anne Kirk in the semi-finals and avenged my previous quarter-final defeat with a 2–0 win. Meanwhile, in the semi-final in the other half of the draw, the reigning Ladies' World Darts Trophy champion, Holland's Mieke de Boer, was up against Francis. Francis defeated Mieke 2–0 to set up yet another titanic dual between us. We both wanted to win the trophy so badly.

The atmosphere was electric, with 3,000 darts fans attending each session, which really was a great indicator of how the sport had taken off over there. Francis started like a train and took the first set 3–0, finishing each leg on double twenty scored with her first dart at double. I pulled myself together and then took all the remaining sets 3–2. I hit a magical 156 out-shot in the third leg and had an eleven-dart game in the fourth to make it 2–1 in sets. In the fourth set, I scored a 120 out-shot and had the chance to shoot out on 64 to win the title but, as usual, Francis pulled it back level at 2–2. The final leg was very close, but I took it and the title with a 64 checkout. I was presented with a magnificent glass trophy by the Mayor of Utrecht, Mrs Annie Brouwer, and the cheque for the biggest purse in ladies' world darts. Afterwards, Francis, Clare and I, and some others, went back to the hotel and celebrated with a few glasses – sorry that should be *bottles* – of champagne.

After winning the World Darts Trophy I realised that I was actually on course for the Grand Slam. The BDO and the WDF had introduced Grand Slam events for 2003 that consisted of the Women's World Championship, the World Darts Trophy and the WINMAU World Masters. All I had to do next was to win the WINMAU title and I would be the first woman ever to be crowned the Grand Slam winner. I say *all* I had to do ...

Could I do it?

Before then I had to captain my country in the World Cup XIV in Epinal in France. Once again, the girls did their country proud and we finished the competition with three gold medals. I won the Ladies' Singles against Sweden's Carina Ekberg by a margin of 4–0, while Clare and I won the Women's Pairs, beating Francis and Karin Krappen of The Netherlands 4–2. Then, to cap it all, seventeen-year-old Kate Dando (Somerset) took the Girls' Singles title 3–2 against Shunet Luke of South Africa. It was a great tournament for all of the England teams. In the celebrations that followed I ended up on stage playing drums, transported there by Holland's Co Stompe in a shopping trolley! I *think* I played drums, at least. (If I had been able to see them it might have helped!)

The WINMAU World Masters held at The Spa in Bridlington was hailed by many as the finest weekend of darts ever seen on television. Tony West (formerly a Hertfordshire County player but now living in Holland) and Raymond van Barneveld fought out a magnificent final, which Tony eventually won 7–6. What the ladies had produced before that was exceptional and was a great advertisement for women's darts. My journey to the final saw me beating Jan Robbins in a very close game and then taking out Carina Ekberg in the semis. Meanwhile, who was making her way through the second half of the draw? Yes, you've guessed it. It was my good friend ...

... Crissy.

Darts World called our final a 'ding-dong battle'. I couldn't have put that better myself. The match went right to the wire. In a best-of-seven final, Crissy and I traded high scores, but I went 3–1 up, only to see Crissy level at 3–3. The crowd at The Spa were on the edge of their seats. One minute they were quiet as the darts were thrown and the next they were on their feet screaming encouragement. The loudest response was when Crissy was down to a 64 finish with me back on 101. I knew Crissy could easily check out on 64, so I also knew that I needed to hit that three-figure out-shot. It was my last chance. I had to hit it. As I stood on the oche psyching myself out for the throw, I said to myself, 'Cor blimey Trine. You don't half put yourself through it sometimes!' I aimed for the twenty bed. Yes! Single twenty. Now treble fifteen. Yes! And finally double eighteen ('Please go in.'). Yes! I leapt up in the air, landed and then turned to Crissy to shake her hand. As she held my hand she said, 'Well done mate', and then added, 'I was ready for that sixty-four'. She knew I was well aware of that.

So I retained my WINMAU World Masters title and became the first to win the BDO Ladies' Grand Slam. Next up would be what used to be called the Embassy but was in future to be known as the Lakeside World Professional Darts Championship, with Bob Potter OBE, owner of Lakeside, becoming the main title sponsor. It was very sad to see the Embassy title disappear but of course everyone in the sport was thrilled that Bob had stepped forward.

The line-up for the fourth Ladies' World Championship was formally announced in November. I was the number one seed and had been drawn against Barbara Lee in my quarter-final match. I was thrilled that Barbara had made it through the qualifiers to earn a shot at the title. In the other quarter-final in my group, Karin Krappen would be taking on Scotland's Anne Kirk. Clare had also made it through to the finals via the tough qualifiers and was drawn to play the number three seed, Carina Ekberg. The remaining quarter-final would be an all-Dutch affair with Francis (the number two seed) up against the impressive Mieke de Boer.

As if winning the Grand Slam and the WINMAU weren't enough, the rest of the year simply got better. First of all, I went to the Jersey Open and won the Ladies' Singles against Sally Smith, won the Ladies Pairs *with* Sally Smith and then took the Mixed Triples title with Sally and James Wade. That weekend was also the time that England won the rugby World Cup. A large group of us gathered in the bar at the hotel after breakfast. What a match – and that Jonny Wilkinson, just how cute was he!

I spent the following weekend at the Swedish Open. Clare stopped my progress in the last sixteen. She played brilliantly. However, it was Sandra Pollet who won the title, beating Francis in the final. I did make it through to the final of the Ladies' Pairs with Francis but we lost to Sally Smith and Crissy. Perhaps the birthday celebrations affected my game. I mean, it was Barbara Lee's birthday on the Saturday and Crissy's daughter Michelle Jackson's that same day, then it was mine on the Sunday. All in all, it had been a tough weekend of darts but we had a great time off the oche.

The year was going so well, but could it get any better?

Yes it could.

A phone call from the BBC informed me that I had been nominated for the title of BBC *Midlands Today* Sports Personality of the Year. The other nominees were the footballer Robbie Savage (then playing for Birmingham City FC and a Welsh international), Ashia Hansen (the World Triple Jump Champion), the cricketer Gareth Batty, the jockey Richard Johnson and multi-World Darts Champion, Phil 'The Power' Taylor. I was thrilled to be nominated alongside such well-known names. Needless to say, several shopping trips with Mum and my sister Denise were necessary in order to find an appropriate outfit for the occasion. (You may find this strange, but I *hate* shopping!)

Phil Taylor won the Sportsman of the Year award, but you can imagine how I felt when it was announced that I had been voted BBC *Midlands Today* Sports Personality of the Year. Chuffin' 'ell! I'd polled one-third of the votes and beaten Robbie Savage who was runner-up, with Ashia Hansen third. My win entitled me to attend the fiftieth anniversary BBC TV *Sports Personality of the Year* in London. I remember thinking, 'I wonder if Jonny Wilkinson will be there? I hope so!' As it turned out, I did meet Jonny and had my photograph taken with him, although unfortunately, I didn't get a chance to snog him!

On the eve of the World Championships, I attended the inaugural IDPA Player of the Year Awards at Lakeside and was thrilled to be awarded the Lorna Croft Memorial Trophy as IDPA Women's Player of the Year. That certainly brought tears to my eyes and you can imagine how I felt when I was named as the IDPA Players 'Player's Player of the Year', too. I certainly had had a great year and so I was determined to maintain the pace and retain my world championship for the fourth consecutive year.

My campaign began with a 2–0 victory over Barbara Lee in the quarter-finals with an average of 28.20, compared with Barbara's 22.12. Francis made short work of Mieke (2–0) in her quarter-final and Clare beat Carina Ekberg 2–0. Holland's Karin Krappen beat Anne Kirk by a similar margin and was my semi-final opponent. Karin was really up for it and raised her game and her average in the semi. Even though Karin's average per dart was 27.50, it wasn't good enough and I won six of the seven legs, recording an average of 30.08. In the other semi-final, Francis' experience saw her through with a 2–1 victory over Clare, although both players' averages exceeded 26.5 per dart. So, here we were again – Francis and me in the World Championship final.

Although I surged into a two-leg lead, I knew Francis would retaliate and so she did, with back-to-back maximum 180s silencing the Lakeside crowd. The nine-dart perfect game was on. You could have heard a pin drop. Then there was a sigh from the crowd as Francis missed the seventh treble twenty and the dream of a nine-darter evaporated. I managed to take the first set 3–1. In the second set, we both went up a gear and traded 140s and 180s, but I took the set and the match with double five, having just previously hit my seventh maximum of the tournament.

I was on top of the world (again) and to cap it all, my good friend and 'big brother', Andy Fordham, took the men's world title, beating Mervyn King 6–3. I was so pleased for him.

It was also great to have my mum, Muriel, and my sister, Denise, stage-side spurring me on to my fourth World Championship. They have been such an important part of my success. In fact, Mum nearly didn't make the final. She suffered a fall earlier in the day and nearly missed seeing me play. Graham Reeves, one of my sponsors, and his friend Tuffrey (who both love taking the piss out of Mum), ably assisted by Gerry Walters, Francis Hoenselaar's manager, carried her to the car and drove her to Frimley Hospital. (Gerry has always been very good to me. If I ask him to do something for me, he will. He's Francis's manager, not mine, but he's always been so helpful to me.) After the doctors had looked at Mum she was told that, luckily, nothing was broken. The worst she suffered was some bad bruising. But Mum's a tough old girl and there was no way she was going to let a fall get in the way of watching her daughter play – and win. I suppose that's where I get my toughness and resilience from.

I was going to need all of that and more because, during the summer, Gully and I had separated.

Chapter Twenty-two

From Stamford Bridge to Las Vegas

Although 2004 had started well darts wise, in my personal life things were very different. Gully and I were living apart and within a year we were divorced. Darts was my life and it's possible that I focused on this to the exclusion of everything else, especially Gully.

It was work, work, work for me. February was a very busy month and there was more of the same to come. I paid a visit to Stamford Bridge, the home of Chelsea Football Club. It wasn't to watch a match; it was to do with a promotion for the Argos catalogue and WINMAU products were in the book. To be honest, I'm a Manchester United supporter although I've never seen them play. I had a personal tour of the ground once. In 2005, I think it was, John Gwynne, the Sky Sports darts commentator, arranged it for me while I was up that way doing an exhibition with him. I took my nephew Dan with me, as he's a huge fan of Man U. Dan was like a big kid.

Anyway, back to Stamford Bridge. Also at the event, promoting themselves and their sponsor's products, were two of the greatest darts players the world has ever seen: the five-time World Champion Eric 'The Crafty Cockney' Bristow and, at the time of writing, *thirteen*-time World Champion Phil 'The Power' Taylor.

Part of the day consisted of an event where you played four different games – 'dartboard tennis', golf, squash and hockey. The 'dartboard tennis' was played with Velcro balls which were aimed at a target, while in the golf game you had to chip the ball into certain scoring zones. The squash game was a bit more physical because you had to hit and return the ball as many times as you could within a minute. So, too, was the hockey game in which you hit the ball as hard as possible and a meter measured the speed of it. All the points scored from these games were counted up at the end of the day and the player with the highest score walked away with a Play Station.

Eric and I are both very competitive and so took up the challenge and decided to try our luck, although in reality we were only playing against each other. We decided on the best of three for each of the events and that worked well until we came to the squash event. Eric went first and was hitting the ball really hard. By the end he had broken into a sweat, his face had turned a deep shade of red and, to be honest, he looked totally knackered. I suggested that we make it 'the best of one to Eric'. Eric smiled and replied, 'Thank goodness you said that!' I didn't do much better than Eric in the squash and I didn't feel a hundred per cent when I'd finished, but I didn't tell Eric that. But we'd had a great laugh and it was something a bit different from the norm.

I continued to work in London that weekend helping to promote WINMAU products at Earls Court. I then returned home for a few days' rest and then it was time for the Dutch Open in Veldoven. I flew to Rotterdam with Sally Smith and Clare where

Francis, who lives only ten minutes from the airport, picked us up and took us to the venue. Previously, I had always flown into Amsterdam airport and year after year Francis had said, 'Fly to Rotterdam and I'll pick you up from there', and year after year (being a blonde) I'd forgotten her kind offer. However, this year I got it right. It'd only taken six years for her advice to sink in!

I paired up with Francis again for the Ladies' Pairs and met our friends Sally and Clare in the final. It was a repeat of the previous year's final. I think Sally and Clare were hoping to reverse the result this time round but it was not to be, with Francis and me running out winners 2–1. I know this might be becoming a bit tedious for some readers but, yes, Francis and I met in the Singles final. She was out for revenge for my beating her in the World Championship and played out of her skin to record a single dart average of 28.97, the highest ladies' average in the Dutch Open up to then. My average was a creditable 27.58 per dart but it wasn't good enough. Francis was well into her stride very quickly and, before I knew it, I was two sets to nil down. Although I pulled one set back, I had left myself too much to do and fell victim to my great friend 3–1. In fact, the tournament was all 'Double Dutch' as Francis's countryman, Raymond Van Barneveld, lifted the men's title.

While I was in Holland, the England team selections were announced. I was to captain the ladies team, comprising Clare, Apylee Jones and Karen Smith, while called into the squad for the first time were Lisa Stephens (Lancashire), Karen Littler (Somerset) and Dawn Standley (Norfolk). These were the lucky ones. I knew there were others who had not been picked who would be disappointed. There was a lot more talent out there and all I could advise was for them to keep trying. It seemed to me that there was a very fine line between being selected and not.

To celebrate my appointment as captain of the England ladies' team, I decided to have a red rose tattooed on my hip. I'd thought about having a tattoo for ages and this was the best reason and the best time for going ahead with it. Dan came with me to the tattooist and the two of them were laughing their heads off as I winced in pain at every touch of the needle. (I'm such a wuss!) It was a small rose with a stem and a couple of leaves. Even the outline hurt. Dan called me 'a big lightweight' and the tattooist said, 'Do you want me to pretend it's winter and leave the leaves off?' They took the piss out of me during the entire process, but I endured the pain and was very pleased with the result.

The next major event for me was the Finland Open in Helsinki and to say that travelling there was a nightmare would be the biggest understatement, probably, of all time. Instead of taking a direct flight to Helsinki from Heathrow (because the price was prohibitive), I decided to fly from Birmingham via Frankfurt. It was a 6.00 a.m. flight so I had to be up at 3.00 a.m.! Half asleep, I boarded the plane on time and there we stayed for one and a half hours. We were never told what the problem was. Consequently, I missed my connection at Frankfurt but I was soon issued with a ticket for the next flight out, which was due to leave in only a few minutes' time. I had to get to another terminal and, arriving puffing and panting, I was told that the plane had just taken off. So, I went back to the terminal I'd just come from and took out my anger on a poor innocent member of staff on the information desk.

In time I was issued with another ticket but was then informed that, as I had missed the previous flight, the airline had no idea where my luggage was. Great! I had to wait another three hours for the next flight and, as if that wasn't enough, I was then stopped at security where I was frisked with a noisy metal rod and then had my hand luggage searched. Fortunately, previous experience had taught me to put all battery-operated equipment in my suitcase to save any embarrassing moments. That over, I eventually arrived in my hotel room in Helsinki at 7.00 p.m. I'd been up and on the road for over sixteen hours. What a start to the weekend – and it didn't get any better.

Francis and I were well beaten in the semi-finals of the Ladies' Pairs by Crissy and Karin Krappen and I was deservedly beaten in the Ladies' Singles by the up-and-coming young Russian star, Anastasia Dobromyslova. I said at the time that Anastasia had the ability to be a senior champion one day; after all, she already had one world championship under her belt, the 2001 WINMAU World Youth Girls' title. In the years that followed, I was proved right. A few days later, I was runner-up again in the German Open, this time to Francis, and I began to wonder if this would be the trend for the rest of the year.

In April 2004, the Twenty-fifth (Silver Jubilee) British International Championships were held at Renfrew, in Scotland. My mum and her friend Iris were due to travel with Clare and me to support us. We had a reasonable flight time from Luton Airport of 2.40 p.m. and we arrived in good time. Clare's mum and dad, Marion and Peter, were travelling on the same flight but Clare stayed with Mum, Iris and me as I had booked our flights together. Since we were a bit too early to check in, we sat in the bar area and I started taking the mickey out my mum's passport photograph. We laughed and Mum clipped me round the ear, so I moved on to Iris. 'Come on Iris', I said, 'Show us your passport photo.' There was a pause. Iris then revealed that she had not brought her passport with her. At first you might have thought that that was OK but, since 9/11, photographic ID was compulsory. Panic? Iris's face said it all. It had 'PANIC!' written all over it. It was also Mum's seventieth birthday that weekend and we were all going to celebrate in style up in Scotland, but now …

While Iris panicked, cool, calm and collected me touched her arm and said, 'Not to worry Iris. These things happen. I'll sort it out.' I rang her daughter Veronica and told her what had happened. She then went to Iris's house to retrieve the passport while I phoned my sister Denise and asked her to pick up the passport and bring it to the airport. Job done?

No.

Iris couldn't remember where she had put the passport! She sat there thinking for ages and I couldn't stop myself from laughing. Mum, Clare and I were in fits. Then, all of a sudden, it came to her like a bolt out of the blue. Iris told me that, just before she went to bed the previous night, she had placed her passport under a tablecloth in her dining room just in case she was burgled. Well, that did it for the three of us. We collapsed in laughter and I laughed so much, I nearly wet myself.

The problem solved, Denise arrived at the airport with the passport. It was too late to catch our original flight but, and I'll give Easyjet their due, the staff there sorted out seats for us on the next flight out so we arrived in Scotland just a little later than planned.

Mum's seventieth birthday celebrations went well. Mum, Iris, Clare, Marion, Peter and I went for a meal in the hotel. We consumed a few bottles of wine and Mum had a few vodkas. It was lovely. A super surprise birthday cake that a friend of mine, one of the Scottish International players, Jackie Sharpe, had sorted topped off the celebrations.

What a weekend of darts it was too. The England Ladies went on a rout, beating the Scotland Ladies 6–0 and the Welsh Ladies 5–1. Again, I was so proud of my team. There was simply no stopping us as we won the title for the sixth consecutive year and for the seventeenth time since the Internationals were first played in 1979. The men's team was also victorious, winning for the twenty-fourth time since the inception of the tournament.

Back in county darts, Peter Prestidge, treasurer of Warwickshire County darts, presented me with an award to record my fiftieth consecutive victory for Warwickshire Ladies' A in the BDO Inter-County Championships. I achieved that milestone in the final match of the 2003–04 season against Cheshire and it meant that I had remained unbeaten at county level since October 1998! I believe that I am the only county darts player – male or female – to record such an achievement. Looking back at the time, I noticed that I had played sixty-seven times for Warwickshire since the start of the 1996 season and had only lost twice. By the way, Peter is an absolute top fella. He's also manager of the Leamington Spa Super League team Leamington Sureway for which I play and he has worked tirelessly for us Warwickshire girls for years – and he never complains. (We all love him to bits.)

During May and June my fortunes improved and I won the Isle of Man Festival of Darts Ladies' Singles title, beating Dawn Standley in a final that went to a deciding leg. Then Sally Smith and I won the Ladies' Pairs. At Pontins at Hemsby, I regained the title of May Day Darts Festival ladies champion, which I had previously won in 2002, with a 3–0 win over Dorset's Caroline Carter. I then completed the weekend double by winning the England National Singles at the same venue, this time defeating Staffordshire's Emma Pearce 3–0. It was my fourth win in that event in ten years.

I decided to take the May Bank Holiday off and treat my great-niece Leah (then aged seven) to a day out at Alton Towers. Clare and her friend Michelle came along, too, and Michelle was accompanied by her two kids, Ella (who was then five), who was company for Leah, and Josh (who was about ten). Josh also brought his friend Oliver. Between them they ran me ragged. My God, I've never felt so worn out in my entire life. 'Auntie Trine, can I have this?' 'Auntie Trine, can I have that?' It was relentless. At one stage, the kids were looking after me because I was about to throw up. No, not because I'd been on one of those huge and dangerous rides. I'd only been on the kiddies' roller coaster!

However, I did find time to use my camcorder and filmed the kids falling off the rides and crying. I thought it would be a nice memento for the parents. In any event, after such an exhausting day, I promised myself that the next time I took kids out for the day I'd book myself on a crash course in child-minding first.

In June, I won the Red Dragon Sports Welsh Ladies' Open at Pontins, in Prestatyn. It was a tough match against the home favourite, Jan Robbins. Jan went ahead 2–0, but I pulled the game back level and then, thanks to a missed double by Jan, I took the title.

In July, Clare ousted me from first spot in the Women's Inter-County Averages. I was very pleased for her and it was great to see Warwickshire ladies taking first and second places in the table. I think that, by playing for the same county, we spur each other on with our friendly rivalry. But I soon had other things on my mind as I and other top lady darts players journeyed to the Six-In-One Club in Tonbridge in Kent for the inaugural Ladies' British Pentathlon. Sam Hawkins, who has worked unceasingly for the BDO for many years, had come up trumps and obtained sponsorship from Retriever Sports in Slough not only for the men's pentathlon but also for one for the ladies. I was up for it. I had learnt from previous years playing against the men to pace myself throughout the long day. It worked and I eventually came out the clear winner on 410 points, with my nearest rival, Karen Smith, over 70 points behind.

The next day I was bound for Las Vegas.

I had two very good reasons to fly to Las Vegas. Firstly, I was entered in the Desert Classic for the first time and secondly, and more importantly, I was to be maid of honour at the wedding of my good friends Crissy Howat and Peter 'One Dart' Manley. Twenty girls were there at the start of Crissy's hen night but only five remained at the end. It was a real fun event, spent at the Ghost Bar which we were told at the time was often frequented by Britney Spears. Being at the hen night reminded me of how a practical joke backfired on me when Crissy and Peter were engaged in 2000.

Their engagement had taken place during the Isle of Man Open. Before I left home I popped into Leamington Spa to a joke shop and bought a couple of items. I bought Pete a 'collar and cuffs' set, which was literally a pair of cuffs, shirt collar and a dickey bow, the idea being that the guy wears them – and nothing else. The thought of Pete just dressed in that – well – the mind boggled! Then I searched for something appropriate for Crissy and eventually settled on a 'Willy Water Pistol'. I secured the presents in my hand luggage and at Birmingham airport purchased a bottle of champagne. My plan was that, on arrival at the hotel, I would gain access to Crissy and Pete's room before they arrived and place the presents on their bed together with a card and the champagne.

Martin Adams travelled with me over to the island and, in a way, I'm glad he did. What followed was to be one of the most embarrassing moments of my life. My hand luggage went through the x-ray machine and – to my horror – I saw the Willy Water Pistol on the screen, lit up – veins and all! I was *so* embarrassed. I went bright red. I held my head in my hands – I think I was trying to hide – as the security people (and Martin) stood there laughing. To add to my embarrassment, I said, 'It's a Willy Water Pistol for a friend.' The laughter seemed louder then.

The serious side was that, as the pistol had a trigger mechanism, it had to be checked, so a security bloke took me and Martin (still laughing) into a side room where the present was carefully opened, the guy taking care not to rip the paper. Amid further laughter, he inspected the Willy. He looked up from the Willy and said, 'You know, technically speaking, I shouldn't really allow this on board as it has a trigger mechanism.' 'Yes,' I replied sheepishly. Then he said, 'But you're not likely to get it out on board are you?' 'Definitely not', I replied. By this time I was having a fit of the giggles. In between bouts of laughing I kept apologising and saying how embarrassed I was, as the man carefully wrapped the Willy back up. He told me he was as embarrassed as I was. His other two security colleagues were women and they had let him deal with me – as a wind-up – when strictly speaking one of them should have seen to me. As I walked away the security man spoke again. 'Oh, one more thing' he said, 'They ain't really that big you know.' I began laughing again and left the room.

As the security guy had been finishing with me, Martin had wandered out and rung the 'Fat Man', MC Martin Fitzmaurice, who was already in the Isle of Man, to tell him the story. (Bastard.) So when I finally arrived at the hotel, everyone knew that I'd been pulled at customs with the chuffing Willy Water Pistol. When I entered the bar, everyone was winding me up, coming out with innuendos and generally taking the piss. Not for the first time that day, I was very embarrassed – but it was very funny.

After all the fuss had died down, I put the presents in Pete and Crissy's room as planned and waited. Later Pete came downstairs to the bar wearing his present – but, thankfully, he was fully clothed. When I told Crissy about my experience with the customs, she had hysterics and said, 'How embarrassing for you Trine, but that's what you get for playing tricks on me.'

Crissy and Pete's wedding in Vegas was a really emotional occasion with hardly a dry eye in the place. The wedding service was held at the chapel at the Flamingo Hotel although the actual ceremony itself took place in the beautiful hotel gardens under a large gazebo. The bridesmaids were Crissy's daughter Michelle Jackson and Pete's daughter Sarah. Crissy was given away by another close friend of theirs, the Essex professional darts player, Wayne Mardle. As I stood in the gazebo watching Crissy and Pete, I couldn't help thinking how happy they both were.

During the reception round the hotel pool, Donna (Wayne's wife) and I decided – for whatever reason I forget – to jump, fully clothed, into the pool. Donna was convinced that I wouldn't go through with it. She ran towards the pool with me and then, hand-in-hand, in we went, posh dresses and all. What I didn't realise, until I saw the photos much later, was that the water had made my dress see-through. You could see everything, including the small red rose tattoo on my hip that I had had done to celebrate my being selected as England captain.

We had some great laughs at the wedding and I was so happy for Crissy and Pete, but inside I felt sad at my own situation.

Chapter Twenty-three

Happy Times, Sad Times, Five Times

My time in Las Vegas in 2004 had started off really well with Crissy and Pete's wedding, but I was suffering terribly from jet lag and it was several days before I recovered from it.

Fortunately, I was feeling better in time for the semi-final of the Ladies' Desert Classic III at the MGM Grand Hotel. I was up against Canada's Gayl King, who you will recall as the first woman ever to play in the PDC Skol World Championships. I spoke to her about her game against Graeme Stoddart and told her that she had done a great job and had done women's darts proud. However, I was soon down to business and ran out the clear winner 4–1. My three-dart average for that semi was 83.26 and I also hit a fifteen-dart leg of 501 that included a maximum 180.

In the other semi-final, Stacy Bromberg had beaten her fellow American Carolyn Mars by the same score. Stacy, a resident of Las Vegas and one of the greatest American lady darts players of all time, had won the title the previous year by beating England's Deta Hedman 6–4.

In the 2002 final against Deta, Stacy opened up a 2–0 lead – and she did exactly the same thing in our final. However, I came back at her, winning five in a row – the second leg in fifteen darts and the fifth in only thirteen darts (140, 100, 100, 137, double 12) – and there I was needing only one more to secure victory. But Stacy wasn't finished yet. In front of her home crowd, she won the next three, one with a brilliant bull finish. So, once again, I found myself having to play a deciding leg when I should really have wrapped it up, but then Stacy never really gave me a chance.

The decider was very tense, with both of us nervous and making mistakes. With a maximum 180, I was down to a finishing double before Stacy but I couldn't take it out. I missed a winning shot out with five darts and bust my score with another three, but, fortunately for me, Stacy was experiencing similar problems. Eventually, we were both left needing double two for the title. I hit it at my first attempt.

After the presentation, I walked off the stage at the MGM Grand and on to a plane back home. Landing at Gatwick, I stayed there overnight and the next morning I was on my way up to Inverness for the IDPA Masters. I drew Martin Adams in the first round – so it was the England Men's captain versus the England Ladies' captain – and he annihilated me 4–0. I thought my average per dart was good (nearly 28 per dart) but Martin was on superb form with a 35-plus average. He didn't miss a thing. All I wanted to do after that was to go home, have a good kip and overcome the jet lag.

In the Gold Cup (now renamed the BDO Gold Cup following the banning of tobacco sponsorship) at Frimley Green, Julie Gore of Pembrokeshire won the Ladies' Singles title, beating Surrey's Apylee Jones 2–1 in the final. Clare did well and made the semi-

final but I was literally not in it. I didn't go, but I had good reason
– a very special reason. On that very same weekend, on 17 July,
Crissy and Pete were holding a reception at the Pinegrove Hotel
in Carlisle to celebrate their marriage and Crissy had asked me to
make a speech.

I sat down and thought about it. I was OK with standing up
and talking to folk so a speech wasn't a problem, especially
when I would be talking about such close friends, but I wanted
to make this different for them, make it *really* special. It didn't
take me too long to decide what to do. I decided to write
a poem about them and, with a little help from Clare, here's
the result:

> Just a few things I would like to say
> How truly honoured I feel today.
> You see Crissy makes friends so readily
> But above all others she's chosen me.

> I've known Crissy for about ten years
> And through that time we've shed many tears,
> Not for sadness but for fun
> Too many to mention but I will just some!

> Now a trip to Germany we took one year
> A trip Crissy will never forget I fear.
> Jagermiester that day was her tipple
> The drink that makes you sick a little

> Or, as the case may be, sick as a parrot
> (Don't you just hate it when there's loads of carrot?)
> The taxi drive home was one of a kind
> 'Would you pull over please? If you wouldn't mind.'

'For the Lady up front is about to throw up.'
'Quick!' said I, 'Throw in this cup.'
The taxi stopped and out she leapt
To throw up on someone's doorstep.

At the hotel and into the lift
Three of us it took to get her to shift.
We got her to bed on that extraordinary day,
'I'll just have a nap,' she said. 'And I'll be out to play.'

Needless to say, we let her be
But the next day what a sight to see!
Three days it took her to feel well
But don't worry, mate, I'd never tell.

Now picture the scene of one sunny day,
Crissy on her phone chatting away.
Now Pete is driving on that fateful ride
When Crissy spotted the police coming along side.

As quick as a flash she sets the phone free
Saying 'That was close there', looking straight at me
Pete was laughing but he did take the time
To explain he was driving so it wasn't a crime.

Now saying something nice about Pete
That really has to be a great feat.
We never got on that's clear to see
But after so long he's growing on me.

The day they first met is still so clear
Crissy saying 'Look at that Custey bara charva over theyer'
So I said, 'Excuse me Pete. Can you step aside?
I want to look at what Crissy has eyed.'

'Custey bara charva' for those that aren't sure
Means good-looking fella, I'd hoped for more.
Another blonde moment for me I feel
'Cause it was Pete she meant and that's for real.

Seriously, though, I would like to say
I hope they have both enjoyed their day.
And may they share a long and happy life
With all the joys of husband and wife.

This is my plea to you 'One Dart'.
Please look after Crissy with all your heart
For she is a great friend to me,
One I hope in return I will be.

I have a lot of love for those guys and I hope it showed in the poem. It certainly went down well. Everyone had a great day.

Back to the darts: I had met Crissy in the semi-final of the Norway Open and beaten her to reach the final. Clare also made the semis where she met Hampshire's Jane Monaghan, who was playing for the first time in that competition and was doing really well. Jane battled through against Clare to meet me in the final where I came out the winner, 4–2.

I think some people believe that I tend to win everything, but I'm sure you're seeing now that that is simply not the case. There are a lot of talented lady darts players, like Jane, out there challenging me and desperate to beat me, keen to take my world crown. For example, at the British Classic at Kettering Leisure Village in August 2003 I met Yorkshire's Dee Bateman in the final. Dee's another great player and, in a tough, close-fought contest, Dee ran out the winner 3–2. (I hate double ten and hated it with a vengeance that day!) However, I soon returned to form by winning the Denmark Open, beating Finland's Tarja Salminen in the Final.

I never seem to do things by halves. I either comprehensively beat my opponents or the game goes to the deciding leg or set. Such is the quality of ladies' darts that I can never allow myself to rest or fall below my best. Being the number one in my sport is everything to me and anyone who planned to take my crown would have to work very hard to achieve it. The Bavarian World Darts Trophy in Utrecht illustrates my point.

I've already mentioned Anastasia Dobromyslova as a potential world champion for the future. Well, Anastasia was a wild-card entry (that is by special invitation of the sponsor Ad Schoofs) and I was drawn against her in the first round. As reigning champion, I was expected to win but Anastasia hung me out to dry 2-0. My average was a very respectable 27.68 per dart but Anastasia really turned it on against me and recorded what turned out to be the highest average in the entire ladies' tournament that year, an incredible 29.88 per dart! I believe that our match was the best of the tournament.

I had no answer to that on the day and neither did Mieke de Boer who met Anastasia in the semi-final. Anastasia began with a maximum and finished the first leg in thirteen darts! Mieke had no reply and was beaten by the same margin as I was, 2-0. Meanwhile, in the other half of the draw, Francis made good progress, making it to the final, beating Jan Robbins and Crissy along the way. In the final, experience finally triumphed over youth as, in a tightly fought game, Francis took the title by three sets to one. However, everyone agreed that Anastasia had laid down her marker and would soon be challenging for the number one position in ladies' darts.

During the late summer I fulfilled one of my life's ambitions to drive around a proper motor racing circuit. When an opportunity to go round the famous Silverstone circuit presented itself, I jumped at the chance. My brother Andy arranged for Andy Fordham, Clare and me to go for a spin. Mike Swinnerton of

National Supersports Cars and Paul Gibson, proprietor of GPS Racing supplied the car – a £170,000 Aston Martin Vantage.

Unfortunately, Andy had to withdraw because of an injured wrist, so off Clare and I went cornering at 100 m.p.h. and hitting speeds of 155 m.p.h. on the straight. We almost lost it on one bend. Andy heard the tell-tale screech of tyres and knew that we were having a hairy moment, but we were OK. Mind you, I nearly needed a change of underwear when I was told how close we'd come to crashing!

After meeting Jane Monaghan in the Norway Open final, Dee Bateman in the British Classic final and Tarja Salminen in the final of the Finland Open, it was the 'old firm' contesting the final in the British Open – Francis and me. Francis should have beaten me at Bridlington that weekend. She missed countless doubles in the deciding leg which let me in to take the title 3–2. Even with that poor final leg our averages were still around the 28–29 per dart mark. I suppose our problem is that we know each other's game so well and have so much mutual respect on the oche that neither can afford to give an inch. Sometimes I feel that just puts more pressure on both of us.

Another thing on my mind at this time was where I was going to live. Gully and I had sold the house and I'd moved in with my mum. Everything I owned – more or less – was in boxes and I feared that it would be months before I could find anything. I spent hours scouring the newspapers for a suitable new home but there was little around within my price range. But then a solution presented itself.

Clare had recently parted from her boyfriend Ian and was looking to sell her upstairs flat. (She also had one of the most annoying neighbours on the planet, whom she and the other neighbours called 'Victor Meldrew'.) Clare really wanted to move up the property ladder a bit and I certainly didn't want to drop down it. I wanted to buy another three-bedroomed house but I couldn't afford it on my own. To me, if I had bought something smaller it would have been like going backwards and I didn't want to do that. So Clare and I talked about it and after some time we agreed that it would be a good idea if we combined our resources. That way Clare got a bigger place and I stayed firmly on the property ladder.

The next thing to decide was where to buy. It was to be either in Warwickshire, my home county, or Oxfordshire, where Clare lived. With my job as a darts professional, it mattered little where my base was – I could work from anywhere – although I didn't want to be too far away from my family. It seemed more practical for me to move to Oxfordshire where Clare's job was, so we started looking round.

We decided beforehand that we were either going to buy a complete wreck of a place and then do it up, utilising my carpentry and building skills – always something I've wanted to do – or buy something that needed nothing or very little doing to it. At one stage, I even went to look at a plot of land on which to build from scratch, but that was disappointing and the idea was shelved.

We put in an offer for the third house we viewed in Marcham, not far from Abingdon in Oxfordshire. We thought our offer was a good one but they turned us down. When the estate agents told us the news, Clare admitted that she was glad because she wasn't really that keen on it! I hadn't really liked it that much anyway. We'd agreed to put in the offer because we both thought the other liked it so much. What a couple of plonkers! Next time we had to be sure. The house we eventually bought came up by chance. We were looking in the local property pages and saw it. It looked very impressive from the outside and we actually thought the price was a misprint. We though it was at least £100,000 more than the price shown but we thought we'd take a look. Clare and I went along to the estate agents and asked for details and if the price quoted were correct. It was! We immediately made an appointment to view.

When we were let into the property, both Clare and I fell in love with the place straightaway. It was lovely. It had all the mod cons and even the decoration was to our taste. It was a large three-bedroomed house, too, so there was plenty of room for both of us. We put in an offer that was rejected. We then decided to make a better offer and that was accepted. That was on a Wednesday and the people who owned the house were actually moving out on the Friday, so it was just a matter of sorting out the paperwork and we would be in. Clare had her flat on the market and it had sold within a week.

Result!

Before going ahead with the joint purchase, we had spoken to our families and friends about buying a place together and there were some obvious concerns, but once we explained our reasons, they seemed to be fine. After all, it was an investment. I suppose two girls buying a property together might seem a little strange and I suppose that, in our hearts, we knew some people who would question our motives. We had people coming up to us in the pub and saying 'So ... er ... are you two ... er ... together ... er ... together sort of thing?' To begin with we explained politely to folk what we were doing but, to be honest, both Clare and I became sick with the same question and the innuendo.

It came to a head when I was in a darts competition. A bloke, a complete stranger, walked up to me and asked me outright. To say I was taken aback would be an understatement. My first thought was 'Who the hell are you?' and my second, 'You cheeky bastard!' but neither came out of my mouth. Instead, I glared at him and said, 'What makes you think I would tell you if we were anyway?' He replied, 'Well, it's just that everyone is asking me and I don't know what to say?' Why were they asking him? I hadn't seen him before in my life! Shocked by this approach from someone I had never met before, I took a few seconds to compose myself. I then replied, 'Well, you can tell them to mind their own fucking business for a start and then, once you've done that, tell them if they want to know, to be brave enough to come over here and ask us their fucking selves.' With that, he turned and walked away. I never saw him again.

Clare and I moved into our house on 5 November 2004.

November was also the month in which I defended my WINMAU Women's World Masters title at Bridlington. Once again, Francis and I met in the final. I know that it seems we always meet in finals but there are two reasons for this. For so long Francis and I have been either number one or number two in the world. In the draw for ranking tournaments run by the BDO, the two top players are always in different halves and, therefore, in theory, the top two should eventually meet in the final. The second reason is that we have achieved those positions by hard work and endeavour, travelling the world for ranking points to maintain our status. Only if one of us drops into the number-three-ranking position would we actually meet in earlier rounds of those competitions.

I was in fine form. I think that recent victories in the WDF Europe Cup (Gold medals for the England Ladies (Clare and me) and another for winning the Ladies' Pairs with Clare) spurred me on as I took care of Dawn Standley in the quarter-final (4–1) and Anne Kirk by a similar margin in the semi-final. In the other half, Francis had a slightly more difficult ride, beating the Australian international Natalie Carter (Tony David's girlfriend) 4–1 and then defeating Yorkshire and England's Karen Smith 4–3 in a close fought semi. Francis had beaten me in the Europe Cup singles 4–2 so I had some ground to make up – and I did – with another 4–1 victory. My defence of my title was complete. I had won the World Masters, completed a hat-trick of consecutive victories *and* kept my sponsors WINMAU happy.

On the Saturday before the ladies' finals I was asked by the television production company TWI to interview the players' wives in between sets during the men's competition. I had been hoping for ages that I would be given the chance to do something like that and, now it had arrived, I was very nervous – and it was live! Being interviewed and being the interviewer are two totally different things. I was more nervous doing that than I was standing up on the world stage. But it all went very well and I have to thank the ladies concerned – Tracey King, Sarah Hankey (wife of the 2000 Embassy World Champion, Ted Hankey), Gill O'Shea, wife of professional darter Tony O'Shea, and Natalie Carter – who really helped make the job so easy.

Despite continuing to prepare for the world championships, at the turn of 2005 I felt less confident going into that year's tournament than ever before. I knew I could win but I was less sure than in previous years. My form was OK but that was all. There had been a number of off-stage distractions that affected my game and I felt vulnerable. However, once I had won the world title I became very possessive of it and simply was not prepared to give it up. This had been demonstrated in previous years when I had successfully defended *my* title no less than three times. I had to be focused on the job in hand. I told myself that, whatever problems I had, must be forgotten the moment I stepped up on stage at Lakeside.

I began the fourth defence of my title against Scotland's Ladies' captain Anne Kirk and won 2–0 with a 28.43 average per dart and beat Crissy in the semi-final 2–0. Once again, Francis was on her way, clinically disposing of her compatriot Karin Krappen 2–0 and then accounting for Wales' Jan Robbins 2–1 in her semi-final. So here we were again. Would it be Francis' year? Would all the other stuff inside my head and outside of darts affect my performance in the final?

Francis had the throw (by which I mean Francis threw first in the opening leg) and she quickly took the first leg. I then levelled the game and then won the next leg against the darts with a 135 checkout. I then had the advantage of throw in the fourth leg and played well enough to secure the first set. The 135 finish spurred me on and despite Francis scoring a maximum 180 in the second set, I shot out on 31 (single fifteen, double eight) and became the Lakeside Women's World Champion for the second time to add to my three Embassy triumphs. I was the five-time World Champion.

Once again, I had done the business, but, clearly, I hadn't been firing on all cylinders.

Here's why.

Chapter Twenty-four

The Most Difficult Decision of My Life

Gully and I were divorced in March 2005. It had all come to a head two years earlier. There was no major falling out. I didn't have another man and Gully didn't have another woman. We grew apart. It was as simple – and as difficult – as that. You don't see or feel it happening, not at first anyway. Unknowingly, your paths drift off in different directions and then, when they meet up again, you just don't know each other. Relationships are so complex. In the end, I really had no choice but to finish it, but I can't say that it didn't hurt.

I'm still hurting now.

My life had rapidly changed. I was four-time Ladies' World Darts Champion. I was in demand and on the road playing many tournaments and exhibitions. Gully had continued to support me over and above his own day job but even though he was there, there was something not quite right. He had always been supportive of me, especially at exhibitions when I had the staging to put up. He would finish work and jump in the shower quickly. By the time he was dressed, I'd have the car loaded up with all the gear and we'd shoot off to the venue where we'd set it all up and we'd have a great evening. But major tournaments were a totally different matter.

Gully always had trouble watching me play in key competitions, like the World Championships at Lakeside. When I was playing in preliminary rounds of competitions on the floor of the venue he was very happy to be in the same room but he never ever watched me play. He would gladly watch other people play their matches, but not me. As soon as I made it to the stage finals, when the focus was totally on me and there wasn't any other game to divert his attention, he was gone. He simply couldn't bear to watch me play, so he left the venue and waited in the car park, biting his nails until an official went out to tell him how I'd fared. It was always five minutes later when he'd come in and I'd get my hug. 'Well done!' he'd say, but the moment had gone. Plenty of others had hugged and congratulated me before the one person I wanted to hug and congratulate me above all others, to congratulate me *first*, actually appeared. Yet all the time he behaved like that I never mentioned how important his presence was to me, how I felt about it. I was always thinking about his feelings and what he would say rather than how I felt myself.

Wrong.

I had often said, 'I would like you there,' at such and such an event, but was always happy if he refused because Gully was quite a nervous person. He wasn't a very confident person either and that had become worse since his illness. Simple things like walking to the bar in a pub worried him. He always had visions of tripping over. He was always frightened to death of embarrassing himself and I guess that's why he didn't want to watch me play; he was concerned about getting carried away and possibly having a panic attack. I tried so hard to understand it from his point of view but found it difficult to come to terms with. What man wouldn't want to witness his wife winning a major championship or even *the* highest prize in her sport – the world championship? I let Gully handle his problem as he thought was best for him. I often said that I'd rather he was there, but, foolishly perhaps, I never emphasised just how important it was to me. He'd say 'No. I can't handle it. I want to be outside in the car park. I'll be in as soon as I can afterwards'.

Even so, when the winning dart had gone into the double, I still used to turn and look for Gully, hoping he'd be there, but, of course, he never was. As the years went by, I retained both my number-one position and my world (and other) titles and it became more and more important to me for him to be there. I wanted him to change his mind and just be there for me. I grew more impatient, more frustrated at his absence. I was consistently winning so Gully sitting in the crowd now three or four years down the line wouldn't have affected me at all. No pressure, Gully. In fact I am convinced that it would have made me an even better player if he had been there. Nervous at first or not, I'm sure he would have soon got used to it.

Gully was a steady nine-to-five person. He'd work very hard all day, do overtime and everything *and* be there for me whenever he could when I needed him for exhibitions and tournaments, but he was not, and could not be, there all the time. He was selective. Rather than him thinking, 'Right, I'll do that one', I'd have preferred it if he had said, 'Well, do you want me to come to that one, or would you rather me go to that one?' Because there were times when I used to say 'Well, come with us to that one'. He'd just say 'No'. If he didn't want to do it, he wouldn't do it. Then there were other venues that he'd say he'd come to and I'd say 'Well I'd rather you came to the next one if there's a choice because the next one is really important to me', but he wouldn't listen. He came along when he felt like it, when it was best for him – which I suppose is fair – yet I felt that he was pleasing himself rather than trying to please me. I said little – which was probably a mistake – and that led to a breakdown in communication. We didn't listen to each other; didn't appreciate what the other wanted or why, so our conversations became thinner and more meaningless. Sometimes we didn't talk at all, sitting sharing the silence between us.

I often wondered if Gully was envious of my success but I never really came to any firm conclusion about that. Sometimes I thought, 'He's really proud of me,' and then on other occasions I felt that my success didn't bother him at all. I suppose if he ever did feel envious, it was more out of self-pity, by which I mean nothing hurtful but just that he was so good at rugby and had so much potential which had suddenly been torn from him by his terrible illness. I couldn't blame him if he felt that way. I think I would have felt exactly the same in his place. He lost a huge part of his life. Sport was his life. Apart from rugby, he used to play basketball and football and to have that ability ripped away from him had been a devastating experience – for both of us.

When I was away from Gully either in tournaments or on the exhibition circuit I used to ring home regularly and tell him how I was getting on. He'd say 'Oh, well done, love' or 'Sorry about that, love'; always very encouraging but as time went on, I thought that something was missing. The telephone conversations became so ordinary, so dry, so passionless, so routine, so lacking in ... I didn't know what. I just felt that we were changing, both somehow falling out of love. Over time, I believed that he didn't love me anymore, that he was disinterested in me, but I know now that that was only my impression; the truth was quite the opposite. It wasn't until after I decided that we would split up that I discovered that it was only me who felt that way.

The longer we stayed together, the more I felt that we were drifting apart and the more uncomfortable I felt. Whatever you say about hindsight, I knew at the time that my love for Gully was growing stale and changing its form. We were no longer lovers. We were more like brother and sister or just friends rather than husband and wife, and I naively thought that if I didn't love Gully, then he didn't love me either. I thought this was the way thousands of relationships ended up. Gully's words and actions never challenged my assumption that he'd fallen out of love for me, too. He would say now and again that he loved me, but it was just like a throwaway line; no passion. It was as if it were an obligation – 'I love you' – an everyday line – 'I love you' – uttered in the same way as you might say 'Is that the milkman?' or 'Pass the remote'. I honestly thought he didn't care for me anymore.

But apparently he did.

When I eventually plucked up the courage to tell Gully that I didn't love him anymore he was completely gutted. I wasn't expecting such a reaction. What was I expecting? I suppose a look of relief on his face and perhaps the comment 'Gosh Trine, that's how I've been thinking for ages but never had the guts to say'. He told me he loved me, always had and always would. How did I react? Well, to prepare myself for our discussion, I had known exactly what I was going to say. I'd put this huge protective wall up inside my mind, so nothing he could say could change it.

I had convinced myself that he didn't love me and I had told myself over and over, 'Right, I know I'm going to get hurt. I don't want him anymore and he doesn't want me anymore so this must all stop. This relationship must come to an end'. By this time I was out of love with Gully. I still cared about him. I still loved him, but I wasn't *in love* with him and inside my mind was this huge wall that neither he nor anyone else could knock down. God knows how long it took me to construct that wall but it held out despite my tremendous feelings of guilt (which still remain today) and Gully attempting to break it down – he tried his hardest, bless him. Mind you ... it was close. Gully stayed in the marital home for a while longer and then moved out in July 2003, just after the British Pentathlon.

The British Pentathlon is probably the most difficult darts competition ever. It's not like any other. Twenty players start out and as well as playing each other over two legs of 501-up, they also play one leg of 1,001, one leg of 2,001, 'Round the board on doubles', 'Shanghai', and 'Halve-It'. Points are awarded not only for just winning but also for high scoring, high finishes and finishing in the least number of darts. At the end of the day the player with the highest score pockets the first prize, which is usually about £1,000.

On this particular occasion, Gully and I set out for the Six in One Club in Tonbridge. I played an exhibition on the Saturday night and then played in the Pentathlon the next day. It was my third Pentathlon and as usual Gully was very supportive and for once stayed to watch my progress. He recorded my scores and checked with the referees and even gave me the odd telling off – 'You know you need to get a few more points in this one' – that sort of thing – but I had no idea what was going on in his mind at that time.

On the Sunday, I was the only woman darts player out of the field of twenty. I played as well as I could given the way I was feeling, but ended up in a disappointing fifteenth place and well out of the money. Perhaps if so much had not been going on in my private life, I might have done better but I clearly enjoyed myself for a while at least. Sam Hawkins, stalwart of the BDO, reported his 'Game of the Day' as being the match between former World Champion Andy Fordham and me. Sam wrote in *Darts World* that we were both enjoying our match of 'Halve-It' and that 'to see both players laughing and playing brilliant darts against each other was a joy to watch'. Sam also promised that he would do his best to ensure that in 2004 there would be a separate women's Pentathlon – sponsorship willing – and, as you know, he was true to his word.

'Brilliant darts' or not, I had other things on my mind. Inside, I was angry with Gully. He was annoying me for no reason, no reason at all. I had to do something, but as it happened it was Gully who made a surprise announcement towards the end of the tournament. Unexpectedly, he said, 'When we get home I'm going to move back to my mum's.' My jaw dropped. Stuck for any other words, I said, 'Why?' He replied, 'Because things aren't right and perhaps you need some space.' I said to him, 'Perhaps I do. I don't know.' I mean ... what was *that* all about?

We didn't speak to each other in the car on the way home; the only sound being the car engine. When we arrived home, Gully went upstairs and packed a few bags. Unbeknown to me he had rung his mum while we were at Tonbridge and told her of his plans and asked to come home for a while. Saying goodbye was a horrible, horrible experience. I was sobbing my heart out. He was very upset, too. We just hugged each other, then he picked up his bags and left. And that, as they say, was that. He's been at his mum's ever since.

As Gully disappeared from sight I just stood there, staring into the distance. For how long I couldn't say. At that moment and long afterwards, I really didn't know what I wanted except that, whatever it was, Gully wouldn't be part of it. To make the decision was tough. I'd found it very, very hard; so tough that, looking back, I probably did it completely the wrong way, but what's done is done and I had to get on with my life.

I never contacted him much after he left. My theory was that if I didn't talk to him or see him, he would forget me and get over me quicker. He could then move on.

Gully never contacted me either. I found out later that he had been sitting at his mum's waiting for me to contact him. His not contacting me merely reinforced my notion that he had fallen out of love with me, too – but, unbeknown to me, Gully still loved me. Between us we had made a right pig's ear of it. Shit! If I had known that, perhaps I *would* have approached things in a different way.

I knew I couldn't live with him anymore because otherwise I'd be unhappy for the rest of my life. I'm not saying he was a bad person or anything like that – far from it. I'm not saying that he and I couldn't have lived out our lives together as 'Mr and Mrs' like thousands of people do, tolerating each other 'til death doth them part. We could, but for me that wasn't an option. The way I felt, and had felt for ages, it just wouldn't have been fair on either of us in the long run, so something had to give and I had been brave enough to do it.

I instigated divorce proceedings against Gully. Of course, I retained solicitors and they advised me to do this and to do that but, for whatever reason, I never did anything they advised me to do. That was pretty stupid, I know, but Gully and I sold the house and split the contents between us without my heeding my solicitor's advice. Looking back, I guess this could have led to major problems but in practice it didn't. At the time, I wouldn't really have cared if Gully had taken everything, but of course with hindsight I'm glad he didn't.

Since Gully and I split some people have asked me whether having no children was part of the reason for the breakdown of our relationship. At first I answered that it had nothing to do with it, but now I'm not so sure. Writing this has made me think harder about many things, so perhaps you can judge for yourself. By my mid-to-late twenties, I was ready to start a family. Gully and I had been together for nearly ten years and it seemed to me to be a very natural course to follow. So we discussed it and the upshot was that he didn't feel ready. As I've said before, Gully was a worrier; he fretted about everything so I guess he fretted about parenthood and was concerned that perhaps he couldn't cope. I understand that's not an uncommon concern; after all, having a family is a huge step and one hell of a responsibility. Put simply: I was ready for that responsibility and Gully wasn't. My response to Gully was not to argue. He'd made his mind up and so, if I couldn't focus my attention on a child, then I needed to turn that attention to something else. I said to him, 'Well, in that case then, I want to do some darts.' Which is when I started taking my darts even more seriously. I needed an alternative goal. I'm the sort of person who needs to aim at something. I was ready for a family and that would have been my goal if Gully had said, 'Yes, let's do it!' But he didn't. He said 'No' and I accepted his view without question but had to move on to something else, so I thought, 'Right. I'll do the darts circuit. I know I can do it.' So darts, and not Gully, became my life and all thoughts of starting a family faded while I pursued a career in the sport I loved.

Then, a few years later, when I was at the pinnacle of my career, having just won my third Embassy World Professional Ladies Darts Championship, Gully turned round and said, 'Right, I'm ready now. I'm ready to start a family.' I was gob-smacked and confused. However, I didn't find myself replying 'Oh right, so *you're* ready now. So the time suits *you*, does it?' I wasn't angry with him either – not immediately anyway. I know this for a fact because after I'd won that third world championship, I was interviewed by the BBC at Lakeside and when I was asked if I'd be back to defend my title the following year, I found myself saying 'I'll definitely be back next year although I may have a little bit of a bump.' Smiles and laughter all round the studio at the time but shortly afterwards I thought, 'Hey. This is the wrong time for me.' I was literally on top of the world with a successful career in darts and there was Gully deciding that he was now ready to start a family.

This time it wasn't what I wanted.

I'll admit that if I had not retained my title that year I might – just might – have agreed. It's possible that I would have bowed out gracefully and had a family. However, having said that, I would have entered into it begrudgingly because I still wanted to be world champion. I wasn't simply going to hand over my world title. I wanted to continue being the top lady darts player and so, as the year went on, I focused on retaining my number-one position and my world crown, defending them against all-comers. Eventually, all thoughts of having children with Gully faded from my mind.

That, I suspect, was when Gully and I really started to drift apart. Although I was off the pill, nothing happened, absolutely nothing. You have to have sex to get pregnant, don't you? The subject of children was rarely raised again but whether that was just Gully being thoughtful or not wanting to put pressure on me, I couldn't say. Every aspect of our relationship began to fall apart from that point. Nothing was ever the same after that and I know that if Gully had said to me one day 'Come on Trine, are we going to have this family or what?' I would've plumped for the 'what'.

Chapter Twenty-five
Same Old Faces?

At the beginning of 2005, the debate about how players qualified for the finals of the Ladies' World Championship was raised again. The question was something like 'How can someone claim to be Women's World Darts Champion by winning three games on stage?' Comments like that deeply upset me because I know the effort that I, and other dart players, including Fran, Clare, Crissy, Anne Kirk, Karin Krappen and many others, put in to earn the right to step up on that world stage.

I've dealt with many of the defensive arguments in another chapter and have set out my case time and time again. In a letter to the editor of *Darts World* magazine one dart player wrote:

'There are hundreds of good lady darts players in the UK alone, but how many can up and away at weekends, leaving their husbands and children to get on with it whilst the wife is away to Finland and Holland, etc., to earn ranking points?

Is it not time that there was a better way to select players for these tournaments so that every lady player has a fair chance of taking part without travelling the world to earn ranking points?

To get a true ladies' champion, the event should be open to all, not a handful of ladies fortunate enough to have sponsors paying for them to travel the world.'

The suggestion that the rules should be changed just for the women is ridiculous. Both men and women qualify for major tournaments in the same way. As for players like me being 'fortunate' to have sponsors, I ask them to remember how hard I worked to obtain and retain mine. Being professional at anything demands your full attention at all times and that means that professional darts players are away from their partners and family for days, even weeks, at a time.

To succeed, players must be totally committed to their sport and if in order to succeed in women's darts that means that the husband spends some time tending the children for a weekend or three, then that's how it must be. Being a professional darts player is a great life – most of the time – but as you have already seen in mine, it can be fraught with problems. Success is never easy. There are no easy solutions.

Trust me on that.

Anastasia Dobromyslova sent us an early warning when she won the Dutch Open, beating Clare in the final. Francis and I only made it to the last eight. Anastasia was swiftly climbing the world rankings and at the time of her success in the Dutch Open was ranked ninth in the world.

In early 2005, I spent some time in the Netherlands at the new Masters of Darts tournament in Holland. The format pitched four BDO players against four PDC players; that's four men from each organisation, not ladies. As far as I could see there was no divide between the two camps, the lads were just there to play darts and try to earn a decent living, regardless of any politics. That's how it should be. As it turned out, the match everyone wanted to see actually happened. Phil 'The Power' Taylor met Andy 'The Viking' Fordham in the final, which Phil won 7-1. P & H Promotions ran the event very well indeed and, although the ladies were excluded from the actual competition, I was very pleased to be invited with Francis to entertain the VIPs during the week.

By 'entertaining the VIPs' I don't mean pole dancing or anything like that. I did try to persuade Francis but she wasn't having any of it! (Only joking.) Seriously, we played darts against a few of the VIPs and answered questions about the sport. It was a great way to spend the week. We met some interesting people – and some mad ones, too! Then on the Sunday evening, before the final, Francis and I played a demonstration game to warm up the crowd. It was a great opportunity to show our worth and we put on a good show.

Back home, I was invited by SKY Televison's darts commentator, John Gwynne, to play an exhibition match at Baldy Bob's Club in Failsworth in Greater Manchester. What a night that was! The crowd was great and I really enjoyed the night. I beat all but two of the sixteen challengers but how I beat them! I had the audience up on their feet cheering and applauding loudly as I clicked into exhibition mode. I could tell immediately that the crowd was really up for a laugh and that's what exhibitions are all about. I played well, finishing one match on forty, with two double tens, then a little later I hit a 100 checkout, twenty-five, twenty-five, bull and later still another 100 out-shot, this time with two bull's-eyes. All of these games were played on the standard dartboard. I mention this because Manchester has its own smaller dartboard called the 'log-end'. It's ten inches in diameter, is numbered differently and has no trebles. John thought it a good idea for me to play against the best 'log-end' ladies at some stage. If you're reading this John, I'm still up for it.

The Isle of Man Darts Festival in March attracted around 120 hopeful lady darters, seeking to relieve me of the title I had won for the first time the previous year. I made the last sixteen with ease but then met Clare in the quarterfinal. Clare won the first leg, but a 130 checkout brought me back level and I went on to win 3–1. My reward for beating Clare was a meeting with Francis in the semi-final. I played dire darts. To say I played below par would be praise indeed. I scored low and missed doubles and Francis cruised through to the final 3–0. There she met Cumbria's Dee Bateman and beat her 3–1, which gave Francis her third win in the tournament, her previous victories being in 1999 and 2000. Francis and I then went on to win the Ladies' Pairs against the former world number one and England international, Mandy Solomons and Welsh International Gaynor Williams. Mandy had been off the scene for some time, so it was great to see her back and doing a few more tournaments.

After the Manx championships, I was back on the Continent again for the German Open. I won the Ladies' Singles and lifted the Ladies' Pairs with Francis. Then it was back on the road for a few more exhibitions at venues up and down the country.

In April, it was time for the British International Champion-ships at Bridlington and, once again, the England teams triumphed. The England Ladies, captained by me, won the title for the seventh consecutive year (eighteen in total), as we whitewashed the opposition, beating both the Scotland and Wales ladies 6–0. This had never been achieved before. All the England Ladies played magnificently, producing consistently high averages which made my job as captain so much easier. Despite high averages throughout the England side, I won the 'Lady of the Match' awards for both games, but only just. My average against the Welsh ladies was 27.83, just 1.46 ahead of Clare. It was even closer in the matches against the Scotland Ladies. My average there was only 0.06 ahead of Apylee Jones. The England Men made the weekend by taking the men's title with a win against Wales and a 6–6 draw against Scotland.

As mid-year approached, I was thrilled that my sponsorship with Reeves Boatbuilders was renewed, making it an eight-year association. Graham and Julie Reeves have made it possible for me to succeed in darts. Car Consultants renewed too and presented me with a new car, a Nissan Primera. Of course, I had to test it first – to see if all my exhibition equipment would fit in and then it was taken away again so that Midland Graphics could paint my name on the side.

But the big darts story of the summer was the official recognition of darts as a sport by all four Sports Councils in the UK. Announcing the decision, BDO Managing Director, Olly Croft said, 'This is one of the greatest days in the history of darts, and is just reward for the players, officials and supporters who can at long last call darts an official sport.' It had been the result of many years of hard work and importantly the Sports Councils' decisions would allow the BDO to apply for Sports Council and Lottery grants. At last, dart players could call themselves sportsmen and sportswomen, something we had all known for a very long time. Olly added, 'The prospect of darts being part of London's 2012 Olympic bid may be more of a reality than a dream.' Was that possible? *Could* darts be featured in the Olympics? What would recognition do for ladies' darts? Only time will tell.

On the county side, the Warwickshire Ladies' A came top in the Premier Division. At around the same time, the Inter-County Averages for 2004–05 were announced and I was pleased to see that I had regained my number-one position, which Clare had taken from me the year before. Clare was still in there but was runner-up this time. My average score per dart thrown was 28.74 compared to Clare's 25.56. My average score plus a bonus point for each set won totalled 35.74, only 2.18 ahead of Clare.

On the exhibition scene, I was booked for a couple of appearances on the Isle of Wight. (I love that place. It's so pretty.) I had a fun night at the Simeon Arms in Ryde – well that was the case until the moment I fell over. No. I wasn't drunk! If I had been pissed, then perhaps it wouldn't have hurt so much! When I had entered the pub earlier I had noticed that there was a ramp in the entrance, but, unfortunately, I had not registered that there was also a step. At the end of the evening, after having had a great time, I walked out laughing and joking, missed the step completely and down I went. Thankfully, nothing was broken. However, at an exhibition the following day at the Cowes Liberal Club, I did spend a good deal of time explaining to people why I was hobbling about.

My next stop was back across the water at an exhibition in Bristol. The Somerset and England international player Marie Geaney has a pub there called The Airballoon in the St George area of the city and had invited me over to give an exhibition for her customers. It was a brilliant night and all the money raised went to my chosen charity, the Julia Raggett Memorial Fund. The highlight of the evening was the sweepstake where customers had to guess what score Richard, the barman, would have left when I checked out against him. His mates had a lot of faith in him, didn't they? Surely, they should have been betting on how many *I* had left! By the way, Richard is a great fan of Francis Hoenselaar and, whenever I visit The Airballoon, he always gives me grief! So I beat him. Marie's customers were very generous throughout the evening and raised an amazing total of £250.

As far as tournaments were concerned, the summer was a mixture of success and disappointment. After a very tiring day, I won the Welsh Open, beating Lancashire's and England international Lisa Stephens in the final. Then I attended the Swiss Open and was beaten in the semi-finals by Karin Krappen who was then beaten in the final by Francis. In the England Open at Brean Sands, Somerset's Sue Biddle put a stop to my progress in the last eight by dumping me out of the competition 3–0. Sue then disposed of Welsh number one Jan Robbins 3–1 in the semis only to fall at the final hurdle to – yes, you've guessed it – Francis. I picked up £35 for making the last eight, but I did manage to win something that weekend. Mervyn King and I joined forces and won the Mixed Pairs, beating John 'Boy' Walton and Anastasia 3–1.

The following weekend I was back in Kent to defend the Women's British Pentathlon title that I had won the previous year. I retained my title with 359 points, a massive 81 points ahead of my nearest rival who, on this occasion, was Apylee Jones. Dawn Standley and Clare were third and fourth respectively. I think the Pentathlon is unique in that it offers the same prize money to the women as to the men. It's thanks to the foresight of the event sponsor, (the late) Tom Pope of Retriever Sports, that this was the case. It was Tom who had the insight to acknowledge the quality of the ladies' game. If only such was the case in other major darts events!

Then it was off to Las Vegas again to defend my Desert Classic title. On this trip I was accompanied by one of my sponsors, Julie Reeves. I have to say that I had never before been led astray so much by a sponsor! We had a brilliant time. Well, apart from my being sick in a helicopter. We did about everything we could do in Vegas. We went to see Celine Dion in concert. She was just brilliant. We had wonderful meals in the revolving restaurant at the top of the Stratosphere Hotel from which you can see for miles.

Then we took Crissy and Pete to the Monte Carlo Hotel to celebrate their first wedding anniversary. For some unknown reason Pete seemed to think that I was a wine connoisseur. He handed me the wine list and asked me to choose. Eventually I decided and called the waiter over to our table. I went to order and he asked me for my ID to prove I was over twenty-one. I couldn't believe it! I had the feeling that I was being set up and so wasn't sure at the time whether to feel insulted or complimented. As it happened, it wasn't a wind-up and we were able to convince the manager that I was over twenty-one.

The helicopter ride over the Grand Canyon was Julie's idea. The views were absolutely stunning. The sheer size of the Grand Canyon takes your breath away. But soon I was flagging a bit. It didn't take long before I was feeling dreadfully ill and, I'm sorry to say that, unintentionally, I left something of myself in the Canyon. I think I must have had too much sun.

In the Desert Classic itself, played at the MGM Grand Hotel, around sixty ladies lined up to try and take my title. The semi-finals and final were played out on the Desert Classic stage and I had to come back from 3–2 down against Stacy Bromberg in my semi to level the match with a 101 checkout and then hit a seventeen-darter to win through. In the final I met one of the women who had encouraged me to play and who had helped me get where I am today, Deta Hedman. Deta had beaten Tricia Wright 4–0 in her semi.

I hit two maximums in the first leg of the final and went 1–0 up. Then I went 2–0 up, only for Deta to break back in eighteen darts. I then hit a thirteen-darter to make it 3–1, only to lose my form in the next leg and allow Deta to close the gap. I couldn't let that happen again and I shot out the next three legs in 17, 15 and 18 darts to take the title. My overall three-dart average for the match was 85.20.

I'd come a long way to defend my title but it had been so worthwhile; to win such a prestigious event against Deta, whom I consider to be one of the greatest women darts players of all time.

Chapter Twenty-six

Hit for Six

Throughout the summer of 2005 I continued to throw myself into my darts. I was now a single woman again but still hurting from my break-up with Gully, so I focused on the darts.

Some might say that I took it out on the Welsh when I more or less made a clean sweep of the available titles at the Welsh Classic at the Robin Hood holiday camp in Rhyl. A few weeks earlier, I had retained my Welsh Open title, but now I was back in the Land of Song to wreak havoc.

I met the Welsh number one, Gwent's Jan Robbins, in the semi-final of the Lyons Robin Hood Classic Ladies' Singles. I raced into a 3–0 lead but Jan, in front of her home crowd, pulled two legs back which some incredible darts. Fortunately for me, she couldn't maintain that standard and I came out the winner, 4–2. I met Clare in the final. She knows my game so well but that didn't help her on this occasion as I won the title 4–1. However, we were all friends again when we teamed up for the Ladies'

Pairs and found ourselves in the final where we whitewashed Norfolk's Dawn Standley and Amanda Brown. As if I weren't content with that, I then went on to partner Durham's Mick Nixon in the Mixed Pairs and won that, too, against Jan Robbins and Cheshire's Tony Eccles.

I didn't make the BDO Gold Cup Ladies' Singles this time round. I was absolutely slaughtered in the finals of the Warwickshire play-offs by Clare. But I did go as Clare and I qualified for the Ladies' Pairs. Clare played amazing darts all day at Lakeside and made the Ladies' Singles final, only to fall at the last hurdle (3–0) to Surrey's Apylee Jones. Clare and I got nowhere near the title (or the money) in the Pairs, going out early to the Norfolk pairing of Dawn Standley and Janice Butters.

Then it was approaching the time of the British Classic at Kettering. Before that, I drove down to Stansted Airport to pick up Francis Hoenselaar and Roeli Bakker (an up-and-coming Dutch darter) and drove them back to Wantage to the house Clare and I were buying together. It didn't take us long to decide to have a little party which basically consisted of nothing more complicated than getting pissed. We started it off down at The Shears where Clare and I play darts on a Wednesday evening, and introduced Francis and Roeli to the landlord Paul (nicknamed 'Cockle') and the landlady, Gill (nicknamed the 'Dragon' by those who are brave enough). To begin with, the conversation was about darts but that was too much of a busman's holiday and we were there to party. As the alcohol took effect, the conversation turned to anything at all. We eventually went home and drank into the early hours. God only knows what time we went to bed.

The next day, we decided to go to Kettering and book into a hotel in readiness for the tournament the following day. After a nice meal, a few glasses of wine and good company, we all retired to bed, much, much earlier than we had the night before.

As always with the British Classic, I had to produce great darts to get through. In particular, I had to deliver against one of the toughest opponents, Norfolk's Dawn Standley. Dawn is so consistent and you just know that you have to play well against her every time or she will make you pay. Another tough opponent is Essex's Viv Dundon, whom I met, and defeated, in the semi-final. In the other semi, Hertfordshire's Linda Searle beat Karin Krappen. In the final I quickly went into a 2–0 lead and thought I was cruising to victory but, for whatever reason, I seemed to fall asleep as Linda upped her game and brought herself back level 2–2. In the deciding leg, Linda had six darts at a double to win the title but missed. I stepped up, struck the winning double, and lifted the British Classic Ladies' Singles title for the fourth time. I'll admit I was very lucky to have won it.

Then it was back home, where Roeli and Francis nearly managed to burn the house down after deciding to redecorate the living room with red candle wax! Clare and I love having lighted candles around the house. The subtle light is very relaxing. On this occasion we'd all had a few drinks and Roeli decided to throw a cushion at Francis. It missed its target and knocked one of our red candles over, splashing red wax over part of a wall. It was only a little accident and on viewing their lovely, spontaneous artwork, Clare and I decided to keep it as a unique example of Wantage 'Art Deco'. Later, we did try to remove it but only partly succeeded. Some of it is still there. We just can't get rid of the bloody stuff!

After my non-appearance in the BDO Gold Cup and my near defeat in the British Classic, I began to realise more and more that my world title was under threat and that I was being constantly challenged by a growing number of talented lady darts players. And, of course, Francis was *always* there or thereabouts.

One such talented player is Karin Krappen who provided an excellent example of a key threat when she knocked me out of the World Darts Trophy in Utrecht in the semi-finals 2–1. Taking nothing away from Karin, it was 117 degrees on stage. Karin dealt with that so well, seemingly untroubled by the heat. But her darts were 'hot', too, and she went one step further by defeating Francis in the all-Dutch final 3–1. It was Karin's biggest victory in darts up to that point and a well-deserved win.

Previously, it had been all Francis and me – mostly me! I beat Francis in the Norway Open 4–0. Francis was really out of sorts that day. My delight at winning was frustrated by yet another incident at an airport. Apparently, on the incoming flight, our plane had collided with a flock of birds and so a technician had to be sent for before we could carry on to Torp. I don't know where the technician lived but it must have been hundreds of miles away. He took an absolute age to get there. Perhaps he thought it was such a nice day that he'd walk in!

On the Bank Holiday weekend in Copenhagen, I defeated Francis 4–1 in the Denmark Open thus retaining my title. Francis was back to her old self by then. It was a fantastic game. The final score doesn't do justice to how good and how close a match it actually was. Usually, after the Denmark Open, Francis and I visit Copenhagen's famous Tivoli Gardens but this year we were too shattered and just chilled out.

At the British Open at Bridlington in September the tables were turned again and rather than becoming victor, I became victim to the ever-improving skills of the talented Anastasia Dobromyslova. Anastasia displayed impressive form against me in the semi-final. The last leg saw us both throwing for a match-winning double after only twelve darts each and Anastasia hit hers first. I thought perhaps this was going to be Anastasia's biggest win to date, but in the other half of the draw Clare was hitting a purple patch and had made it to the final, where she defeated Anastasia 3–1. What a great result and what a way for Clare to warm up for the World Cup only a couple of weeks away.

This result also meant that Clare qualified as the third seed for the forthcoming World Championships and I knew that she would present a significant threat to my retaining my title. For Anastasia there was victory, too, at the British Open, as she and Karin took the Ladies' Pairs by beating Jan Robbins and Dee Bateman in the final.

Next up was the World Cup XV held in the Challenge Stadium in Perth, Western Australia. The worst thing about this event is the length of the flight. I suffer a lot from jet lag and this time was no exception. In November, the headline in *Darts World* magazine screamed, 'ENGLAND'S LADIES SAVE THE DAY!' The men's team had been soundly beaten into third place in the final table, well behind the victorious Dutch team of Raymond van Barneveld, Dick van Dijk, Niels de Ruiter and Vincent van der Voort, who had scored 103 points overall to England's 74. In between the two was the Finland Men's team, who were runners-up with 83 points.

Clare and I routed the opposition with outstanding performances on the oche. We were favourites to win the Ladies' Pairs and we didn't disappoint our supporters as we powered our way into the final to face the American duo of Stacey Bromberg and Marilyn Popp. It was a very hard-fought final and at 3–3 it was into the deciding leg. Clare and I had first throw in that leg and I hit the winning double with my first dart.

In the final of the Ladies' Singles, who should I meet but – Clare. Fresh from her win in the British Open, Clare played so well. Not surprisingly, as in the Pairs, we found ourselves in yet another tie-break situation, this time against each other. We matched scores all the way down and then I missed three darts at double eighteen. Clare stepped up to the oche and carefully claimed the title with double eight. The England Ladies finished top of the final table with 66 points, 37 points ahead of the runners-up, the USA, while the team from The Netherlands shared fifteenth place (with only four points) with teams from Wales, Northern Ireland and the Philippines.

I was very pleased with my form in Australia and, although I missed a number of important shots along the way, I felt as though I was building up nicely to my next challenge, the WINMAU World Masters. As for Clare, well, she was really beginning to shine on the world stage and, once again, I made a mental note of the threat she posed in January in the forthcoming World Championships. Would Clare be the one to take my crown?

For the entire weekend of the WINMAU World Masters at Bridlington, 21– 23 October, it rained. However, that didn't dampen my enthusiasm for fighting to retain my title – and I really had to fight this time. However, during the week running up to the World Masters something, and I couldn't exactly put my finger on what, had left me with a lack of self-confidence. I took some valued advice from Eric Bristow, a friend and a legend in the game. I spoke to Eric about not feeling confident and, in his own unique way, he reassured me that everything would fall into place when I needed it to. If I needed to step up a gear, I would. I was so grateful to him. Everyone needs a boost every now and again and his words certainly worked.

In my semi-final at the World Masters, I came up against Apylee Jones. As usual, it was a very tough match but I managed to win it 4–2. In the other semi-final Francis was having a similar match against Finland's Sari Nikula, but finally scrapped through 4–3. Once again, it was the 'old firm' in the final and I made it my own again by defeating Francis 4–1 with an average per dart of 30.27. That made it four World Masters in a row for me, and five out of the last six, as I had won my first Masters back in 2000. Once again, I had produced the goods for my sponsors, WINMAU. I was really pleased with my overall performance and I was thrilled that the BBC showed the entire ladies' final on *Grandstand*.

On the charity front, I continued to be involved with events for the Julia Raggett Memorial Fund, raising money for local and national cancer charities. One day I received a phone call from Val Steele, the Chairwoman of the Southam Ladies Lions Club, asking me to help raise funds for the Julia Raggett Memorial Fund and the Warwickshire Air Ambulance. 'How can I help?' I asked. 'By being a model' was the reply. A model! Oh God! Immediately into my mind sprang images of me tripping over on the catwalk, falling off the stage, and later seeing the replays on *You've Been Framed*.

The Ladies Lions were organising a fashion show with Essentials, a clothes shop in Southam, and wanted me to be part of it. Of course, I agreed and my sister Denise joined me. The show was held at my old school, Southam High School, but by then it had been renamed Southam College. In the end, there were twelve models featured in the show – all ladies – each having to model six outfits. The schedule was very tight, with only three minutes between coming off the catwalk and walking back on stage in the next outfit. That was virtually impossible for me. I usually take hours getting ready, although it's probably the application of the war paint that takes the time, but I have to say I did it and enjoyed it. I didn't fall over or even trip. In fact, the organisers told me afterwards that another one might be planned. (Perhaps I should have fallen over after all!) Still, it was all for two very good causes although I have to admit that I would rather throw darts in front of a crowd of 2,500 people than walk along a catwalk in front of 250.

Back in darts, I was thrilled and delighted to be awarded the 'Sportswoman of the Year Award' in the inaugural Coventry, Solihull and Warwickshire Sports Awards. The ceremony took place at the Ricoh Stadium, Coventry. I was in good company as England cricketer Ashley Giles was named 'Sportsman of the Year'. My award not only recognised my personal achievements, but it was marvellous for darts as a whole and women's darts in particular. I was the first woman to receive the award and that really felt good. Shortly after that, Clare and I were named 'Team of the Year' in the 2005 BBC TV *South Today* Sports Awards for our outstanding achievements in the World Cup in Perth.

Next up was the BIG ONE, the World Championship. Clare was seeded number four, while I was number one, which meant that we were both in the top half of the draw and so would never meet in the final. With our next visit to Lakeside just around the corner, Clare and I decided to chill out and fly to Los Cristianos in Tenerife. We had a lovely time. We stayed in a hotel instead of our usual choice of self-catering. I wanted to relax and be pampered a little and return to England refreshed and ready to defend my title successfully for the fifth time.

In the quarter-finals at Lakeside, I had a comfortable 2–0 win over Bath's Karen Littler, who was playing in the World Championship finals for the first time. The game was all over in fifteen minutes. That win secured me a semi-final match against Clare, who had swept aside another championship debutante, Switzerland's Sabine Beutler, in her quarter-final by the same score line. I knew I had to play well against Clare as she knew my game so well – and I did just that. I won the first set 3–1 with an eleven-dart final leg and then in the second set hit four maximums and another eleven-dart leg to secure another 2–0 victory. Sorry Clare. Well, no. I'm not really! I was there to do my job and defend my title, although it was an extremely difficult match to play psychologically.

Meanwhile, in the bottom half of the draw, Francis had disposed of Yorkshire's Karen Lawman (previously known as Karen Smith but who had by then reverted to her maiden name) in the quarter-final and Wales' Jan Robbins 2–0 in the semi. So – here we were again – England versus The Netherlands, the 'same old faces' meeting on the oche of the world stage. The crowd was expecting quality darts. Francis and I were expecting to throw quality darts, but that final turned out to be the worst on record. As *Darts World* reported, 'the expected fireworks fizzled out as both players suffered double trouble and big match nerves'.

My first throw, a maximum 180, was probably the highlight of the entire match. The first set was a right scramble but I managed to scrape home 3–2 with double ten. In the second set, I was 2–0 up in legs but *still* missed six darts at a double to take the title. Then Francis, playing to save the set and the match, missed double eighteen and then double nine to let me in and this time I made no mistake, checking out on double one. I still believe that, if Francis had taken that second set, the result would have been entirely different.

But she didn't and I was the Women's World Darts Champion for the sixth time!

Chapter Twenty-seven

The Magnificent Seventh

Never in my wildest dreams did I imagine that I could retain my title for a fifth time. I kept pinching myself. It was true. I'd become World Champion for a sixth successive time.

There had been a fantastic atmosphere at Lakeside and it really is the greatest of all stages to play on. I also think it gives me home advantage. As usual, the home crowd had been behind me, giving me great support and that always means a lot to me, especially when I'm playing Francis. It makes such a difference, just as she benefits from the partisan crowds over in Holland when we play there. I just wish I could have given my fans a better final to watch. If Francis had raised her game just a fraction, or hit those illusive doubles while I was missing mine, or if she had taken the first set, the outcome could have been so different.

For me the best game was the semi-final against Clare. We have had some great games in the past, but on this occasion she was on the wrong end of an on-form me. Everything had fallen into place in that game. I only wish I could have continued that form into what turned out to be, by mine and Francis' usually high standards, a rather drab final.

In the Men's final, an exciting new Dutch talent, twenty-one-year-old Jelle Klassen, beat Raymond van Barneveld 7–5 to become the youngest ever winner of the world title. Within a few weeks it was announced that Barney would be joining the PDC and while much of the darts world was stunned, it was probably one of the sport's worst kept secrets. So the future of men's darts, it seemed, now lay in the hands of Jelle and other young men coming up through the Dutch ranks.

A short time later, news also broke that women's involvement in the World Darts Trophy in Utrecht was being dropped and replaced by a youth tournament. This was one hell of a blow to women's darts. Not only were we to lose one of the great showcases of ladies' darts but we were also losing the biggest prize purse in our sport. We were all devastated.

The ladies were good enough to have been included four years previously to get the tournament off the ground and during that time it had produced four different champions. Now we were being dropped. I guessed that the decision was made in response to Jelle's fantastic win. It was certainly a great opportunity to promote the youth game, which was (and is still today) particularly strong in Holland, but why at the cost of the ladies?

It could not have come at a worse time for our sport. Just when there had been an increase in the number of ladies playing, we were hit with this decision. We were stunned. (What happened to equality?) Frustrated? You bet! The World Darts Trophy (WDT) Ladies' tournament had been a giant step forwards and now we'd taken about twenty steps backwards. Over the next few weeks, I spoke to many people about the decision to axe us from the WDT but while everyone agreed with me and was very supportive, nothing more was to come of it. Each side blamed the other – it was the usual cop-out – so we never learnt the truth. Then the organisers confirmed the decision and the women were out.

True to my post-world championship form, I was runner-up (to Anne Kirk) in February's Dutch Open Ladies' Singles and only made the last eight of the Pairs with Francis. Then, as usual, I recovered and won both the Isle of Man Darts Festival Ladies' Singles (beating Francis in the final) and a new tournament, the Isle of Wight Open where I met Dawn Standley in the final. We both threw some great darts and Dawn came out the winner, 3–2. In April, at the British International Championships, the England Ladies were once again victorious, but not by such a large margin as the previous year. We beat Scotland 5–1, but could only draw 3–3 with the resilient Welsh girls.

While I moved on from success to success, then failure, then success again in my chosen sport, the 'same old faces' issue raised its ugly head again. I wrote, by my standards, a fairly angry column in *Darts World* in which I defended my position and that of other successful professional lady darters and asked the readers to come up with ideas as to how the women's game could be improved. We all knew the potential was out there so – come on! I wrote, 'If anyone has any ideas they'd like to share with me and with the readers of *Darts World* then please write to me care of the editor.' No one contacted me and no one wrote to the magazine with any ideas. It all fell silent. Perhaps the level of commitment was simply not out there. Perhaps when they read my explanation of how I had struggled at first to make my name in the game without sponsors and how hard I had had to work to secure backing, they all decided that it was, literally, too much like hard work.

I gained no pleasure from the total lack of response and tried to put those harsh comments at the back of my mind, but I never really succeeded. I was at the top of the County averages, top of the WDF World Rankings, I was Captain of England, and I was reigning world champion and yet ...

I don't think I had ever felt so low during the summer of 2006. Despite my world champion status, I wasn't that busy. Surprisingly, exhibition work was scarce, but the bills still had to be paid. I pottered around the house doing some DIY. I reached the stage where I felt as though I was losing control of everything. I still felt guilty about separating from Gully. I'd hurt him big time and found that very hard to deal with. I also felt that I was losing everything I had worked so hard for over the years. I lost about a stone in weight, which wasn't a healthy thing to do. I was missing my family and friends back in Warwickshire. I kept in touch by phone and visited them regularly. I only lived a one-hour car journey away from my family but often it seemed like a million miles. I was feeling isolated and depressed.

I went for counselling. It took a lot of nerve and determination on my part to make the phone call but I did it and attended several sessions. I was so lonely and talking to a counsellor, who saw people like me every day and had the experience and training to help me, make me feel better, but it could never take the place of true friends. Everyone needs their friends and family around them during troubled times. I was at such a low ebb and of course my real friends were there for me.

One of those true friends is Gill Cox, the landlady at The Shears. I've lost count of the number of times I've gone to Gill for a chat about everything and nothing. She's like a big sister and a second mum rolled into one. Gill can always tell if there's something troubling me and she helps me put things into perspective. Sometimes I just need to have a good moan or, just jokingly, slag a few people off and put the world to rights.

The support of friends like Gill and my natural determination not to be beaten, enabled me to soldier on with my darts and I managed to claim more titles including the Swiss Open.

However, there was a flip side (as usual). I was beaten in the semi-finals of the England Open by Yorkshire's Dee Bateman and then fell victim to Anne Kirk (3–2) in the Granite City Open. I also participated in the Portland Open – one of the few opportunities for me to play against the men – and was beaten in the last sixteen by Scotland's number one, the very much on-form Gary Anderson.

Then in the BDO Gold Cup Ladies' Singles at Lakeside in July, I was beaten in the semi-final by Yorkshire's Karen Lawman, who went on to win the title. Clare and I managed to win the Pairs, beating the Pembrokeshire team of Julie Gore and Coralie Jones 3–1, a title we had previously won in 2003. I fared worse at the British Classic at Kettering going out in the early rounds to Staffordshire's Sarah Cope. Clare kept the Warwickshire flag flying and made the final of the Ladies' Singles but just could not overcome Dee Bateman, who took the title 3–0. Despite Clare's performance, I was obviously disappointed with my own form. It *had* to improve before my defence of the WINMAU World Masters.

Things did improve during August. I won the Isle of Wight Open. Again, I met Dawn Standley in the final but this time the result was reversed. In the Denmark Open final, I met Finland's Tarja Salminen and beat her 4–0, earning myself some valuable ranking points. After that, I was off to Japan.

In Japan, I was working with a company called DARTSLIVE who are deeply involved in electronic darts in that country. DARTSLIVE had created a programme which enabled electronic darts machines to record not only a players' scores but also his or her stats. Basically, you insert a plastic card into the machine, play your games and it's all recorded on the server. The information produced tells you all your averages and includes the date, time and where in the world you're playing. My part in the promotion was to take part in the DARTSLIVE party with another darts professional, Paul Lim. Our role was to play against qualifiers on stage and to participate in a question-and-answer session.

Around the venue were about ninety electronic darts machines. This method of playing darts is also called 'soft-tip' because the darts, although they have similar barrels and flights as the steel-tip game, have plastic tips, which ensure that the sensitive electronics behind the darts scoring area are not damaged by the entry of the darts into the board. The DARTSLIVE machines were all equipped with this new technology. A staggering 1,500 people attended the party and took part in various games and competitions from 11.00 a.m. to 10.00 p.m. I was particularly pleased that there were almost as many women playing the electronic darts machines as men. The atmosphere was fantastic and I felt genuinely privileged to have been part of it. DARTSLIVE's hospitality was second to none and I will remember that Japanese experience for as long as I live.

My indifferent form during the build-up to the WINMAU World Masters should have warned me of the dangers I would face at Bridlington in October. WINMAU had only recently renewed my sponsorship for another three years and I was duty bound to do well for them, but on this occasion I failed.

My old adversary Francis dumped me out of the Ladies' Singles in the semi-final and then went on to win in an all-Dutch final, beating Karin Krappen 4–3 to take the World Masters title for the first time since 1999. When I walked off stage after my semi-final defeat, I was in despair. The MC then announced as Francis left the stage that she was Champion of the World. I resented that. *I* was Champion of the World. There was a lot of difference between being World Master and being World *Champion*. I spoke to some friends in the VIP bar and one said to me, '*You* know you're World Champion. *We* know you're World Champion. So go on and prove it again at Lakeside in January.' Fuelled by that discussion and the encouragement of my friends, I did just that.

Again, I didn't make it easy for myself. I struggled in my quarter-final match at Lakeside against the Dutch teenage sensation Carina Molema. I missed doubles early on but eventually scraped through 3–2. My semi-final opponent was the ever-improving Anastasia Dobromyslova, who had beaten Sweden's Carina Ekberg 2–0 in her quarter-final match. Anastasia was extremely nervous in the first set, which I won 3–0, but then, in a reversal, *I* was affected by nerves in the second set and fell behind 2–1. However, I power scored throughout the rest of the match and eventually took the second set and the match 2–0 and was set for my sixth defence, but against who? No surprises. For the fifth year out of seven I met Francis in the final. Francis had progressed to the final by defeating the Australian debutante Carol Forwood 2–1 in the quarter-final and Surrey's Apylee Jones 2–1 in the semi-final.

The final took place on Friday, 12 January 2007. It was scheduled to start at 8.45 p.m. and a little after that Francis and I were introduced to the crowd and we stepped out on to the world stage. In the final, Francis sent out an immediate message of her intentions in the first leg of the first set with a 151 checkout (treble twenty, treble seventeen, double twenty) and then took the set 3–2 with a double sixteen finish. I came back in the second and levelled the match one set all. In the third set, I opened up a two-leg lead but then Francis came back at me to level and take us into a sudden-death, fifth and deciding leg.

When this situation occurs, the players have to throw for the bull's-eye and the nearest then throws first. It is all-important that you win that bull as it can prove a psychological advantage in such a tight game. I won the bull-up and two scores of 140 and one of 100 gave me a clear lead over my rival. Despite three missed shots at double eighteen, there was still time to have another shot at it. I went back to the oche and hit the double eighteen. I clenched my fist and said, 'Yes!' The expression on my face was one of complete and utter relief. I puffed out my cheeks and murmured to myself, 'Chuffin' hell, Trine. You've done it again!' I then turned to Francis and we embraced each other. I said to her, 'What a great final!' Francis agreed. We had both enjoyed the final so much – and what a great advertisement for ladies' darts it had been. I then stepped to the front of the stage, raised my hands in the air, closed my eyes and soaked up the applause of the crowd.

I really was in seventh heaven!

Chapter Twenty-eight

What's Next for Me...
and Ladies' Darts?

There are certain things that happen in life that show how vulnerable we all are. In early February 2007, I was shocked to receive a phone call from my sister Denise to say that my mum, Muriel, had had a heart attack.

I was in Holland at the Dutch Open and wanted to pack my bags and come home straightaway, but Denise said there was little I could do and that I should stay where I was. The doctors had checked Mum over and had managed to stabilise her but the next twenty-four hours were going to be crucial. I felt so helpless. However, I was under strict instructions from my family to stay in Holland and win the title for Mum, so I did just that. I beat Anastasia 4–3 in the semi-final and then Clare 5–2 in the Ladies' Singles final and also took the Ladies' Pairs title with Francis. However, for obvious reasons, any planned personal celebrations were shelved. I told a reporter, 'I'm going home now to help look after Mum for a while.'

279

I was so pleased to be back home and to see that Mum had been well looked after. As usual, she had been doing too much. The difficulty with my mum has always been to slow her down. She seems to refuse to realise that – like all of us – she's getting older. Having that scare made me stop a while and think about my own future.

What's next for Trina Gulliver, the Seven-time Women's World Darts Champion? I could argue that I've nothing left to prove and call it a day, but that's not me at all. As you know, I've worked extremely hard to get where I am and I have no intention of packing away my darts now, or at any other time in the future. Whatever I do or wherever fate takes me, I cannot imagine darts not being part of my life. My love of the sport keeps me going. I could move into management or perhaps even into television, but whatever happens it would always be darts-related. Only serious ill health would make me give up darts altogether but, touch wood ...

Then, of course, there's that small matter of defending my world title for a seventh time. That's clearly my primary focus for the coming year and there are plenty of contenders coming up on the rails to try and take my crown. The key threats have already been mentioned earlier but I'll name them again now, just to make it absolutely clear whom I think *might* (but not if I have anything to do about it) wrestle my title from me.

The two major threats from Holland remain my great friend and rival Francis Hoenselaar and her compatriot, Karin Krappen. From Russia, but now based in Holland, comes Russia's Anastasia Dobromyslova, who is surely a future world champion. The same can be said of my close friend Clare, probably one of my most difficult opponents, given that we both play for our country, we practise together, play for the same county and even share the same house. Nevertheless, I'm not naïve and I know that potentially any of the seven ladies who make the finals of the

World Championships in 2008 will be hungry for victory. I know that I only have to drop my guard for a moment and, with such a short format, I could be out.

There's still a lot of criticism about the format for the Women's World Championship. With only eight ladies lining up at Lakeside for the final it *looks* as though it's the 'same old faces', but it's not. Sure, Francis and I are there on a regular basis, but then we've been World number one and two for some time now, which means that we are entitled to be there. Of course, I'd love to see more ladies participating in the finals. Don't think for one moment I haven't asked the BDO to consider expanding the numbers to sixteen or even thirty-two players. I am all for longer games, too. The format of best-of-three sets was, and remains, a very short format and, to be honest, you have to be on top of your game from the start to stand any chance of being successful. A longer format, like the men's competition, would allow the ladies to get into the scoring groove and really show their worth. Such a change would also help improve the standard of ladies' darts at all levels.

Then there's the prize money. Chuffed as I was to receive a cheque for £6,000 for my 2007 Lakeside World Championship win, that's relatively small beer when you consider the men's top prize is over *ten times* as much, £70,000. I'm not saying that the purses should be the same like they've recently agreed for grand slam tennis finalists (although that would be nice) but simply a larger sum that would encourage even more women and girls to play darts and which might help to attract the much needed sponsors to the ladies' game. Without more sponsorship, more prize money, more television and more publicity, the ladies' game will go nowhere fast. I'm lucky: I earn a living from darts but I want to see more ladies participating and more sponsors coming forward to back their skills.

I worked hard for my world-ranking points and spent an

enormous amount of time searching for sponsors. I eventually found them and I have delivered the goods for them time and time again and my success has been rewarded by the renewal of their backing of me. Without my sponsors, I think I would still have been a success in darts, but not so quickly. I believe that my determination would have seen me climb to the top of my sport. However, whether I could have sustained the momentum without sponsorship ... I doubt it.

The year 2006 saw the ladies' event in the World Darts Trophy removed and replaced by a youth event. That was such a blow to the ladies' game. The organisers' action generated much interest in a new darts organisation formed in Holland called the Ladies Darts Association (LDA). The LDA's main goal is 'to be fully committed to promote, stimulate and improve the sport of darts nationally, internationally and worldwide for all women participating in darts'. Its long-term aims are to create a range of tournaments for the ladies and eventually hold its own independent world championship.

The Association is still in its formative stages but its membership is increasing. Both Francis and I have signed up to be directly associated with it, although how the BDO will eventually react is, at the time of writing, not known. But, surely, anything that helps bring attention to the ladies' game and brings in more sponsorship can't be a bad thing. It must be a positive step forwards. I've always said that our sport needs to be taken in hand by professional marketing people. Give us the backing and lady darters will deliver every time.

And what about the 2012 Olympics? Wouldn't it be marvellous if ladies' darts made it to the Olympics before the men's, maybe just as a demonstration sport? What a privilege it would be for me to lead the England Ladies' team out into the arena and take on the world on our home soil! However, I'm not holding my breath on that one!

WHAT'S NEXT FOR ME ... AND LADIES' DARTS?

The great thing about darts is that it is such an easy game to learn to play. It doesn't matter if you are male or female, able-bodied or have a disability, you can play darts. In darts, women and girls are technically and physically on a par with the men. You have to train hard to win, like in all sports, but there is no reason why women shouldn't be as good as the men in our sport – no reason at all. In addition, darts is such a good game. It's such a sociable recreation whether it's played in your local pub or club, in Super League or for county or on a board hanging in your garage or spare room. There are still, thankfully, hundreds of places in which to learn to play and to develop your darting skills and progress.

However, there are still so many more opportunities for men than women to earn a living from darts. The Professional Darts Corporation (PDC) has substantially increased the number of competitions over the past few years but few women actually join the Professional Darts Players' Association (PDPA). I've thought about it, but prefer, for the moment, to stay where specific provision is available for the ladies. Don't get me wrong, I don't mind mixing it with the men. As you have read, I've done that in competition including the Pentathlon and at the IDPA tournaments and played well. I also have my responsibilities in relation to my captaincy of the England Ladies' team. I would undoubtedly lose that if I 'changed sides' and I'm not prepared to let that happen.

Captaining your country in the sport you love is one of the greatest privileges and one of the greatest feelings on earth and I'm not prepared to give that up or, for that matter, hand over my world title to anyone just yet.